CONTEMPORANEITY OF CLASS AND CASTE IN INDIA

From Text to Context with Special Reference to Mulk Raj Anand

Sunita Arya

ATLANTIC
PUBLISHERS & DISTRIBUTORS (P) LTD

ATLANTIC
PUBLISHERS & DISTRIBUTORS (P) LTD
7/22, Ansari Road, Darya Ganj, New Delhi
Tel.: +91-11-4077 5252, 2327 3880
E-mail: orders@atlanticbooks.com
Web: www.atlanticbooks.com

Published by Atlantic Publishers & Distributors (P) Ltd 2024

Printed & bound in India by Atlantic Print Services

Preface

Our lives all across the world are dominated by different prejudices such as class, caste, race, ethnicity, colour, and religion. In India, there are conventions and codes on the basis of race, colour, religion, caste, and class. India has a multiracial social set up. Class and caste are the two most important proportions of any society. Class and caste are timeless topics. It is like the perennial Himalayan River which is ever flowing. And in this regard, India holds a very special place.

The present study proposes to discuss the class and caste consciousness in Indian society through the works of Mulk Raj Anand in particular and other eminent writers in general such as Sharankumar Limbale, Arundhati Roy, Rohinton Mistry, U.R. Anantha Murthy, Arvind Adiga, Shashi Deshpande, Toni Morrison, Bhabani Bhattacharya, Baby Kamble, Bama, and others. Mulk Raj Anand has elucidated the class and caste consciousness in his novels, short stories and other non-fictional works. He reviewed the institution of class and caste by vividly and forcefully describing the sufferings of million voiceless, unheard Indians. Every novel of his seems to have been designed by him to arouse the social conscience. There is hardly any ugly or depressing aspect of fiction which has not been attacked by him in his writings. He is one writer whose works are still relevant after decades of Independence in modern Indian society. A comparative study of Mulk Raj Anand's works with other contemporary writers provides a broader and comprehensive understanding of class and caste in literature.

The study has been divided into five chapters. The first chapter titled "Class and Caste: The History, The Authors and Texts". The chapter foregrounds the statement of the study, the problem to study. The chapter is followed by a short introduction of caste and class as a concept which will be elaborated in the succeeding chapters. The chapter also discusses in detail about Mulk Raj Anand, his journey as a writer, his area of interests, and his life long quest as a writer of social change and human equality.

The second chapter titled "Historiography of Division: The Class System" analyses the key concept of class in western as well as Indian society. The term *class* first came into widespread use in the early 19th century, substituting such terms as *rank* and *order* as metaphors of the foremost hierarchical groupings in society. In Indian society, the evils of capitalism became manifest immediately after the British introduced modern industries. In introducing the mechanical mode of production, the British did not aim to end ills of medievalism, which afflicted the Indian society, but were motivated by the sole objective of earning profit. The devil of capitalism, which settled down in the cities of India, grew into a monster on the blood of shriveled workers, with its dark shadows spelling doom in the traditional rustic life in India. The brunt of the attack of the forces of capitalism had to be borne by the poor and lower middle classes in cities and villages. It is in this context that Anand looks at the Indian society in *Coolie, Two Leaves and a Bud* and *The Big Heart* with Marxist perspective of class structure and class struggle. In this chapter, I have discussed the two novels i.e. *Coolie* and *Two Leaves and a Bud* in detail besides some short stories by Anand.

The third chapter titled "The Indian Inferno: Caste Propagation and Consciousness" analyses the factors of social disjunctions in Indian society through *Untouchable, The Road* as well as some short stories by Mulk Raj Anand, and narratives by other writers. Caste is known as *jati* in common parlance. In this chapter, I have discussed the origin, nature, complexity of caste in detail through sociology. The class and caste system of India is the direct product of religion. In the next section, I have discussed the dimensions of caste and class explored by different writers in literature. Mulk Raj Anand is the foremost writer to write about the outcastes, the pariahs, the underdogs and to resurrect them from the obscure lanes and alleys of India. The narrative form of Mulk Raj Anand's novel *Untouchable* (1935) shows a skillful organisation of the various tools of narration i.e. point of view, focus, atmosphere, characterization, etc. Apart from the novels, I have also taken some prominent short stories written by Anand. His short stories like *Silver Bangles, The Barber's Trade Union, Old Bapu* also beautifully portrays the caste system. Anand probes the social maladies of contemporary times with rare insight. These tales are social products shaped by their times. In the last section of this chapter, I have done a comparative study of *Untouchable* with Sharankumar Limbale's *Akkarmashi* (an autobiography).

The fourth chapter titled "Literature of Dissent: Breaking Hegemony" analysis the efficacy of literature as a weapon of social protest. Literature is produced in specific socio-historical, cultural and ideological contexts. The creative writer reflects, echoes and at times reacts in the process of his interaction with the society. The writer depends on the social and cultural institutions and he drives his sources from everyday world. Especially in modern novels, the writer focuses his attention on the social world and its complexities ruled by many historical factors. Society is made up of institutions, practices, customs, and beliefs; it is divided by class, caste, ethnicity, race, gender, religion. In this chapter, I have discussed social protest throughout the globe. I have in brief discussed the European protest literature, African protest literature particularly Nigerian literature, South African literature, Afro-American protest literature. I have also discussed in details certain text such as Arundhati Roy's *The God of Small Things* which *is* set within the southern Indian state of Kerala. Another novel which talks about the decaying caste system is *Samskara* written by U.R. Anantha Murthy and translated by A.K. Ramanujan. Next, in the line, I have analysed Rohinton Mistry's *A Fine Balance.* Moving forward in this list Arvind Adiga's *The White Tiger* needs to be looked as novel defining the class system prevalent in modern contemporary India. In the next section of this chapter, I have also discussed women's protest literature.

The fifth chapter deals with the "Conclusion: The Vicious Circle Continues" which states that Class and Caste consciousness in Indian society is still intact as it is being explored by contemporary writers also. Since Class and Caste are timeless topics. Anand's fictional world does not come from the dominant groups of the indigenous society but the subaltern classes and groups such as untouchables, coolies, farmers and industrial labourers, servants, waifs. It is history as it affects these large masses that are narrated in Anand's text. History here is not the representation of the glorious achievements of the heroic, but records of the suffering of millions of poor and helpless people who had no place in earlier, elitist historiography.

Dr. Sunita Arya

Contents

1

Class and Caste: The History, The Authors and Texts

1.1 The History of Class and Caste

Though race, class, ethnicity, and caste are different factors, the divisive role they play in different societies is more or less the same. Colour played a dominant role in deciding one's fate. A black colour could never be human; he was considered to be treated and suffered like an animal. India has a multiracial social set up. In India, there are conventions and codes on the basis of race, colour, religion, caste, and class. The practice of such restrictions prevents a smooth relationship among the people of different groups. This, in turn, becomes a sort of social rejection which leads to a lack of space for living and few opportunities for earning and finally drives them to hunger and poverty. Class and caste are the two most important proportions of any society.

Class and caste are timeless topics. The day human beings came into existence, came with existence the fatal question of survival, and survival means to compete and withhold other human beings. It is just like the jungle law either you become the hunter or the prey. The vicious circle of being a hunter and prey once onsets it decides who is the master and the slave. It is like the perennial Himalayan River which is ever flowing. And in this regard, India holds a very special place. Our lives all across the world are dominated by different prejudices such as class, caste, race, ethnicity, colour, and religion. Fragmentation of the world is a very common feature all over the globe. We see relation of the master and slave, the exploiter and the exploited, the poor and the rich, the capitalist and the labourers and so on.

Since at the universal level, the world is divided into two classes i.e., 'rich' and 'poor', but in India, we go for one more level and that is segregation based on caste and it is further divided into four prominent castes, then thousands of sub-castes. So, Indian society is deeply stratified with class and caste consciousness. The literal meaning of class is rank, status, position and wealth is the economic indicator which gives a person "class" whereas caste is something which is related to birth and the status, position, rank of the person depends on which caste he or she is born and the economic prosperity also correlates with the caste. Today We find divisive forces operative in many parts of India. India is a land of oddity. Here we find very rich, upper caste and class people on the one hand, and extremely poor, lower caste and class people on the other. There are people belonging to different castes, religions, regions and linguistic groups spread all over the country. Even the so-called majority group, the Hindus, are divided into several sects, castes, clans, and linguistic groups. These groups have certain aspirations for their members in regard to better education, employment and a certain standard of living.

Religion in India has never been static. Today it partakes through the pitches of politics and economic life. Religion is really a complex phenomenon in India. For example, elements of Aryan Sanskrit and Dravidian tribal religion are found in a mixed form at various levels. So is the interaction between the 'great' and the 'little' traditions according to Milton Singer and Robert Redfield. The class and caste system of India is the direct product of religion. The *varna* system on which Indian society is based is very much correlated with religion. The Literal meaning of *varna* is 'colour'. India has always been the meeting and melting point of the world. Different races came to India and thrived. According to the ancient history of India, after the decline of Indus valley civilization the Aryans prospered. With the Aryan came the term *varna* which means 'colour'. So, the initial difference was based on 'colour' of the skin since the native Indians were brown coloured people known as the Dravidians.

The Aryans as they expanded in the great Northern Indian plains the indigenous people shifted to the southern forested areas. There is a well-known belief amid orthodox Hindus that *chaturvarna,* or the hierarchical four-tier social composition of ancient India, had a religious origin. In reality, however, the support to *chaturvarna* given by the religious texts on the pretext of its allegedly divine origin served purely to sanctify and perpetuate an ancient form of unjust division of labour that was based on the coercion and exploitation of the entire working class, which constituted the overwhelming majority of the populace in ancient India, by a small and sponging ruling class. The 'other-worldly' religious injunctions were in the nature of a calculatingly contrived functional ideology that served to camouflage a this-worldly socio-economic configuration of exploitation. In other words, the social roots of the metaphysics of *chaturvarna* were entrenched in the relations of production in ancient India. By the middle of the period of the Dharmasastras, however, most of the peasants, including those who tilled their own land, were demoted to the status of Shudras. Only that diminutive section of peasants who were big landowners and produced a viable agricultural surplus were now counted as Vaishyas.

From that time onwards, the Brahmins and Kshatriyas effectively constituted the ruling class of ancient India, with the Vaishyas playing a somewhat assisting role. Thus, by about the 1st or 2nd century A.D. the entire working class, including all small and marginal farmers, landless labourers, artisans, craftsmen, and all manual labourers, was relegated to the status of Shudras. The Brahmins and Kshatriyas naturally constituted only a small fraction of the population. Since industry and trade were undeveloped in that ancient period, the Vaishyas also constituted an insignificant proportion of the population. The Shudras, therefore, constituted the overwhelming majority of the people of the country. It was this vast class of Shudras that was relegated to the bottom of the socio-economic pyramid and callously exploited by the composite ruling class of the Brahmins and Kshatriyas, using both the power of religion and the power of the state as its instruments of control.

The concept of swadharma was central to the injunctions of the religious texts regarding the division of labour consummated by *chaturvarna*. All major religious texts, including the *Manusmriti*, the *Bhagavad-Gita*, and the interpolated versions of the *Ramayana* and the *Mahabharata*, prescribed the unquestioning service of the three 'higher' *varnas* as the swadharma of the Shudras. The vast working class of Shudras was thus deprived of all social, economic and political rights. The *Manusmriti* also denied the Shudras the right to education, the right to property, the right to carry arms, and even access to religious observances. The *Manusmriti* declared that if a Shudra acquired any property, any Brahmin or Kshatriya had the right to take it away from him forcibly. As regards the carrying of arms, even the Brahmins were empowered to carry and use arms in times of difficulty, although it was alien to their swadharma. But the Shudras were totally prohibited to carry or use arms. The denial of the right to property in a societal structure based on personal property perpetuated the proletarianization of the Shudras, while the denial of the right to carry arms rendered them incompetent of overthrowing the structure of exploitation. The nauseatingly exploitative class structure of ancient India, which was cleverly veiled and sanctified by the Dharmasastras, particularly by *chaturvarna*, has remained virtually unchanged to this day.

The manipulative strategies of ruling classes over many centuries have contributed to the continuation of the ancient relations of production and their socio-cultural superstructure. According to sociologists Yogendra Singh and K.L. Sharma, class and caste represent, to a large extent the same structural reality. According to Yogendra Singh in his classical article "Caste and Class: Some Aspects of Continuity and Change" (*Sociological Bulletin*, Vol. xvii, No. 2, 1968) on the caste and class nexus are quite appropriate. According to Yogendra Singh, the sociologist:

> Classes operate within the framework of castes. Caste conflicts are also class conflicts as the upper and lower castes correspond to the high and the low classes, respectively, in terms of their social placement. (165)

Ghurye in his *Caste and Class in India* (1950) says any attempt to define caste is bound to fail because of the complexity of the phenomenon. Indian Marxist thinker comrade Sharad Patil argued that "the institution of class did not exist in India prior to the British rule. Hence, caste is a pre-class institution of exploitation and administration in India. With the colonial regime, the two modes of production, that of caste and class, came to co-exist with each other" (Mathew and Muricken 223). Indian capitalism since Independence grew on stretches of poverty i.e., the foundation for the prevailing structures of deprivation and inequalities. The poor classes are not only landless peasants and unorganized workers, but also the scheduled castes, backward classes, and scheduled tribes. Caste is a haunting idea and all Indians are conscious of the caste.

The original four *varnas* have proliferated into over a thousand castes and sub-castes due to numerous socio-religious and economic factors. These include counterfeit ideas regarding the hereditary transmission of purity and impurity, differences of rituals and ceremonies, endogamous marriage and other forms of socio-cultural interaction, geographical location, and above all, economic status, particularly land ownership. The process of *Sanskritization* a term given by M.N. Srinivas explains, the vertical and upward movement of the 'lower' castes, have also taken place over the centuries, mainly due to their rise in economic status, change in living condition, basic amenities of life. The innumerable castes and sub-castes of contemporary India cannot in all cases be classified under the original *chaturvarna* of the Dharmasastras, although they have all risen on the matrix of the four-tier hierarchical socio-economic structure of ancient India. Perhaps the most important retrograde development is that the entire caste system has become hereditary and transformed itself into a crystallized bigotry structure.

Although it is still a superstructure of the relations of production, it has over the centuries acquired a measure of autonomy, and in some ways behaves in parallel of the relations of production. This is the foremost distinctive characteristic of sophistication relations in the Asian nations these days. The proliferation of castes, and the comparative improvement of the socio-economic status of some of the 'middle' castes have to some degree diluted the structure of the four-tier hierarchy of ancient Indian society. But so far as the relations of production are concerned, the slave-like condition of the Dalits—descendants of the panchamas and asprishyas—has remained unaffected at the bottom of the socio-economic pyramid. Similarly, the Adivasi—descendants of the shavaras, nishadas and kiratas—have remained the victims of the grossest and most sharp form of socio-economic mistreatment. This is mainly because neither the basic class structure of India nor the crystallized prejudice structure of caste has distorted appreciably for many centuries, including the plentiful years since India's independence. The existential characteristics of the combined historical condition of these two socio-economic classes make them the 'wretched of the earth' who truly belong to the fourth world of nearly total isolation and exploitation. Apart from being the victims of sickening economic exploitation, they also suffer from the stigma of low social status imposed on them by the prejudice structure of caste.

1.2 Mulk Raj Anand: The Marxist and The Thinker

According to Francis Abraham and John Henry Morgan (1989):

> Hegel reasoned that history is the evolution of reason to the consciousness of itself, and the constitutional, legalistic state is the conclusion of history. But Marx adapted only "dialectics" from Hegel. According to Hegel, each statement of truth has its contradictory statement, or antithesis, which is also true. The thesis and anti-thesis may be reconciled on an advanced level of synthesis, but this is not the end of dialectical progression for the reason that it continues as the fusion becomes a new thesis with its antithesis and so on. Contrasting Hegel, Marx claimed the ideas are not the realm of fact, but relatively material is. Where Hegel's system could be called "dialectical idealism", Marx provided himself over to the development of what

came to be called not by him but his followers, dialectic materialism. (25-33)

Marx was concerned in the investigation of nature and meaning as well as the veracity of history, but unlike Hegel, he thought that a materialistic analysis and not the idealistic approach to history would extract the truth. The alteration is echoed in Marx's acceptance of French radicalism and the economic pragmatism of the British theorist Adam Smith. This reworking of Hegelian idealism to historical materialism attached with his acceptance of British monetary theory led Marx to accept as true that the encouraging influence in human existence was not ideas about religion and society but a money-oriented realism having to do with subsistence. This subsistence, the requirement to produce the means of survival, was essential to human life and human action in community and society. It was a principal fact underlying all human communications. History for Hegel and Marx, and for the most European intelligentsia, was the focus of their philosophies of humanoid existence. For Marx, human history was the record of the human struggle between men and human efforts to dominate and regulate the environment, physical and social. Marx acknowledged four phases of anthropological history on the base of modes of production: primitive communism, ancient slave production, feudalism, and capitalism. The association which mankind has with one another differs with the mode of production. Primitive collectivism signified communal ownership whereas the prehistoric mode of production was characterized by slavery, the medieval mode of production by serfdom, and the capitalist system by the bourgeois mistreatment of wage earners. Each of these phases, apart from primitive communism, instituted a distinct manner of man's exploitation by man, and his struggle for autonomy.

Marx supposed that the process of dialectical materialism in which men struggle for existence in the competition would come to termination when the waged individuals of the world, the proletariat, came to be adequately strong and politically cognizant that private enterprise would be finally toppled and socialism would be mounted. The fifth and ultimate state would establish a classless society with no private possessions, and no differences sandwiched between controllers and controlled. Conflict and uprising would vanish. Mulk Raj Anand also fantasized of such socialism where class and status terminated in the ideal land. Mulk Raj Anand was one of the ardent Marxists. Further, Anand appraisal of Marx's Letters on India contributed to *New York Herald Tribune*, 1953 and their conversation with comrade Ralph Fox marked noticeable additional turning point in Anand's career, a culmination of a quest for truth:

> And a whole new world was opened to me. All the threads of my past reading, which had got tied up into knots, seemed suddenly to straighten, and I began to see not only the history of India but the whole history of human society in some sort of inter-connection. The fact that Marxian dialectic had naturally developed out of Hegel whom I had read added to the zest of my preoccupation with it. And, of course, the happiest thing was that Marxism was no dogma of a church militant, in spite of the critics who declared it to be only another religion with Marx as its prophet, but a scientific and rational method for the study of society, a hypothesis which was leading to new discoveries. (Anand 105)

According to Francis Abraham and John Henry Morgan (1989):

> Marx believed that no matter how well a society functions in terms of its own order and structure, it was destined to turmoil and revolution until the final breakdown of all class divisions. Even when a society exemplifies the best that mankind can establish in terms of harmony and cooperation, the established order becomes an obstacle to progress, and a new order begins to arise. Creating a new order of production that is a synthesis of the old and the new. The new order, however contains the seeds of destruction and dialectical process to continue. The certainty of the continued struggle is expounded to the emergence of the division of labour at

> intervals in society, for it is this phenomenon of labour differentiation which forms antagonistic classes that in turn become the centre of competition and struggle against nature as well as against other elements within society.... Marx and Engles emphasized the primacy of economics in human relationship and the centrality of the economic dimension in political structures. The national economy of production and distribution, or the means and relations of production in the Marxian sense, constitute the basic structure of society on which are built all other social establishments, particularly the state and legal system. The mode of production in material life determines the over-all character of the social political and otherworldly processes of life. It is not the consciousness of humans that regulates their being, but, on the opposing, their social reality regulates their consciousness. Under the influence of the forces and relations of production, men spend their lives struggling with and against one another for survival and power. (25-34)

Outlining the development of society and history, Anand too believed that in initial phase the natural procedures went on for long. Then by unexpected bounds, the quantum transformed into value. Afterward man started to use machine-driven, physical and chemical properties to fulfill his subsistence needs. In this course, nature with its enormous potentials converted into a zone for exploiting it. To further meet out his requirements, man's manipulation of nature continued with unrelenting vigour. The advancement of civilization added to his requirements substantially which demanded the harnessing of natural resources on large scale. The unremitting misuse of resources of production gave rise to class hatred. Anand perceives in this connection:

> the exploitation of means of production creates production relations which on account of the constant interaction between man and nature, and between the various parts of society, create those contradictions which are inherent, in the development of society. And, as in nature, so in

> society, when the disequilibrium among the conflicting forces reaches a stage at which it is chocked up for want of further development, there occurs the social revolution which by "Leap" takes the property relations through dynamic opposition implicit in them a stage further. And property being an economic, social, as well as political fact, that is to say the basis of the political power of the state, we find those continual alterations in the balance of power which leave wrecks of people behind as the fade-outs of history; shadows in the obscure background of changing world forces. (101-02)

The learning of Marxian thoughts not only resolved various of his rational thinking but also provided him the foundation of his philosophy in life.

1.3 Mulk Raj Anand: The Journey as a Writer

According to Srinivasa Iyengar (1985):

> The nineteen thirties were the seed time of modern independent India: the Gandhian salt satyagraha movement of 1930 and 1932, the three Round table conferences, the passing of the government of India Act of 1935, the introduction of Provincial Autonomy in 1937, the Gandhian movements of Harijan uplift and Basic education, the organization of Marxist parties of diverse hues (the congress socialists, the Royalists, the communists), the involvement in the war in 1939, the schism in the congress leading to the expulsion of Subhas Chandra Bose and his eventual escape to Europe and Japan—it absolutely was a packed decade indeed. (332-33)

In this dynamite age Mulk Raj Anand was having the most inflammable youth and mind which responded to the age he painted through his writings. Anand touched India after his adventures in Europe. The first five novels appeared in the following orders: *Untouchable* (1935), *Coolie* (1936), *Two Leaves and a Bud* (1937), *The Village* (1939), *Across the Black Waters* (1940), *The Sword and the Sickle* (1942), *Private Life of an Indian Prince* (1953), and *The Big Heart* (1980).

He was connected with the progressive writer's movement in India; and after the war, he lastly returned to India and settled down happily in Bombay. During the last twenty or more years he did the editing of *Marg*, a high-class journal dedicated to the Arts, and one of the finest of its kind anywhere. He also published a standard discourse on Hindu erotic art. The leftist peace movements found a zealous follower in him, nevertheless, it must be accepted that politics claims but a portion, a small slice, not the total, of his life. There are numerous narratives and assemblages of short stories. Anand's literary occupation has been astoundingly diverse. He has to his publication sixteen novels, more than eight anthologies of short stories, countless articles on subjects varying from Hindu art to cookery.

Mulk Raj Anand has so far produced dozens of short stories like *The Lost Child and Other Stories* (1934), *The Barber's Trade Union and Other Stories* (1944), and many more. Apart from short stories autobiographical works are also immensely written by him. In his special preface to the second Indian edition of *Two Leaves and a Bud* (1951), Anand has specified his early fervour and determination behind his first work of fiction. Iyengar (1985) writes that in writing of the pariahs and the lowermost dogs rather than of the chosen and the sophisticated, he ought to volunteer into the terrain that had been mostly overlooked till at that moment by Indian writers. For all their patriotic enthusiasm, Bankim Chandra's novels were but romances abstractedly derivative of Scott, with an ancient or numinous gradient; Tagore was predominantly in the higher and middle classes; and Sarat Chandra in the lower middle classes; and Munshi Premchand picked his theme tune from the peasantry and modest folk of Uttar Pradesh. The million unheard voices resonated for the first time by a writer who was far strong enough to debut his writing by making an outcaste a hero, the unsung peasants, slaves, serfs, the waifs, labour the protagonist of his novels. At that period of time, it was unthinkable by any writer to yield out a protagonist amongst the lowest rungs of society, who were non-existent as a living entity for the so-called upper-class society.

Anand was an insatiable student of literature, art, philosophy and many other branches of training he had. His mind having determinative inspirations both of the European and Asiatic on his cognizance and art as well as on the content and technique of his writings. He truthfully acknowledges in his letters, prefaces, articles and *Apology for Heroism* that he has lived and written under the impression of immeasurable writers such as Aristotle, Rousseau, Marx, Ruskin, Bertrand Russell, the Bloomsbury intellectuals, Locke, Iqbal, Gandhi, Buddha, the ancient Indian saints, the English Renaissance scholars, Tagore, Nehru, Bhai Vir Singh, Premchand, Sarat Chand Chatterjee, Bankim Chand Chatterjee, Tolstoy, Dostoevsky, Gorky, Gogol, Turgenev, James Joyce, Cervantes, Fielding, Smollett, Dickens, Hardy, D.H. Lawrence, Wyndham Lewis, Theodore Powys, Sartre, Camus, Freud, Adler, Jung, Einstein, Byron, Shelley, Keats, Mazzini, Proudhon, Victor Hugo, Goethe, Heine, George W.M. Reynolds, Charles Garvice and Rider Haggard. Anand has not only remained able to comprehend the major movements in world literature, but also appropriately understood the numerous fictional forms approaching into being since the days of Cervantes. Besides, he has prudently examined E.M. Forster's *Aspect of the Novel*, Percy Lubbock's *The Craft of Fiction*, and supplementary books and articles on the art of writing.

Thus, the minute Mulk Raj Anand underwent writing, he unquestionably decided that he would choose the accustomed to the imaginary, he would evade the highways of passion, gothic castles, men-women relations, royalty, superiority but to reconnoiter the bylanes of the outcastes, the farmworkers, the sepoys and the working people. Another momentous occurrence that enhanced Anand's working-class awareness was his coincidental involvement in the Spanish Civil War which evidenced to be a purgatorial experience to him. He acknowledged himself with the cause of the Republican party and penned down a leaflet upholding the cause of the communists, who were unflaggingly fighting in contrast to the daunting forces of totalitarianism. In one of his articles, which served as an authentic article of his proletarianism, Anand (1937) observed:

> I am a novelist, a writer of books, of social documents, about a rather neglected country India. And, as I set from day-to-day writing a long novel about the peasants of my country while news of the Spanish war was coming in. I became conscious that the problem of agrarian masses of India was not very unlike that which faced the Spanish peasants, since both these people are emerging from feudalism, since both have for centuries been oppressed by a capricious landlordism, since both are face to face with the brutal tyranny of an upper class anxious to secure its privileges and possessions even if that involves the virtual extermination of the vast masses of the people. (09)

Anand spent all his life fighting for the underprivileged, the unfortunate, the peasants, the outcaste, the labourers, and the miserable beings in the society. But Anand always believed that literature and art has such dimensions to transform human heart, and make us a sensitive person. As born human, it is our natural right to have human rights. And to live life with dignity is the essence of humanity. Equality and human rights were the cornerstones of Anand's humanistic ideology that would solve India's humanitarian problems. According to Dr. Gupta (1974), he believed that:

> Men must realize and accept the profound importance of man—of man as such, shorn of all considerations of class, caste, creed, race, religion, and wealth. The most vital need of our troubled times is to engender among men a genuine respect for man, love for him, and faith in his ability to live a life full of dignity. Anand believes that man can solve his many problems with the help of imagination, reason, and the scientific method. (Anand 15-16)

According to Gillian Packman (1978) in her piece "Mulk Raj Anand and the Thirties Movement in England", Anand's work was:

> Primarily a literature of protest.... Anand shows sympathy in writing of the working classes.... He describes the

> daily life of the oppressed and provides glimpses of the oppressors.... [The] work is a form of social realism which concentrates on the description of human misery without suggesting the possibility of a better future or describing the dynamics of change which develops from man's own actions. However, Anand did better. His novels mirror a society in transition.... He treats the isolation of the modern revolutionary from the social collectivity. He shows his characters learning to take control of their own destiny and coming to accept the value of brotherly love. (57)

According to K.K. Sharma (1978), Anand is one of India's leading authors, and the most outstanding fiction writers of the world. His books are read and esteemed all over the world. His first novel, *Untouchable* (1935), published in the early thirties has been deciphered into twenty world languages and keeps its curiosity intact to this day. Specialized and academic critics, both in India and abroad—Europe, America, and Australia—have appraised his works. As K.N. Sinha (1995) says:

> The first three novels of Mulk Raj Anand—*Untouchable, Coolie* and *Two Leaves and a Bud*—are in class by themselves. They not only present a mirror reflection of the actual life lived by the less fortunate, the lowly, and the disinherited, but move us also to the catharsis of pity. The range of their realism is unlimited. While *Untouchable* deals with the life and fortune of humble scavenger, *Coolie* and *Two Leaves and a Bud* weave the tragedy of the working class. The human situation in each one comes in for sharp criticism, but the irony is diluted to some extent by a tender, moving pathos. These are, indeed, rich, human documents, having varying degree of excellence. (27)

G.L. Gautam in his exhaustive and descriptive work *Mulk Raj Anand's Critique of Religious Fundamentalism: A Critical Assessment of His Novels* published in 1996 highlights the significance of Mulk Raj Anand as a writer for ages to come. According to him:

> In fact what distinguished Mulk Raj Anand from other fiction writers is the fact that he portrays on his fictional landscape the social, religious, economic and ideological conflicts, in their multi-dimensional manifestations, characteristics of the times of his creative writings. In spite of the fact that his characters and their life situations are rooted in the times of the writings, his creative writings are not dull documentations of reality. Nor are they based on the artifice of romantic imagination.... To be more explicit on this point, he depicts reality without dipping his artistic pen in the glittering ink of romantic imagination. Not only in terms of depiction of the contemporary reality but also in context of, and relation to, a problem, no other writer, among the major Indian English writers, rationally discusses a problem under three dimensions, what Hegel in philosophical terminology described, thesis, anti-thesis and synthesis. (13)

While an overabundance of criticism of Indian Scholars is accessible, only critics such as K.R. Srinivasa Iyengar, S.C. Harrex, C.D. Narasimhaiah, Saros Cowasjee, G.S. Balarama Gupta and some others who have shown astonishing significance in Anand's literary career and have produced noteworthy critical scholarship, taken up for review. Amongst the Western critics, it is, Margaret Berry, Marlene Fisher, Alastair Niven, D. Riemenschneider and Jack Lindsay who have written widely on Anand and of course a score of others who have published fine documented, research articles in leading journals. K.R. Srinivasa Iyengar, in his *Indo-Anglian Literature* (1943) renamed as *Indian Writings in English* (1962), has dedicated a chapter to Mulk Raj Anand. Among all these critics, the most distinguished are K.R. Srinivas Iyengar, M.K. Naik, C.D. Narasimhaiah, K.N. Sinha, Jack Lindsay, Saros Cowasjee, Margaret Berry, D. Riemenschneider, Marlene Fisher, William Walsh, Alastair Niven, D.W. Robertson, S.C. Harrex, Ron Shepherd, Mrs. Gillian Packham, Edgell Rickward, Edward Burra, H.M. Williams, G.S. Balarama Gupta, Satyanarain Singh, Debjani Chatterjee, H.C. Raizada, R.S. Singh, C. Vijaysree, and others.

Manmohan K. Bhatnagar in his volume *The Novels of Mulk Raj Anand—A Critical Study* (2000) writes "Mulk Raj Anand is one of the pioneers of progressivism in India literature. His contribution to Indian English literature is phenomenal" (4). In his *Mulk Raj Anand—The Novel of Commitment,* S.A. Khan (2000) writes:

> We have abundance in the work of Anand on the rigidity of caste system, the tyranny of class system, religious bigotry and the predicament of women as.... Mulk Raj Anand is one of the few Indian English Writers internationally acclaimed as a novelist though his works include short stories, criticism, fairy tales, autobiography, language, history, education, politics, arts, films, folk theatres, dance, music feminism and contemporary Indian culture. (01)

No wonder, in acknowledgement of his involvement to literature, he was bestowed the much sought-after Sahitya Akademi Award in 1972. He is the most versatile of Indo-English writers, for he has written, above and beyond fiction, books and articles on wide-ranging topics, such as painting and art, education, show business, criticism, verse, English language, Indian dishes, female beauty, Indian civilization, the story of man, the story of India, memoirs of ideas, etc.

Of all the Indo-English novelists, Mulk Raj Anand has deliberated the art of the novel most knowingly and comprehensively. They are contained in his Prefaces, letters, articles, addresses, conversation, interviews, three essays. Tolstoy is conceivably the first great writer who has brought about this major change in the novel by concentrating on the inward changes in man as against the superficial effects of the external social phenomena. The modern novel portrays the soul's drama of man, and it deals with the crisis of man in every situation. He designates its exact nature as a dramatic depiction, through space and time, of the internal fluctuations in the lives of characters. The definitive purpose of the novel is to make man recognize himself, to stimulate his consciousness, to strengthen his feelings and to enable him to experience *Rasa* or the flavour of exquisiteness. Great novels are the product of great passions. As a substitute for being sugar-coated pills or narcotics, they are gifted of altering human disposition and revolving the world. No doubt, the novel expresses the writer's ultimate experience, the incipient impulses of his or her body-soul, but at the same time, it presents life in its indispensable forms, with all its ambiguity, conflicts and sicknesses. For Mulk Raj Anand, the novel ought to be an apparatus of examination of societal realism, not in its artificial but in its utmost vigorous form. Social realism in a work of art should be poetic in its nature.

Amitabh Roy in his book *The God of Small Things—A Novel of Social Commitment* (2005) draws a parallel between Arundhati Roy and Mulk Raj Anand in the tradition of committed writing. He says:

> Arundhati Roy follows Anand's concern for the victims of caste and class oppression. Velutha is an untouchable and belongs to the working class. His lot is like the heroes of Anand, Velutha too finds himself helpless before a system based on inequality and exploitation. A tea garden in Assam and a pickle factory in Kerala provide the background of casteist and sexual exploitation of the powerless by the powerful in her novel. Thus, her novel blends together certain traits of the three novels of Anand in it and reminds us of Anand's books. (13)

Dr. B.K. Rawat in his work *Mulk Raj Anand—A Critical Study* (2011) points out:

> Mulk Raj Anand belonged to a generation of writers committed to the democratic ideals of egalitarianism and social justice, including stalwarts such as Shivam Karanth, Thakazhi Sivasankara Pillai, Gopinath Mohanty, Tara Sankar Banerjee, Phaneeshwarnath Renu, Khawaja Ahmed Abbas, Sajjad Zaheer, Ali Sardar Jafri, Kaifi Azmi, Sri Sri, Jayakantan, L.S. Ramamritam, Si.Su. Chellappa, Abdul Rehman Rahi and a host of others—who were inspired by the Gandhian identification with the marginalised and the Marxist Principle of the struggle for class justice...who rebelled against every

> form of hierarchy on earth, created their own epoch of secular and socialist literature with its own aesthetic of resistance. (10)

Dr. Farhana Khan published *Mulk Raj Anand—A Critical Spectrum* (2005), T.M.J. Indra Mohan edited *The Novels of Mulk Raj Anand—A New Critical Spectrum* in 2005, Upendra Prasad Singh's *Class Conflicts in the Novels of Mulk Raj Anand* (2005), Alex Tickell's *Arundhati Roy's The God of Small Things* (2007) are some other works on Mulk Raj Anand. Of all his novels as Mulk Raj Anand says *Untouchable* (1935) is the densest and creatively sustaining, *Coolie* (1936) is the most wide-ranging, arousing variegated action, and rich array in character, while *Two Leaves and a Bud* (1937) is the extremely real as a piece of a disguised indictment. Anand appears in his works of fiction as a campaigner against the unfairness of each kind. He persistently clashes with the exploitation of the underprivileged by any class. This consists of the imposing controllers, the village money-lenders, the crooked traders, the native rulers, priests, and tea-planters. So unfathomable is his worry for the unfortunate and the underdogs that in his novels we find him cry with agony against the inequality so predominant in those times.

Anand took upon himself this challenge of bringing into life the characters which he knew could never exist into the pages of a book. He wanted to celebrate the not-so-celebrated faces of human race. The destitute, the workers, the daily bread earners, a low caste Bhangi, tanners, potters, etc. The difficulties they confronted for their existence unknown to the superior, royal and the affluent upper-class people. To sung their woes, their sufferings so that it could tear apart the heart of the merciless society. The characters starting from Bakha, Rakha, Lakha, Chota, Ram Charan, Sohini, Munoo, Gangu, Hari, Lakshmi, Bhikhu, Gauri, Ratan set the order of exploitation and revelation of the unjust system they all faced. These characters are not figments of his imagination but the grassroot masses fighting down the economically, politically, socially. As a humanist, Anand (1975) acknowledged the need for the forgotten and forsaken to be lifted to a level of human dignity. He said:

> I believe, first and foremost, in human beings, in Man, in the whole man...and in his ability to adapt himself to the highest point in the evolutionary process and to a better dispensation.... He can master himself and the universe, create new values and transcend, through imagination, memory and will, all his own highest and deepest awareness, all his past works and struggle to attain the newest and most vital life. (Anand 93-94)

According to one essay "Introduction" written by Nandini Bhattacharya (2008):

> Refusal to accept food cooked by dalit cooks on the part of students (as a part of mid-day meal scheme) in Andhra Pradesh or Marxist-led West Bengal. Atrocities heaped on Dalits in Madhya Pradesh. Massacre of Dalits and destruction of Balmiki bastis (more than 50 homes torched) in Gohana of Haryana by Jats under the congress-led Hooda government on 30th August 2005. On 3rd September 2005, more than 25 dalit homes burnt down in Akola in Maharashtra. Similar incidents keep occurring throughout the nation periodically. (09)

The myriad ways in which a society dictates the norms of purity and pollution humiliates those whom it considers the "other". More than seventy years after becoming a republic and abolishing discrimination based on caste, gender, race and so on, there is no change on the ground. Introducing Mulk Raj Anand's *Untouchable* (1935), *The Road* (1961) to modern reader seemed the right time to present randomly selected information from newspapers, news journal, and television reports. A reading of Mulk Raj Anand's *Untouchable, The Road* forces the reader to come to terms with, not only an extremely uncomfortable and painful aspect of Indian history but also to recognise the roots of several oppressive structures which flourish in contemporary India. It compels the reader to confront the paradoxes and contradictions at the heart of the Indian struggle for independence as well as the contradictions that mire claims of a modern, egalitarian, equitable society. *Untouchable, The Road* as well as other works of Anand is relevant because, even after so many years of Indian Independence, far from fading out as a primitive, barbaric custom, caste prejudice is a rampant issue in contemporary India, and repeated atrocities heaped on Dalits across the country are a testimony to it. Scavengers (or *bhangis* as they are called in local parlance) are in many insidious ways still 'untouchables', even though untouchability has been recognised in the Indian constitution as a cognizable offence. In spite of giant leaps in technology in many spheres, modes of waste removal in large cosmopolitan cities have still remained repulsively primitive and dependent community of scavengers who have been initiated as *safai karmacharis* (sanitation staff) by the government. According to Nandini Bhattacharya:

> Through his novels Mulk Raj Anand compels the reader to engage in some questions as how is the nation to be imagined at a critical juncture of history, when Indians were fighting for freedom from colonial stranglehold. On whose behalf is the new nation being imagined? Does this demand for independence and equality, this protest against British racism (which renders any person of colour as 'untouchable') have any relevance in a country where a large number of people are segregated, and systematically alienated from the mainstream because of the accident of their birth? Are these marginalized, desperately poor and reviled people, actually included in the act of imagining a new nation? The key to the relevance of Anand's novels lies in the exploration of the 'untouchable'. How could these people who have enslaved millions within their own fold, in the name of religion, and condemned them to live a life worse than animals? How could they root for Independence? How could one speak of, or even 'imagine' one nation, where caste Hindus would not even touch a majority of their countrymen, let alone dine or have other social relations with them? (10-11)

1.4 Early Dalit Writings: Pre-Independence Era

Mulk Raj Anand's writings are an interesting example of early writing on Dalit problems by a writer who himself belonged to the 'upper castes' but whose broad humanistic sympathy was able to expose the inhuman structures of exploitation and deprivation in pre- and post-colonial India, all in the name of 'religion' and 'tradition'. But there were other non-Dalit writers too such as A. Madhaviah's *Thillai Govindan* (1908), T. Suryanarayana's *Himavati* (1913), Venkata Parvatisvara Kavalu's *Matrimandiramu* (1919), Saratchandra Chattopadhyaya's Bengali novels such as *Abhagir Swarga* (1929), Munshi Premchand's *Sirf Ek Awaz*, *Sadgati*, and *Thakur Ka Kuan* in Hindi; Thagazhi Sivasankara Pillai's *Oru Thotiyin Magan* (The Scavenger's Son, 1947); Shivarama Karanth's Kannada novel *Chomana Dudi* (The Drums of Choma).

Mulk Raj Anand's works can be better appreciated if the reader situates it within a tradition of protest literature addressing the caste and class issues in India and considers his writings as a predecessor of Dalit writings, which engages specifically with this reality of marginalisation and deprivation of lower classes in modern India. A comparative reading of Anand's works and writings of later and professedly Dalit writers such as Daya Pawar, Lakshman Mane, Sharankumar Limbale, Om Prakash Valmiki or Bama, could help the reader to assess Anand's progressive ideology, and situate it within this tradition of activist and protest literature. It could also make the reader aware of the difference between these older 'fictions of sympathy' (written within the ambit of broadly Gandhian or progressive Marxists ideologies) which made an appeal to the upper-caste reader's conscience, and Dalit fiction that emerged in the late 1950s and 1960s in Marathi and later in Kannada, Tamil, Hindi, Bengali and other languages to uphold the Ambedkarite dictum of 'educate, unite, organise', and use the experiences in the lives of the oppressed Dalit communities to provoke the reader's anger and violence and thereby mobilise them into action. But there has been allegation also that the so-called upper-class writers who talked about Dalits offered only sympathy and refused to upset the apple-cart of age-old privileges. Bakha in his person prefigures this approaching storm of protest. *Untouchable* reminds us all over again of the necessity of addressing problems of systematic marginalisation and segregation of human beings in the name of religion, tradition, and redressing these issues before they erupt to tear apart the fabric of a so-called democratic and 'modern' Indian nation.

Discussion of the literary and cultural representations of the marginalized and the dispossessed people, such as members of India's untouchable and aboriginal communities, has, for the most part, been based on the writings of upper-caste writers, such as Mulk Raj Anand, Mahasweta Devi and Premchand. For Dalit writers, many of these narratives are part of a 'discourse of pity'. Since most Dalit writing, and discussion of this writing, have been in the various regional languages of India, very little of either is accessible in English. This is a major gap, given that much of the theorizing in India and abroad about Indian literatures, culture and society, whether from Marxist, postcolonial or subaltern perspectives, has been in English. Only some of the theorists have drawn on materials from the regional languages, and even they have taken virtually no note of interventions by Dalits.

1.5 Contemporary Writers: Post-Independence Era and The Quest Continues

Dalits are an important political and social force in India. Their literary and critical writings constitute a major challenge to, and questioning of, the theorizing about Indian politics, society, culture and literature by intellectuals from upper-caste Hindu and other dominant communities, and by non-Indians. To fail to pay attention to this challenge and questioning, is to engage in a hegemonic discourse that excludes the realities and experiences of nearly a quarter of the country's people. Aniket Jaaware's "Eating, and Eating with, the Dalit: A Re-consideration Touching upon Marathi Poetry" remains "the only literary criticism in English from within the Dalit community". Sharankumar Limbale, a pre-eminent contemporary Dalit writer in Marathi and Hindi, came to prominence with the publication of *Akkarmashi*, his autobiographical narrative of rural Dalit life. Originally written in Marathi, it became available to a wider audience when the Hindi translation appeared in 1991 and the English translation, *The Outcaste*, was made available in 2003. Though Limbale's book is concerned primarily with the evolution and features of Dalit literature in Marathi, the conclusions he draws and the case that he makes regarding the distinct purpose, politics and poetics of Dalit literature have wider relevance. Limbale argues that Dalit literature is unique, even though its evolution may be seen in the context of the history of various regional literatures—Marathi, in his own case.

Dalit Sahityache Saundaryashastra is a response. According to Sharankumar Limbale, Dalit writers have insisted that their writing has a particular purpose and audience, that these have an important bearing on their literary/aesthetic decisions, and, therefore, their work should not be assessed by 'universal' criteria, which, in India, carry the markers of caste and class. This has led to a rather heated reaction from upper-caste literary critics. Dalit writing has been accused of lacking in literary merit when measured against universal criteria. Dalit writers have been charged with being divisive and sectarian, using disrespectful and offensive language towards Hindu divinities and revered figures, and engaging in distortions of pre- and post-independence Indian history. It has been suggested that some Dalits were treating literature as simply another arena of affirmative action, and were claiming to be writers even though they did not have the ability to write. For example, Bhavdev Pandey, "Hindi Sahitya kaa Savarna Itihaas: Nahin, Yeh Jaativad Nahin Hai" (Caste History of Hindi Literature: No, This is Not Casteism); Namwar Singh, quoted in Roopchand Gautam, "Dalit Sahitya Par Aur Bhi Bahas Jaroori Hai" (Further Debate about Dalit Literature is Essential).

Limbale's book is dialogically related to these critiques and questionings, insofar as dialogism, according to Bakhtin, involves conflict. Limbale asserts that Dalit literature is distinct. He points out that Dalit reality is a liminal reality in time and space. The content and form of the literature that is about this liminality has its own particular features. In identifying these particularities, his works talks back to the universalist assertions of India's dominant group literary theorists. Limbale's rejection of the hegemony of the caste-based universal challenges the neat binary world of postcolonial literary theory by calling attention to the internal contradictions of Indian society.

Limbale is not the only Dalit writer to have written on the form and purpose of Dalit literature. As the body of this literature grows, the subject has begun to receive considerable attention. His book *Towards an Aesthetic of Dalit Literature* is so comprehensive since it locates Dalit literature within a historical context, foregrounds its ideological concerns, and identifies its literary and aesthetic characteristics in a way that few other writings on the subject do. Critics besides Limbale have been troubled by the treatment of Dalit characters in the writings of such prominent writers as Premchand and Mulk Raj Anand. In their view, these representations do not show Dalits as they are, but as helpless and child-like people who cannot make their own decisions or take actions. In Anand's novel, *Untouchable*, for example, the protagonist, Bakha, instead of opting for radical action, submits to Gandhi's pacifism, and thus confined. But, more or less Mulk Raj Anand played a very important role to bring the Dalits identity not only in India but also to the whole world through his works which were written in English. He played a remarkable part on merging the Dalit cause with Marxism through his exploration of caste and class in Indian perspective. Mulk Raj Anand followed Marxism all his life. He worked for the welfare of the people or the masses.

Mulk Raj Anand being a savarna, and an upper-caste Dalit writer believed that all people, by right of being born human, deserve respect and to live a life of dignity. He believed that man is the center of the universe. By virtue of this egocentric thought, it is then man's responsibility to develop further through individual growth, therefore engaging and inspiring the entire human race to mature in a positive and humanistic manner. This mental expansion must recognize, according to Anand's humanistic philosophy, that man is indeed the hub of all experience; it must be acknowledged therefore that all men—human beings—are morally and justly equal. He believed in the autonomy of human reason and denied any power or moral value superior to that of humanity. He had faith in the advancement of humanity by its own efforts and was committed to the betterment of the entire human race.

People like Laxman Gaikwad, Lakshman Mane, Madhav Kondvilkar, Kishor Kale and Ashok Pawar and many other writes in regional languages were writing much better than Mulk Raj Anand. Much of the Dalit literature is to be found in the regional languages and has to be translated into English on a massive scale. In recent times this rebellion has taken a new form. Some Dalit writers and activists have started using their community surnames, previously meant to humiliate and segregate them from other castes, in order to contest caste hegemonies. For example, in West Bengal the poet-activist Kalyani Thakur has added 'Charal' to her surname indicating that she is proud of being Chandal, one of the untouchable communities referred to in the *Manusmriti*. Similarly, the famous Bengali Dalit writer Manoranjan Byapari has published his autobiography titled *Itibritte Chandal Jibon* (2014; translated as *Interrogating My Chandal Life: An Autobiography of a Dalit* in 2018). A Dalit activist-historian from Uttar Pradesh, Bikram Harijan, who teaches history at Banaras Hindu University, deliberately uses Gandhi's euphemism 'harijan' in order to comment on the fact that a 'bastard' child of India, who, in Hindu parlance is also a god's child, cannot choose either a name or surname without following caste rules. Akhila Naik's *Bheda* (2010), Meena Kandasamy's *The Gypsy Goddess* (2014) are some of the examples of novels. Ajay Navaria's *Unclaimed Terrain* (2013), and Gogu Shyamala's *Father May Be an Elephant and Mother Only A Small Basket, but...* (2012) are examples of anthologies of short stories, and Premanand Gajvee's *The Strength of Our Wrists* (2013) is an example of drama. An entire pool, a huge stream, will have to be created, and a debate should be proved. Dalit literature is action and writers have to engage in action, and it is only through writers being activists that Dalit literature can stay alive. A Dalit writer must possess a particular consciousness and commitment. When we remove consciousness and commitment, he or she will no longer be a Dalit writer. Therefore, the primary requirements for Dalit writers is that they must be committed to their society and must have Dalit consciousness in their hearts and minds. Dalit literature from its inception has come a long way today. But we should not forget that its Mulk Raj Anand's works that struck the chord of the hearts of millions through his classical work *Untouchable* in the pre-independence era where writing about a scavenger was considered dirty as we know very well that his book *Untouchable* was considered a 'dirty book'. There lies the uniqueness of Mulk Raj Anand's work. He through his work in english spoke for the millions of humiliated, voiceless souls across the universe. In this context, Raj Kumar comments (2019):

> English is one of the most sought-after languages in the globalized world, and so Dalit writers and activists feel that Dalits should avail of English education as it can only be to their advantage.... English is also considered to be a language of liberation because unlike Indian languages, which are inherently casteist, english is relatively 'caste neutral'. One of the best examples of this is Mulk Raj Anand's *Untouchable* which refers to Dalit community such as bhangi, mala, madiga or mahar. Each of these denotes a particular and demeaning occupational status in the caste society. Other than that, these groups have no identity. It is in this sense that the term 'untouchable', as compared to bhangi, mala, madiga or mahar, is in many ways neutral because it does not suggest any particular traditional occupation of a Dalit Community.... English has become the language of survival and decolonization for Dalits. (118-21)

Mogalli Ganesh, a Kannada Dalit writer and activist observes that it is the English language that will give Dalits the opportunity to liberate themselves. But there are also contrasting opinions regarding English education among Dalits like M. Dasan, who thinks English being language of the rulers, is hegemonic and therefore discriminates between its recipients, particularly those at the margins.

Anand is brilliant at satirizing the bigotries and orthodoxies of his times which are still relevant in modern Indian society which is in flux and caught between traditionalism and modernity. Anand opposed racial, national, religious, and class prejudices. He crusaded against illiteracy, and in favour of government aided public education and free elementary schools for the poor. He crusaded for proper sewage disposal, cheap and unlimited water supply and regulation of industries vital to health. The entire question of sanitation, disease, and public health was further acerbated with the rapid urbanisation, sudden explosion of population, and creation/accumulation of unmanageable waste in the European as well as Indian urban spaces. All these concerns inform and enrich our reading of *Untouchable, Coolie, Two Leaves and a Bud, The Road*. Anand was after all a westernized liberal intellectual, located for a very long period in the heart of the western metropolis, and shared with the western liberal intellectuals, an abiding concern for sanitation, waste management, and public health of the community, at the juncture of social transition. At the same time, Anand's acute awareness that in a colonised country, the racially 'othered' native subject is overdetermined as 'dirty' and 'polluted' by his colonial masters from the very outset-problematizes any simplistic reading of *Untouchable* as a text dealing with sanitation as a civic issue. He demanded the replacement of slums by decent housing for the poor, pleads for the establishment of playgrounds for children and advocates systematic municipal planning. He insists that industrialists must not be allowed to mutilate and kill their labourers in order to save the cost of preventing accidents, working men have right to organise into unions and calls upon the working class to use its power to turn the indifferent and incapables out on streets and force the government to remedy the ills from which the poor suffer. Therefore, we can say that Anand's novels are still relevant even today. It has not grown outdated or superfluous but is a great work of art.

Works Cited

Abraham, Francis and John Henry Morgan. *Sociological thought from Comte to Sorokin*. London: Wyndham Hall Press, 1989. Print.

Anand, Mulk Raj. *The Bubble*. New Delhi: Arnold Heinemann, 1984. Print.

——. “Why I Write”. Ed. K.K. Sharma. *Indo-English Literature*. Ghaziabad: Vimal Prakashan, 1977. Print.

——. *Apology for Heroism: A Brief Autobiography of Ideas*. New Delhi: Arnold Heinemann, 1986. Print.

——. *Confession of a Lover*. New Delhi: Arnold Heinemann, 1976. Print.

——. *Morning Face*. Bombay: Kutub Popular, 1968. Print.

——. *Seven Summers*. New Delhi: Orient Paperbacks, 1970. Print.

——. *The Invincible Will to Live*, Congress Socialist (29th May, 1937). Print.

——. *Untouchable*. “Introduction” by Nandini Bhattacharya. Noida: Longman Study Edition Pearson, 2008. Print.

Bhatnagar, Manmohan K. and M. Rajeshwar. *The Novels of Mulk Raj Anand—A Critical Study*. New Delhi: Atlantic Publisher, 2000. Print.

Dayal, Har. *Hints for Self-culture*. Bombay: Jaico Publishing House, 1983. Print.

Edward, Paul. Ed. *Encyclopaedia of Philosophy*, volumes 3, 4, New York: Macmillan Co. and the Free Press, 1967. 308. Print. https://www.encyclopedia. com/people/philosophy-and-religion/philosophy-biographies/immanuel-kant.

Gautam, G.L. *Mulk Raj Anand's Critique of Religious Fundamentalism*. Delhi: Kanti Publisher, 1996. Print.

Gupta, G.S. Balarama. *Mulk Raj Anand: A Study of His Fiction in Humanist Perspective*. Bara Bazar, Bareilly: Prakash Book Depot, 1974. Print.

Iyengar, Srinivasa. *Indian Writing in English*. New Delhi: Sterling Publishers, 1985. Print.

Khan, S.A. *Mulk Raj Anand—The Novel of Commitment*. New Delhi: Atlantic Publisher, 2000. Print.

Kumar, Raj. *Dalit Literature and Criticism*. Hyderabad: Orient Black Swan Private Publication, 2019. Print.

Lexicon Universal Encyclopaedia. Volume 4, New York: Lexicon Publication Inc, 1987. Print.

Mathew, Philip and Ajit Muricken. *Religion, Ideology and Counter-Culture*. Bangalore: Horizon Books, 1987. Print.

Niven, Alastair. *The Yoke of Pity: A Study in Fictional Writings of Mulk Raj Anand*, New Delhi: Arnold Heinemann, 1978. Print.

Packman, Gillian. "Mulk Raj Anand and the Thirties Movement in England." *Perspectives on Mulk Raj Anand*. Ghaziabad: Vimal Prakashan, 1978. Print.

Rawat, B.K. *Mulk Raj Anand—A Critical Study*. New Delhi: Omega Publishers, 2011. Print.

Roy, Amitabh. *The God of Small Things—A Novel of Social Commitment*. New Delhi: Atlantic Publishers, 2005. Print.

Sharma, K.K. *Perspectives on Mulk Raj Anand*. Ghaziabad: Vimal Prakashan, 1978. Print.

Sinha, K.N. *Mulk Raj Anand*. New Delhi: Kalyani Publishers, 1995. Print.

Srinivas, M.N. *Caste in Modern India and Other Essays*. Bombay: Asia Publishing House, 1972. Print.

Singh, Yogendra. *Sociological Bulletin*, Vol. xvii. No. 2, 1968. Print.

2

Historiography of Division: The Class System

2.1 Class: The Concept

Even though the term *class* has been functional to social clusters in a wide range of societies, including ancient city-states, early empires, and caste or feudal societies, it is most usefully confined to the societal divisions in contemporary societies, particularly industrialized ones. Social classes must be distinguished from status groups; the former is based primarily upon financial interests, while the latter are constituted by evaluations of the honour or prestige of an occupation, cultural position, or family descent. Theories of social classes were fully expounded only in the 19th century, as the modern social sciences, especially Sociology. Political philosophers such as Thomas Hobbes, John Locke, and Jean-Jacques Rousseau discussed the issues of social disparity and stratification. In the late 18th, and early 19th centuries, this idea was taken farther by the French social theorist Henri de Saint-Simon, Marx. The governing class, according to Marx, gearshifts not only material production but also the conception of ideas; it thus establishes meticulous cultural style and an overriding political canon, and its control over society is consolidated in a particular type of dogmatic system. Rising classes that gain strength and authority as a result of changes in the mode of production generate political doctrines and movements in opposition to the ruling class.

According to the Book *Analysis of the Marxist Philosophy* by Mary Claire, the philosophy of class is at the Centre of Marx's social theory, for it is the societal classes formed within a specific mode of production that incline to establish a fastidious form of state, animate political conflicts, and bring about leading changes in the constitution of society. The construction of a society includes its culture, establishments, political power structures, roles, rituals, and state predominates. In Orthodox Marxism, the base determines the superstructure in a unidirectional relationship. History, for Hegel and Marx, and for the most European intellectuals, was the focus of their theories of human existence. For Marx, human history was the record of human struggle amongst men and human efforts to dominate and control the environment, physical and social. According to Francis Abraham and John Henry Morgan (1989):

> To Marx, the most distinguishing characteristic of any society is its form of property, and the crucial determinant of an individual's behaviour is his relation to property. Classes are measured on the basis of person's relation to the resources of production. It is not a man's occupation however but his place comparative to the tools of production that determines his category. (37)

Succeeding theories of 'class' have been chiefly concerned with revising, refuting, or providing an alternative to Marxism. Many opponents of Marxist theory have focused attention on the purposeful interdependence of different classes and their harmonious collaboration with each other. And in reality, by the late 20th century, it seemed undeniable that the classes in capitalist societies had tended to lose their distinctive character, while the antagonism between them had declined to such an extent that in most economically advanced countries it no longer created serious political conflict. Moreover, Marxism's prophecy of the proletariat's successful revolution against the bourgeoisie class and the replacement of the capitalist system with a classless society has not shown any result, and when we see the miserable record of most 20th-century Marxist governments and their collapse from in-house causes between 1989 and 1991, as Marx claims appear hollow to us. Society is usually divided into three classes: higher or the elite, labour (or lower), and middle.

Historically, the principal disparity with the upper class in industrial societies was provided by the working class, which traditionally consisted of blue-collar workers in the extractive and manufacturing industries. Given the vast spreading out of the service sector in the world's most advanced economies, it has been indispensable to broaden this definition to include in the working class those persons who hold low-paying, low-skilled, non-unionized jobs in such service industries as food service and retail sales. The main characteristic of the working class as a whole is a lack of housing, fooding, property, lack of decent life, opportunities, and dependence on wages.

In Indian society, the evils of capitalism became manifest immediately after the British introduced modern industries. In introducing the mechanical mode of production, the British did not aim to end ills of medievalism, which afflicted the Indian society, but were motivated by the sole objective of earning a profit. The devil of capitalism, which settled down in the cities of India, grew into a monster on the blood of shriveled workers, with its dark shadows spelling doom in the traditional rustic life in India. The brunt of the attack of the forces of capitalism had to be borne by the poor and lower-middle classes in cities and villages. S.K. Bhattacharya (1986) remarks in this connection:

> In the traditional villages people used to produce goods and offer services to meet the domestic needs of the village only. These goods and service were exchanged not through money but most directly to customary rules, and occasionally through barter. Commodity market was unknown except in some urban centres grown in response to administrative needs. These urban centres had very little impact upon the internal life and activities of the villagers. When the British traders came they made serious inroads into those villages by introducing money as the medium of exchange for commodities produced by the villagers. (239)

The culture of selfishness cast its evil shadow on the existing social relations and contaminated them by the love of money. Even the familial ties which, before the private property cast its shadow, were full of warmth and compassions, were drowned... "in the icy water of egotistical calculation" (Marx and Engels 38).

The same happened in India too. The industrial and commercial culture grew up in the environment of naked self-interest by sucking the life blood of workers and low classes. Hence, the thousands of workers who hired out their labour in the factories were paid so low wages as were hardly enough to buy them two square meals a day. The population in industrial cities, therefore, got stratified, to use Marx's words, "...into two hostile camps, into two great classes directly facing each other" (Marx and Engels 36). The bourgeoisie and the proletariat were two prominent classes in cities in India. To the bourgeoisie, the proletariat stands in antagonistic terms, according to Marx because..."naked, shameless, direct brutal exploitation" of the latter by the former. Tracing the origin of the former, A.R. Desai (1966) remarks:

> As a result of the enormous expansion of internal and foreign trade, the establishment of modern industries and banks in India, a new class developed, a class of modern commercial, industrial and financial bourgeoisie. This class was as in other countries, economically the strongest class in India. (200)

It is in this context that Anand looks at the Indian society in *Coolie, Two Leaves and a Bud* and *The Big Heart* with the Marxist perspective of class structure and class struggle. When Mulk Raj Anand read a letter written by Marx on India in *The New York Herald Tribune* of 1853, he judgmentally scrutinized how the historic forces were restructuring the prevailing societal relations, the status and religious splits giving way to class relations. Though Anand has been ambivalent towards the influences that moulded his creative faculty, he owes gratitude to Marx for giving him a clear insight in understanding the historical forces of society. This historical method of reasoning made Anand see through the evils of class-divided society.

2.2 The Concept of Exploitation

The word 'exploitation' sounds the keynote of the themes that Anand proceeds to examine in his novels. In fact, the processes unleashed in the socio-political and cultural realms of a country as a consequence of colonial intrusion, are marked by an overwhelmingly exploitive character. It will be no exaggeration to affirm that Anand has consistently investigated the theme of exploitation. Exploitation in Marxist jargon signifies the iniquitous relationships that prevail in the economic sphere only. It is again from the Marxist perception of poverty and exploitation at the micro and macro levels that we have inherited terms such as class, the proletariat, labour, surplus, means and mode of production, used to analyse a capitalistic system. According to Marx, society is divided into two classes, the poor and the rich, also called the ruled and the ruling classes or the dominated and the dominant classes. Marx predicted a class struggle consequent upon the appropriation and accumulation of surplus value in the hands of owners of capital and the deprived proletariat becoming poorer and poorer. In his views, the history of modern society is the story of the struggle between these two classes. The phenomenon of production of extremes of poverty and wealth, pauperism and luxury will sharpen the class-struggle until it breaks into an open revolution. The end-product will be stateless socialism wherein production will be carried on for the good of all and bring about the classless society.

No wonder then that Anand who came under the influence of Marx's writings and was fascinated by Marxist theory of social change and revolution, set out as a writer to expose the evils of a capitalist society divided into these two polarities or classes. In particular, Anand's attention is focused on the aftermath of the colonial imposition of an alien world order. Margaret Berry (1970) sums up Anand's method of attacking the capitalist system in this manner:

> Anand's attack on the capitalist system is executed in the novels by direct and indirect presentation of the evils of private ownership, private enterprises and the profit motive in business. Even in the first novel, *Untouchable*, Sarshar the socialist calls for a casteless and classless society. In depicting the road to such a society, Anand does more than dramatize the issues with plots, themes

> and settings. His 'approved' characters boldly expound the socialist program and with dialectic and oratory, compound their opponents—villains, 'respectable' compromisers, and sincere but unenlightened men. (63)

Exploitation is a correlative term with society since society is the area where any individual or group exploit any other individual or group on different dimensions. In the simplest of words, the term exploitation refers to the using another person's labour or work without offering adequate rewards including all kinds of abuses as physical, verbal, emotional, sexual, psychological and mental. This thesis is an attempt to bring out some elements of exploitation of underprivileged in Mulk Raj Anand's *Coolie* (1936), *Two Leaves and a Bud* (1937) in particular and some short stories, and narratives by other writers.

2.3 Detailed Analysis of *Coolie*

Coolie (1936) has a very simple linear plot structure. The action begins when fourteen-year-old orphan, Munoo, has to leave his village home to earn his livelihood in the town. The novel follows a picaresque tradition as Munoo goes from misadventures to untimely death. *Coolie* is epical in sweep and landscaping in purview, pictures of the effects that the pervasive evil of class-system has a poor hill-boy, Munoo. *Coolie* published in 1936 is an artistic work depicting the widening gap between the haves and the have-nots, the exploiters and the exploited, the ruler and the ruled. *Coolie* is acclaimed as folk epic of modern India. The novel is ramified into five chapters. It is an exhaustive saga which details on how Munoo, right from childhood, is entangled into hardships unless he precipitates and eventually succumbs to consumption. Munoo and his fellow coolies are exploited by the force of industrialization, capitalism, communalism, and colonialism. Munoo is not only the victim of such exploitation, but the novelist also makes it quite clear, that such exploitation and denial of life and happiness is the lot of the poor everywhere in India, whether in village like Bilaspur or a small town like Sham Nagar, or big cities like Daulatpur and Bombay. *Coolie* the novel is the saga of pre-Independent

India embedded with the detailed sociological, economical, political and cultural history of the nation as well as Munoo. The novel exposes the monster of capitalism, cross-section of Indian society from the lowest stratum to the rich businessmen and the haughty English Colonialists. Peter Quenelle called the novel "India seen third class" other items used for the novel include "The Odyssey of Munoo through India."

Munoo was a young boy of fourteen years and an orphan living with his unloving and uncaring aunt Gujri and his uncle Daya Ram. He is made a servant in the house of Daya Ram's employee Babu Nathoo Ram and his wife, Bibi Uttam Kaur who underfeeds him, harasses and humiliates the poor servant, who is a mere boy of a very delicate age. Munoo as a servant is untouchable within the house of Babu Nathoo Ram. Nathoo Ram's daughter pushes Munoo away when he prances on all fours like a monkey to play with them. Sheila tells him: you are a servant boy; you must not play with us.

He was condemned by the sinful structure of class continuously to remain as trivial object. The community in which Munoo finds himself at Babu Nathoo Ram's is one obsessed by capital. That the head of the family is employed in the Imperial Bank of India is an initial indication of what later becomes clear. Anand through these pages, is again intruding his own views, more directly than he has done in *Untouchable*. He comments thus on Munoo's naiveté:

> He did not know that the superciliousness, the complacency, the assurance, the happiness they radiated was built on the strong foundation of money, that easy, privileged and secure life of theirs: that good wealth was nourished by the food which money brought. (*Coolie* 36)

When he was first taken to Babu Nathoo Ram's house Munoo's uncle has told him that 'Money is everything', and Munoo comes to realize this truth early. He begins to understand that the division of rich and poor is more important even than caste. He begins to come in terms with the belief that there must be more poor people in the world than rich, and that suffering must therefore, be a condition of human life universally as he, a poor individual, is suffering at the hands of a rich family now. Munoo frequently thinks over his sad plight and tries to find out the reason for his sufferings:

> 'What am I—Munoo?' he asked himself as he lay wrapped in his blanket, early one morning. 'I am Munoo, Babu Nathoo Ram's servant,' the answer came to his mind. (*Coolie* 34)

He runs away from the house of Babu Nathoo Mal, unable to bear the cruelty and beating any longer: "a whipped dog hides in a corner; a whipped human seeks escape" (*Coolie* 59). Munoo broods over his own condition: "There must be only two kinds of people in the world, the rich and the poor" (*Coolie* 56), he thinks. After the sad episode at Sham Nagar, Munoo ran to the unknown taking a train trip. He reached Daulatpur where Prabha Dayal fished him out of the train. He was also a man from hills, so he took Munoo into his shelter and provided him employment in the pickle factory. The factory was located in the street called the Cat Killer's Lane. Though the pickle factory life was not easy but Munoo was loved like a son by Prabha's wife Parbati. Anand's description of the pickle factory is realistic, yet highly suggestive. A host of details which Anand had from a first-hand knowledge is hinted in his autobiographical *Morning Face*. He has known such a factory by his house in Amritsar. The workers of the factory working from "day to day in the dark underworld, full of the intense heat of blazing furnaces and the dense malodorous smells of brewing essences, spices and treacle, of dust and ashes.... They ran about bare-footed and naked except for loin-clothes" (*Coolie* 92) show themselves what they are. Anand observed in the novel *Coolie*:

> They worked long hours, from dawn to past midnight, so mechanically that they never noticed the movements of their own, or each other's hands. Only the sweat trickled down their bodies and irritated them into an awareness that they were engaged in strenuous physical occupation. (92)

But tragedy befell soon and Prabha was running on financial difficulties being cheated by his own partner Ganpat. As said earlier by Munoo that money is everything, indeed it is. This lesson is further enforced by the happenings at Daulatpur where Munoo is forced to work as a coolie because his employer and benefactor Seth Prabh Dayal has been cheated and rendered bankrupt through the fraudulent conduct of his partner, Ganpat. Since Prabha is ruined he is advised by the doctor to go again to the hills, so that he can regain his health. Since there is no money and job left with Prabha, he goes back leaving Munoo in Daulatpur with a heavy heart. For some time Munoo works as a coolie at the Railway station but again takes a train to the unknown city of Bombay where he has heard that there is plenty of money for everyone. But as he lands to Bombay, the mirage is broken. Bombay being a crueler city than ever he has experienced. The Exploitation of the gullible Munoo continues unabated at Bombay—the industrial and commercial capital of India.

Coolies in India are a beast of burden more manageable, less expensive. The competition that Munoo faces in the Grain Market shows the inhuman rush for the survival of the existence. Each coolie tries to compete with other in asking less money and promising heavier load on his back. But there is God's plenty and Lalaji goes on refusing them all. In the night, the coolies fight among themselves for a share of the market courtyard to rest their naked bodies. The way they rest their mortal bodies to spend the night in the courtyard is also a horrible picture of what man has made of man:

> The bodies of numberless coolies lay strewn in tattered grabs. Some were curled up in knots, other lay face downwards on folded aims, others were flat on their chests, pillowing their heads on their bundle of boxes, others crouched into corners talking, others still huddled together at the doorsteps of closed shops, or lay on the broads in a sleep which looked like death, but that it was broken by deep sighs. (*Coolie* 162)

Munoo somehow manages a job at Sir George White's Cotton mill there and meets Hari Har and his wife Lakshmi who are the fellow dwellers in the hell cotton factory. The description of the working conditions is deeming and darkening:

> ...congested with the bodies of the coolies, coloured like the earth on which they lay snoring or crouching round a communal hubble-bubble, or shifting to explore a patch clear of puddles on which to rest. The smell of stagnant drains, rotten grains, fresh cow-dung and urine, the foul savour of human and animal breath and pungent fumes of smouldering fuel cakes, all combined to produce an odorous atmosphere in the compound, sickening until you were used to it,...the of sprawling naked bodies, glistening with sweat, or sheeted like ghosts, in a vain attempt to escape the flies and mosquitoes that hovered like an invisible plague in the darkness. (*Coolie* 116-17)

The above passage throws enough light on the Indian Coolies living in unhygienic condition and lacking even the barest room to lay their tired bodies. They are transported to animal world, the world of rotten grains, fresh cow-dung and urines. Anand here poses the question—Are these Coolies not human beings? In fact, they are living with the same senses—passions, affections, food and diseases as other human-beings on the planet. But in spite of their strenuous labour, they are deprived of even the basic needs and rights. Anand discovers in life of Coolies a real world of shocking miseries.

Munoo's plight is symbolically presented by Anand as he makes his child-hero wander from place to place in search of a job, a livelihood. Munoo's experiences in Sham Nagar in the family of Babu Nathoo Ram are evidence enough to bring out the kind of ill-treatment meted out to a poor wretch just because he is destitute. He is told clearly that he is no more than a servant and hence cannot hope to mix with people of the rank and dignity of Babu Nathoo Ram's family. His sojourn in Daulatpur, working as a labourer in the pickle factory owned by Prabha, a former coolie and Ganpat a crooked and villainous partner who eventually swindles him, has been described by Anand with a keen eye for details of Munoo's psychological reactions, revulsions, and final disillusionment. He is made to realise that it is only the likes of Ganpat and Sir Todar Mal who have access to big money and therefore to influence and power, who can lead a comfortable, easy-going and pleasure-seeking life while honest and hard-working poor have no chance of survival. Anand further pits his waif-hero against the powerful and unscrupulous world of the rich mill-owners in Bombay. Over to Bombay, the new exploiters is the foreman, Jimmi Thomas (Chimta Sahib) in Sir George white cotton mills. He is even crueler than Ganpat at Daulatpur. He beats and abuses the workers and considers their wives as his own property. He is a thoroughly repulsive character. He calls Hari, a mill worker, 'a stupid bullock' and treats the factory workers as if they were animals. Anand has beautifully described the life of the coolie in Bombay factory:

> The atmosphere though, the atmosphere, the wild hum of the machine, the jig-jig-jigging of its pistons, the tick-tick-ticking of its knobs, the furious motion of the broad conveyor belts across its wheels, the clanking of chains, the heat they all generated, and the heavy, greasy odour of oil mixed with the taste of the fresh cotton thread, not offensive by itself, but sickening like bile in the mouth—from all this seemed to rise a black shadow, strangling one at the throat with its powerful invisible fingers.... There was nowhere for the coolie working in the factory to wash, except at a pump in the grounds at the back, among huge drums of oil and bales of cotton, where a hundred men crowded round to get a drink. (*Coolie* 187-88)

Here again Munoo wilts and withers under the heavy oppressive weight of a system biased in favour of the rich and powerful. Still the flames of life burn in Munoo, under the company of his new friend Ratan, a fellow worker in the mill spend his hard days in the factory. But once more, tragedy materializes in Munoo life, a strike is organised by the workers which end into a catastrophe. The strike organised by the workers is put down with an iron hand and the revolt quelled mercilessly by the unilateral decisions of the British management aided by their Indian henchmen. The worst irony of it is that the whole strike is undermined and debunked as sparking off communal clashes. Before any decision can be taken the rumour spreads that Muslims have kidnapped Hindu children, and gathering workers spit up into the religious communities. This is another device through which the workers are misguided and their plans nipped in the bud. In point of fact, communal riots were engineered by the anti-worker management in order to blacklist and denigrate the striking workers and the labour union leaders. In Indo-Anglian fiction, *Coolie* is perhaps the first novel to touch on the communal relationship between Hindus and Muslims. Industrialism and the market economy don't seem to be the sole forces that exploit Munoo. Communalism also lends its evil hand. In *Coolie*, the relationship between capital and labour is extensively presented which shows the masses of workers and their leaders on one hand and the management of a capitalistic enterprise on the other hand. Finally, we see a hunted and hounded out Munoo is run down accidentally by a car and is again shifted to the hills in the household of an Anglo-Indian, scrupulous and over-sexed Mrs. Mainwaring at Shimla. Here again, Munoo becomes a victim of all the whims and fancies of this rootless caricature of an Anglo-Indian woman. The last days of Munoo as he wastes away under the effects of consumption are one long night of sorrow and pain only terminated by his untimely death.

Anand contrasts solidarity, endurance and friendliness of the pavement dwellers in Bombay and the poor coolies in Bombay and other places with the sordidness, complacency, self-righteousness, and superciliousness of the rich. The novel is a severe indictment of the capitalist system that spawns such inhuman monsters without a trace of concern for the deprived, side by side with hosts of workers, coolies and destitute like Munoo whose life is one long nightmare of thwarted ambition, unrewarded honesty and hard work and unrequited love and service. They are condemned to a life of slavery and abject poverty with no way out, however much they may struggle and strive. As Anand describes their state in these words:

> But they were broken, dispirited, docile and reticent, and they stared blankly through dim brown eyes, or

> mumbled a conventional phrase, in a meek and holy manner.... The misery of their lives had robbed them of all energy, till their souls seemed to have disappeared and only a bare suggestion of the memory of pain hung round their faces, like helplessness about the limbs of a sick man, tenderness about the face of a child, and weakness about the eyes of a dumb animal. (*Coolie* 218-19)

The most pathetic scene when Hari with his family and Munoo goes to seek room and passes through a crowd of coolies, beggars, and lepers. A half-naked woman sitting beside her dead husband, sobbing and begging for the funeral clothes breaks the attention of Munoo: "'My husband died there last night!' 'He has attained release,' said Hari. 'We will rest in his place'" (*Coolie* 164).

The last part of the novel deals with the life of Munoo in Shimla. Back home, Munoo feels better. He has been passing from bad to worse. His desire to live among the 'Sahibs' now drives him to other works. His mistress, Mainwaring, is not as harsh and rude as Thomas, the English foreman of the cottage Mills, in Bombay. Munoo had to pull rickshaw on the winding road of Shimla. He coughed incessantly and sput out, the fact which he concealed from his mistress. But the very sight of blood frightened him. Though his new mistress is kind to him, he is not entirely free from the exploitation, however, different in nature. Mrs. Mainwaring is a kind of nerve broken Anglo-Indian woman to whom sex and seduction mean everything in life.

Munoo's budding youth is crushed. Just a boy of fifteen (15) dies a tragic death. His tragedy is not a Nemesis or God's anger; it is a question of economic determinism. Munoo becomes all the more tragic because he is a child. There are many social forces that regularly contribute to Munoo's tragedy. His poverty makes him an easy target of this merciless capitalist society. As a child, he had dreamed of many things in his life. Munoo as an innocent child had his dreams as Anand says:

> He had dreamed, of course, of all the wonderful things which the village folk spoke about when they came back from the towns, the Lallas, the Babus, and the Sahibs from beyond the black waters; the silk clothes they wore and the delicacies they ate. He was especially interested in machines such as he had read about in the science primer of the fourth class. But he had meant to go to town when he has passed all his examinations here and was ready to learn to make machines himself. (*Coolie* 3)

Anand describes a child's psychology in most poignant words. It tears our heart to think what Munoo gets in his life instead. His poverty drains life out of himself. And as mature he comes to true realisation of his life and others. Saros Cowasjee rightly says:

> Unlike Bakha, the negative hero of untouchable, it is not his place in the old caste system that is questioned, because he belongs by birth to the second highest order. What is questioned of his place in the new caste system, on the basis of cash nexus...poverty forces him to leave the "high rocks, the great granite hills grey in blaze of the sun, and the silver line of the Beas" and "the greenery of the ferns and weeds and bushes that spread on either side of the stream against the purple gleam of the low hills." He could never go back to his village and at simla he dies "watching the tiers of blue sage and barely on the slopes of the valley before him". (17)

The novel highlights the loss of precious childhood, the hardships, and privations experienced at the hands of adults motivated by greed for gain, selfishness, heartlessness, and callousness in destroying irrevocably that tender shoot of humanity that ought to find protection and nurture from the adult world. The story of Munoo finds all too familiar replays in the present. While child labour laws exist, and the Indian constitution bars the employment of children below the age of fourteen, it is well known that the daily plight of millions of children is no different today than that of Anand's Munoo in 1936. So, while many films today assert that their characters are purely fictitious and do not bear resemblance to real persons living or dead, Anand's protagonist Munoo could be any one of millions of India's children trapped early in an unending and vicious cycle of bondage and debt, finding release only in premature death. The description of his illness and death by tuberculosis is oppressive. It is understandable only in the sociological and historical context: This was the fate of many like him at the time. Bringing the story up into the present—that seems justified considering legislation and time have brought little change. Hemenway has rightly assessed the essence of Munoo's personality:

> There is dignity in Munoo's senseless suffering, but no dignity in the system which conditions those born into coolie families never to aspire to anything else, with the possible exception of soldering with the prospect of certain death before them. (11)

Not much has changed from the modern point of vantage. Munoo represents the typical victim of circumstances that push children into the workforce. And India is one of the countries in the world having the largest workforce of children. While child labour laws exist, and the Indian constitution bars the employment of children below the age of fourteen, it is well-known fact that the daily plight of millions of children is nc different today than that of Anand's Munoo in 1936.

2.4 Detailed Analysis of *Two Leaves and a Bud*

Two Leaves and a Bud published in 1937 and marked the first occasion on which Anand's novel was greeted in Europe, at least, by something less than ecstasy. *Coolie's* tone of moral indignation becomes sheer outrage and even diatribe. *Two Leaves and a Bud* is authentically based, perhaps too much so. Saros Cowasjee (1973) has written:

> ... The picture (Anand) paints is more than substantiated by the report of the Royal Commission on Labour, familiarly known after its chairman as the Whitely Report. Anand has drawn much of his information from this Report, and far from exaggerating matters

> he has minimized the brutalities of the English planters and the hardships inflicted on the coolies. (35-36)

It takes its name from the simple catchphrase, almost a threnody, which the tea-plantation workers recite as they pick two leaves and a bud, two leaves and a bud, two leaves and a bud, during their daily routine. This monotony is particularly effective when we remember that these people are leading unrewarded infertile lives. They are moving parts in a machine. Structurally the novel runs in two parallel directions. On the one hand, it follows the misfortunes of Gangu, a peasant whose perceptiveness is the direct product of embittered experience. He is lured to an isolated tea-plantation with an alluring offer of a large salary and a free home. He has sold his own plot of land to take up the new job since his brother had mortgaged the land and his house and the Angrezi Sarkar confiscated his hut and three acres of land as debt. He has to leave Hoshiarpur with Buta, the Sardar who promised him a good job in the plantation. Gangu with his family travels twelve days and night from Hoshiarpur to reach Assam. Buta Ram paints a rosy picture about the plantation workers living in Macpherson Tea Estate:

> If anyone needs money for something special such as the purchase of a cow, for marriage or for the propitiation of the ancestor ceremony, the sahibs advance it free of interest, and recover it only gradually. The manager sahib knows and cares for all his people. He attends to their well-being, and he keeps them happy and contented.... Besides, they hold sports and distribute prizes every now and then. (*Two Leaves and a Bud* 7)

But it is all white lie which Buta Ram is speaking as we come to know in the novel with succeeding tragedies. From his first glimpse of his new house, which with rural insight he knows it will be too hot for summer and too cold for winter, he has a feeling of being closed in, entrapped, by a system which will take everything from him and give minimal returns. Reaching the tea plantation, Gangu says "there was again a vague perturbation in his soul, the ache of an apprehended doom" (*Two Leaves and a Bud* 12). As Narain, a fellow worker, observes, "This prison has no bars, but it is nevertheless an unbreakable jail that is death can only give one release from it" (*Two Leaves and a Bud* 34). Gangu quickly settles into the dreary life of a plantation worker and Anand presents the picking of the crop as annihilation of nature.

Anand's *Coolie* (1936) and *Two Leaves and a Bud* (1937) portray the scandalous gulf existing between the rich and the poor in pre-Independence India. Hence, Anand aims at highlighting the role of the British in bringing about this ill-fated situation. Industrial capitalism was imported from the West by the Colonial rulers. This upsets the applecart of the Indian social and cultural relationships and polity and this development were made possible by the British who introduced Commerce and trade based on mere profit-seeking and cut-throat competition. And it should be noted that the Indian soil was just ripe for accepting this western product as it had been preconditioned by forces such as mechanization, industrialization, and scientific materialism. As a direct result of the interplay of these forces, the Indian society of the thirties was losing its cohesion and stability. Money became the principal symbol, measure, and means of well-being and happiness. Moreover, all relationships and interactions began to be scrutinized and judged by the criterion of possession or non-possession of money. Munoo, the central figure of *Coolie* and Gangu the hero of *Two Leaves and a Bud* are both Kshatriyas, the second highest in caste-hierarchy. But they come of a poor background and, therefore, become victims of the cruelty and marginalisation that is associated with the lower classes.

Munoo and Gangu are represented as labourers or coolies who depend for their livelihood on the wages paid to them for selling or hiring out their labour. Munoo is driven from his home in the sylvan setting of the Kangra Valley merely because "my aunt wants me to begin earning money Munoo said" (*Coolie* 2). Anand makes sure that we are briefed about the havoc played by the landlord in his father's life by seizing his five acres of land in return for the interest on mortgage not paid, Munoo's family was a hapless victim of unscrupulous landlord, Thus Anand underlines the role of feudalism in wrecking the lives of innumerable, unlettered, ignorant, unwary villagers who sought the help of the landlord moneylenders for loans.

S.J. Patel (1992) in a study of agricultural labourers in modern India and Pakistan traces the evolution of landless labour in British India. He provides the social background and valuable insight into the period of Anand's *Coolie* which help us better appreciate Anand's achievement as a social writer and also to empathize more fully with his fictional characters. Patel asserts that pre-British India was a self-sufficient, inter-Independent agrarian society in which landless labourers as a class did not exist. Census returns for the first four decades of the twentieth century, however, reflects drastic changes in Indian rural society in the late nineteenth and early twentieth century. Census returns for 1931, prior to the period of publication of *Coolie* shows that:

> by then agricultural labourers came to form close to two-fifths of the agricultural population of India; their proportion virtually tripled from nearly thirteen (13%) percent in the late nineteenth century to thirty-eight (38%) percent in 1931, thus indicating that they had become numerically the largest group, a remarkable increase that reflects the most dramatic social transformation in the entire history of Indian rural society. (Patel 49)

This disintegration of the traditional agrarian society and the increase in the size of the newly born class of landless agricultural labourers are attributed to the land policies pursued by the British in India from the late eighteenth century onwards. The British introduced the Zamindari settlement, which created large individual landlords in the eastern region in 1793; the Raiyatwari settlement, which dealt with individual small peasant landlords in the southern triangle; and the Mahalwari settlement, which dealt with the village elders in their capacity as landlords in the north. They completely sidetracked the traditional institution of the village community in all these settlements and overhauled the manner and mode of revenue payment. Given this background, it is not difficult to contextualize the life story of Anand's Munoo who, at the opening of the novel, recalls the circumstances in which his father is divested of his five acres by the landlord to whom he owned rent money and interest on his mortgage. The loss of the land leads the family to rack and ruin and catapults the orphaned boy into his own interminable struggle as a child labourer. Child labour is one of the evils of the capitalist system as it provides the factory owners with cheap labour in most inhuman and abominable conditions. Anand's description of this most heinous practice endorsed by the rulers is as pathetic as it is mind-boggling.

In *Two Leaves and a Bud,* Anand is largely concerned with the socio-political function of British colonial attitudes. He devotes much of his attention to a whole range of British characters while he is equally anxious with the exposure of violence and bitterness under which Indian coolies are imprisoned. The locale of *Two Leaves and a Bud* is a tea plantation in Assam. The atmosphere of suspicion and strike, the racial intolerance and prejudice, the private talk in the club, the reign of prejudice and unreason prevails here. It is against this idyllic background that the drama of exploitation is enacted. *Two Leaves and a Bud* is another novel that is devoted to the theme of exploitation built around cash-nexus of the capitalist mode of economic organisation. This novel is more concretely about the class of coolies represented in the novel by Gangu the central character, who is a hapless peasant lured to the plantations of Assam with false promises of better material prospects. Gangu was a poor but happy farmer until he and his family are lured into a virtual prison camp—the tea gardens of Assam. He was copiously convinced by Buta Singh, the Sardar, that 'sahibs' were just like 'mai-baap' (mother and father) who could loan him money free of interest to buy a cow or a piece of land. The Sardar also tempted him by saying that there is a real affection between the labourers and sahibs as they attended to their well-being and prized their honesty and labour. But very soon an atmosphere of twisting and whirling prevailed. Narain, a fellow coolie tells Gangu:

> you will soon know, brother said Narain. First water, afterwards mire! This prison has no bars, but it is

> nevertheless an unbearable jail. The chowkidars keep guard over the plantation, and they bring you back if you should run.... The chowkidars go round at night with a lamp and open every door to see if we are all at home. There used to be roll call every night before I came. (*Two Leaves and a Bud* 34)

On reaching the tea plantation, Gangu realises that Buta had been a liar in all his big talk about high wages, free gifts of land, etc. He is now in 'an unbreakable jail' and has to lead a lifeless life. The irony of it all is that apart from being cut off from his roots, losing his freedom and self-dignity in serfdom and bonded labour, he eventually dies at the hands of his diabolical boss. Although Gangu is skeptical of the exaggerated overtures of Buta, he is finally beguiled by Buta who uses the peasant's strong love of land as a decoy. Gangu's destiny is inextricably wedded to the plantation from now on. He will lose his wife after an epidemic of cholera takes a heavy toll of the coolies. The filth and squalor of the coolies' lives defies description. As if these hazards at the work places were not sufficient, the coolies and their children are exposed to untold health hazards. The British overlords have not an iota of sympathy or concern for the workers. Anand tries to be objective by showing how the British attitude to the Indian can be both imperialistic as in the case of Reggie Hunt and Croft-Cooke or liberal as in that of Dr. John de la Havre.

Professor Iyengar observes that the novel *Two Leaves and a Bud* "culminates in tragic clash of interest and destinies" (343). Anand here seems to be much more ambitious than in *Coolie* to expose the colonial system. Apart from the British characters save de la Havre, few of Indians like sardars, Babus and mistris are the exploiters too. They all together form a group to subjugate the simple and ill-informed coolies. The British owned tea plantation is headed by Croft-Cooke, the manager, Reggie Hunt, the assistant manager and de la Havre, the Doctor or welfare officer. *Two Leaves and a Bud* with all the violence and bitterness has "the atmosphere of suspicion and strife, the racial intolerance and antagonism, the small talk in the club, reign of prejudice and unreason" (Iyengar 346).

The syndrome of racism has become second nature to people such as Croft-Cooke, the manager, and he completely blocks his mind to de la Havre's arguments: "you know as I do.... These coolies are sub-human, and do not altogether value the benefits of hygiene..." (*Two Leaves and a Bud* 27).

Anand analyses the relationships prevailing between the white masters and the coolies. It is a condescending and contemptuous attitude with no concern whatever for their well-being, safety or happiness. The coolies are herded together in plantations as if they were cattle and have no need for the higher pleasures of family life and human camaraderie. Reggie Hunt, the assistant planter is an embodiment of the cruelty, heartlessness, and frivolity of the white planters and the class of planters as a whole. He prowls around the plantations seeking for a prey to devour. He is not only brutal in terms of his treatment of deviant coolies but a sexual wreck who seeks to satiate his lust by preying on any coolie woman. He has no moral qualms about his unethical behaviour and immoral exploitation of the plantation workers.

De la Havre is an exception to the general apathy, cold-heartedness, and ruthlessness associated with the planters. De la Havre is one of the many intellectuals who play important roles in Anand's novels. He is largely the mouthpiece of the author himself who shared with the intellectual role in a capitalist society of the 'Thirties Movement' in England. He has a dissimilar perception of the deplorable plight of the coolies and the injustice and sinfulness of the system that is operating. However, he is powerless and finally deported after being labelled as a non-conformist, anti-British humanitarian. He is not only a compassionate doctor but a champion for the cause of the coolies. Coming to the coolies, we find them averse to any protest or reaction. They are uneducated and ignorant and it is their crass stupidity that makes them resigned to their inhuman situation. Most of the Indian characters are represented as naïve and innocent victims of the British colonialism, with the exception of a few British characters like Croft-Cooke and Reggie Hunt, the assistant manager, who represented as the stooges of British imperialism; crooked and nefarious Croft-Cooke and

Reggie Hunt are the very embodiments of evil, pressing the very phantasmagoria unleashed by the forces of imperialism.

Soon after his arrival at tea plantation Gangu realises that he has been trapped in a pandemonium without escape routes and he seems to loose grip on his innate potentiality. Suddenly malaria breaks out in the colony and his wife Sajani becomes its first casualty. Gangu does not have money even to perform the last rites to his wife:

> The fuel for the cremation would not cost anything because there was plenty of firewood in the jungle, but the performance of the last rites required by religion was imperative. He must buy a red cloth and get a bamboo hearse made. And he had spent the entire sum earned by the family and the remainder from the bonus, during that ominous shopping tow in the bazaar.... As he stood with his head weighted down over his chest and avoided looking towards the dead body which lay sprawled under the sheet, lest the sorrow which filled him nowhere there had been his love, should break down in another agony of despair, he recalled that Buta had told him that the Manager Sahib was a sort of Mai-bap who lent money when coolies were in need. (*Two Leaves and a Bud* 93)

He approaches Croft-Cooke, the plantation owner, for help but returns empty handed, after having been abused and kicked out. How cruel and heartless fate is towards Gangu as Anand paints the apathy:

> Get out! Get out! Exclaimed Croft-Cooke, turning purple with rage, and kicking at the coolie. You bloody fool, get out! Get out! You have been spreading infection all over the place! Didn't you know that you were under segregation? By whose orders did you come here? (*Two Leaves and a Bud* 98)

Gangu meets Buta and asks for help. Buta advises him to approach the bania; but Gangu rather hesitates to approach the bania because of the higher interest rate. He laments his tragedy in these words:

> Oh, friend Buta Ram, if only I had known things were going to turn out this way, I wouldn't have come here and he took his hand to his eyes to wipe the tears that had welled up in them with the reproach against the sardar that he had suppressed into self-pity. (*Two Leaves and a Bud* 101)

After the death of his wife, Gangu loses his composure and interest in life and passes from bad to worse with no peace in his heart. He starts living at the mercy and kindness extended to him by his masters, with his future blacked out. Disenchantment and disillusionment turned him a destitute, and he tries to embattle with the malevolent forces of continual repression and exploitation. A minor scuffle takes place between two mistresses of Reggie Hunt Chambeli and Neogi's wife and the plantation owners think mutiny had broken out. The coolies are ruthlessly beaten up, maimed, bruised and subjected to innumerable forms of unspeakable repressions. The coolies run helter-skelter, crying, shouting and sobbing, and prophesying that "the end of the world had come". Havre advises them to see the Burra Sahib even as he attends on the badly pawed coolies. The coolies thus proceed to captain Croft-Cooke to seek his help. They also meet Reggie Hunt who roars:

> Hands up! You swine roared Reggie, pointing his revolver at the ringleaders.... Step back, or I will shoot you dead! Let de la Havre mind his own business. Back you go, swine, back you go to the lines!... warders, march these men back to their houses. Take them off before I shoot them all! (*Two Leaves and a Bud* 170-71)

This small protest is treated as a mutiny by the tea planters. They are abused, beaten and charged with fifty rupees fine. De la Havre is terminated from his job by Croft-Cooke instantly. Now, they are left all alone without help. They are incapable of making any protest, ran down, abused, beaten mercilessly they tried mobilizing the group to wage a battle against the consistently anti-labour policies and practices of the British planters but all in vain. Life on the plantation is full of disgust and indifference. The coolies easily develop a sense of disillusionment that drives them towards defeatism and death. Life in the plantation turns normal and Gangu continues his life of slavery living under the loan of money he had incurred from the Sahukar, and the fine. The Seth words to Gangu:

> I can't help it if your wife has died, and you have been fined. I want my money, do you hear, you son of a bitch, and if you don't return it, I will get the sahib to cut it at the office. (*Two Leaves and a Bud* 216)

Gangu's realisation is the same as Munoo in *Coolie*. In utter sadness, he says "'Money is everything', he kept on saying, 'Money is everything' as if the phrase were loaded with all the suffering he had endured" (217). As the time moves on Charles Croft-Cooke becomes busy arranging the details of a hunting expedition arranged for Geoffrey Boyd, the Governor of Assam. The coolies get busy in their work. Gangu continues to live for his daughter and son numbed by the cruel fate unaware of the biggest tragedy which awaits him. One day Reggie Hunt taking the round of the tea estate sees Leila. Reggie Hunt lusts for Leila, the daughter of Gangu, plucking 'two leaves and a bud'. Lured by her personal charms, he craves her indulgence. The girl, apprehending the danger, runs home only to be hunted down by Reggie Hunt. Wild with anger, Gangu comes out from his neighbour's house to rescue her but is shot by Reggie Hunt, and thus he ends the saga of his pain and suffering. This also gives us the information that sexual exploitation of the Indian coolie women and girls were also rampant at that time. There succeeds a mock-trial, comprising of seven European and two Indian members of the jury, who declare Reggie Hunt 'not guilty'. Thus, Gangu 'is more sinned against sinning', his pathetic end only confirming the "tragic waste of his life". The novel vividly projects the miserable plight of the hapless individuals as they are caught in the vortex of social malaise and the fact of their ruthless repressions and subjugation which are the structured truths of the contingent social order. As Premila Paul rightly observes: "*Two Leaves and a Bud* is a grimmer tragedy: the world of Assam plantations is too dense a jungle for the ray of love to penetrate" (33).

The mild protest organised by the leaders of the group ends in a fiasco as they are overawed by the presence of the white masters, particularly Reggie Hunt. Gangu is a typical character belonging to this group. He is fatalistic when it comes to the crunch, be it his wife's death or his daughter's narrow escape from the rapacious grasp of Reggie Hunt symbolised by her escape from the python. The climax of this story of subtle satire on the white bosses in relation to the natives is achieved when the court finally acquits guilty Reggie. This, in other words, is symbolic of the ultimate triumph of evil in the capitalist world of the ruling class suppressing the working class and treating them as the scum of the earth. Anand's portrayal is grim and is a vehement plea for the subverting of this system so that the workers will not only get adequate wages and recompense but will come in possession of the means of production. This is what is declared by Anand through his mouthpiece de la Havre. As perpetrators of an unjust system of capitalist exploitation and the resultant furtherance of social stratification, the British administrators have no right over the land of the Indians. Through a Report on Labour Condition in India by A.A. Purcell in the novel de la Havre brings the true picture:

> The present system of plantation labour is a curse and a crime. It is a monstrous crime against humanity.... 75% of the coolies on Assam plantations suffer from caratomalaisia (bad eyesight) for lack of proper nourishment, fats and greases. 50% of the population of India suffers from dental diseases for lack of any milk in diet. Two million women die in childbirth in India as a result of malnutrition. 20% Anglo-Indians and members of upper of upper classes of India die of gluttony, overeating—another form of malnutrition... wages of coolies on the Indian Plantations have not changed for the last seventy years. The wages of a coolie in 1870, were five rupees per month. In 1922, the maximum wages of a coolie on the Assam tea plantations did not exceed seven rupees per month. It should be remarked in this connection that the price of rice—the coolies only article of food—has more than

> doubled during this period.... (*Two Leaves and a Bud* 106-07)

A composed analysis of the situation of the unbridgeable gap existing between a small group of the wealthy and the overwhelming majority eking a subsistence level or below poverty line existence, unfolds the undeniable fact that the British were the leading cause as they introduced the capitalistic form of trade and commerce. Of course, later it became an unavoidable and inevitable phenomenon any country or society has to reckon with. Saros Cowasjee (1976) in his, *Coolie: An Assessment* remarks:

> But the plight of Munoo and his kind is the direct result of the British rule and the industrial revolution they introduced without paying sufficient heed to social reforms, Munoo's position in life raises the question of freedom in a capitalistic society. As Anand sees it, freedom to Munoo, as to millions of others, means no more than being beaten from pillar to post. (17)

Anand's spokesman de la Havre in *Two Leaves and a Bud* verbalises Anand's own perception and anger in the following crisp words:

> And when, after enjoying the monopoly of Indian trade for generations, our Britons, who never, never shall be slaves, found they had cut their own throats by introducing the steam engine into India, not only because their home manufactures competed with their colonial manufactures, but also because the Indian moneyed classes were pressing for a share in the industries of their country, they began to bully the coolies and bleed them as much as they could before the judgement day arrived.... Three cheers for the man who imprisons old Gangu on the plantation by false pretences, keeps him well guarded and refuses to give him a strip of land which he promised by contract. But what's a contract with a slave? Less than a scrap of paper! And that's your System! (118-19)

De la Havre seems to have gone to the origin of the question of exploitation and squarely placed the blame for it all, on the British colonisers. His perceptive insight is not altogether bereft of sympathetic concern for the sweat and toil of the condemned coolies. He says that "a single cup of tea contains the hunger, the sweat and the despair of a million Indians". If this was true of India during the British Raj, it is more poignantly descriptive of the contemporary Indian predicament. Anand exposes the seamy side and the horrendous injustices and oppression unleashed by the class distinction and consciousness, an intrinsic part of the capitalist world. Hence, we have some moving, pathetic, gruesome, mind-boggling and tragic scenes and details of the social underdog's experiences at the hands of the rich and powerful people who call the tune in a capitalist set-up. Anand is out to disparage not only the system as a whole but also the individuals and groups that manipulate the system in order to turn it in favour of their personal aggrandizement and profit-seeking. Anand is realistic in his approach to this theme, often reminding one of Dickens. Nevertheless, his purpose is first and foremost to expose the insincerity and one-sidedness of this class character of a capitalist society. In order to highlight the inhumanity and injustice of it all. He sometimes exaggerates the cruelty and barbarity of individual capitalists, particularly the British colonial masters in relation to their lowly subjects or employees and in this Odysseus quest Anand is true to his proclaimed social convictions.

In Marxian analysis of social systems, class plays a crucial role in maintaining the exploitive character of a capitalist society. Class conflict or class war eventually yields to proletarian rule and the stateless and classless society according to Marx. Anand probes the class character of exploitation in several novels, the chief among them being, *Coolie, Two Leaves and a Bud* and *The Big Heart*. Anand seemingly subscribes to the Marxist view of class struggle preceding final liberation in the form of a classless society and stateless socialism. Munoo and Gangu, although they are kshatriyas, are discriminated against and exploited simply because they are poor and downtrodden. *The Big Heart* (1945) is a moving and heart-rending tragedy of Ananta who dies a martyr for the cause of educating and conscientizing his people to accept the inevitability of modernity. Anand portrays the heinousness and dissects the per se evil of casteism and untouchability in *Untouchable* and *The Road*. The twin sin and shame of India are projected by Anand as equally responsible for the social and economic inequalities that still persist since so many years after Independence.

2.5 The Subaltern Class

The term 'subaltern' is drawn from Gramsci's "on the margins of History: History of the Subaltern Social Groups" (*Prison Notebooks*, 1971). Gramsci uses the term 'subaltern' inter-changeably with "Subordinate" and "instrumental" in his class descriptions (Gramsci 26). This is generally used in reference to the subjugated and oppressed groups. The subaltern studies group describes 'subaltern' as individual "of inferior rank" (Guha, Preface, *Subaltern Studies*, Vol. 1, 1982). Anand's fictional writing acquires additional significance, viewed as a sort of subaltern historiography presenting fictionalized accounts of peasants, labourers insurgencies in colonial and post-colonial India. Anand's foremost and original novel *Untouchable* deals with a hegemonic structure peculiar to India-caste. The target of Anand's attack here is the bigotry of Hindu orthodoxy, and the contestation is launched from the subject—position of a member of the exploited group—the untouchables. Anand flings open a heterogeneous field where different kinds of exploitation are at work and different systems of domination (caste, class, gender and colonial) operate in a crisscross manner. Bakha occupies a position of subalternity in more than one scheme of exploitation: caste, class and colonial subjugation. Anand conceptualizes the entire complexity of the colonial condition by describing a day in the life of Bakha. As Robertson (1977) rightly points out: "The greater effect of the novel is in its archetypal presentation of colonial situation" (Robertson 05). He is also convinced of the need to act, the urge for a change. This change in Bakha symbolizes the arousal of subaltern consciousness.

The theme of colonial relationship obliquely touched upon in *Untouchable* receives greater attention in Anand's next novels

Coolie and *Two Leaves and a Bud*. Anand's focus here is on the economic exploitation of the Indian peasant and worker by the oppressive forces of capitalism and colonialism. The author makes it clear that the so-called civilizing mission of the colonizers is a myth and that the economic self-interest of the empire has been a major motivating factor for colonization. In *Coolie*, Anand shows how the policy of industrial capitalism promoted by the colonial power spread its tentacles over the poor and helpless, often claiming their lives. As the novel progresses, its statement about the nature of capitalist power with its destructive effect on the working-class community is increasingly insistent in tenor. Anand portrays the predicament of the industrial workers through the tragic tale of the protagonist, Munoo, a village lad turned an industrial worker. The novel adopts the structure of journey-quest, and traces Munoo's journey of life beginning in his native home in the Kangra Hills, through the trials and tribulations of living in the impersonal city of Bombay, and the agony of working in the oppressive atmosphere of the industrial town of Daulatpur and coming to an untimely end on the cold hill slopes of Shimla.

In this quest, Munoo moves from one affliction to another. Munoo's journey is more in the form of a flight, desperately looking for safe shelter in the moral wilderness of contemporary society, and his one aspiration all along was that he wanted to live, he wanted to know, he wanted to work. The central conflict is between the protagonist's will to live and the hostile landscape's unrelenting effort to hurt. The various attempts Munoo makes at earning a livelihood include working as a domestic servant in the household of a Baboo at Sham Nagar, as a worker in a pickle factory at Daulatpur, as a labourer in a cotton mill in Bombay, and as a rickshaw puller in an Anglo-Indian household in Shimla where he contracts consumption and meets an untimely death. What is important is the uprooting of the village lad from his familiar rural world and setting him abroad the alien landscape of an industrial world. This may be read as a case of forced exile, dispossession and estrangement. The subaltern's struggle for survival against all odds of life is itself a mark of strong will to fight and eventually succeed.

Mulk Raj Anand's *Coolie* is not only a story but truth based on the life of an orphan boy Munoo and God knows how many several different Munoos. The central character emerges as a figure whose personal experience crystallizes the experience of the entire community—the community of peasants and workers. The novel suggests that the crippling effects of colonial rule and capitalist economy are all-pervasive and as varied as life itself. The negative effects of these oppressive systems are identified over and over again. But this very repetitiousness-enacted in the experiences of Prabha, Parvathi and the workers in the pickle factory, Hari, Lakshmi and others, the industrial workers in Bombay, Mohan and the other rickshaw pullers in Shimla—reiterates the sufferings of the subaltern in a forceful manner, and makes their voices, however, feeble, unmistakably audible.

In *Two Leaves and a Bud*, Anand once again turns to the theme of economic exploitation, this time against the background of tea plantations in Assam. The novel draws upon the real-life account of plantation labour in British owned tea plantations in Assam. Dwarakanath Ganguli (1972) gives a graphic account of the life of Bengali plantation labour in his study on the subject in *Slavery in British Dominion*. Assam then was practically inaccessible and organizing the labour was no easy task for the British estate owners. Special recruiting agents of the Sarkar used all sorts of bait to lure the landless peasants from remote villages into working on these estates. The most important of all was the promise of a piece of land. Once these workers were recruited and transported to these uphill estates, they found themselves practically prisoners, left to the mercy of ruthless planters and greedy middlemen.

They were constantly ill-treated and flogged to work, their women were often insulted and molested, and these families were condemned to live in tin sheds with no basic amenities. The topography of Assam besides the cautious vigil kept by the employer made escape impossible. Any sign of revolt was dealt with a heavy hand and the poor peasant had no support of any kind. The British planters could get away with anything including murder, as the English jury could acquit them of any crime on grounds of paucity of legal proof. Anand's novel is an unvarnished tale of the sufferings of peasants in this British plantocracy.

Gangu represents this unfortunate community of uprooted peasants trying to negotiate their destiny in alien landscape of tea plantations. Falling prey to the false promises of a coolie-catcher Buta, Gangu allows himself and his family to be transported to the distant, unfamiliar tea estates in Assam. He soon finds that it is a prison without bars, an unbreakable jail. Gangu's life here is one of unrelieved suffering: his wife Sajani dies of malaria; unable to meet the expenses of her funeral he falls into the debt-trap of a moneylender; meanwhile his daughter, Leila, draws the attention of the roving eyes of the lusty manager Reggie Hunt; and in a melee, that follows, he is shot dead by the manager.

Many of the themes and concerns of his novels are reflected in the wide range of his short stories as well. These are vignettes of life presented in snapshots with little emotional or intellectual interference from the author. In his short fiction, Anand recreates the lives of the people he had known intimately since his childhood—the untouchables, peasants, workers and suffering women—in order to achieve a variety of purposes:

- (i) Exposing the injustice of the existing order,
- (ii) Articulating the agony of silently suffering subaltern women,
- (iii) Attacking the greed and inhumanity of feudal lords and imperial authority,
- (iv) Satirizing the vanities and follies of different classes of men and women,
- (v) Spreading the message of reform and revolution.

Thematically, Anand's short stories show a rich diversity. A large number of these tales are women-centered texts and present poignant account of the tragic lives of peasant women. The subaltern women hardly entered the domain of literature till Anand has forged the lives of peasant women in the Centre space of his narratives. "Lajwanti" a short narrative of a young women, without mother raised by her father, rustic maiden whose husband is away at university. She finds herself an easy target of the sinful eyes of her lascivious pockmarked brother-in-law and wicked mother-in-law. She runs away to her father's house hoping to find refuge in her parental home. But in her heart, she knows the burden of her father is too much:

> Lajwanti was sad for her father. She knew that a man who had borne the grinding pressures of years of survival on one *bigha* and a buffalo, and whose wife had died leaving him with two small children, was in no condition to receive a grown-up married daughter, who had returned without even the proverbial bundle of clothes to change into. ("Lajwanti" 18)

She doesn't want to go back to her in-laws but as it is disgraceful in the Indian village community if a daughter runs away from her in-law house. So, the father is worried about his respect in the community and turns back Lajwanti, her father turns her out saying: "I will take you back to your parents-in-law's house. I shall fall at their feet and ask them to forgive you. The disgrace of your widowhood without becoming a widow is unbearable..." ("Lajwanti" 20). Her father takes the poor Lajo to her in-laws: "... And now I leave her in your care. Kill her if you like. But don't let her come to me without her lap full of a son. I shall not be able to survive the disgrace if she comes again..." ("Lajwanti" 25). Lajo's pathetic condition is shown by the Maina which is trapped inside the cage which Lajo carries with her always. In a desperate bid to seek release from the pain of living she tries to kill herself, in vain. Her pathetic reconciliation: "Alas, she said in a wordless word, above the ache of the head and the thumping of the heart, "there is no way for me...I am...condemned to live..." ("Lajwanti" 27). It marks the height of her tragedy and Lajo like women in our society. In "Naina", Anand shows how marriage entraps woman for life making her a ready victim to the sexual excesses of an ever-demanding husband.

Anand shows a special concern for peasant mothers who suffer a great deal for the succor of their young ones. In "Birth", Parvati a poor working woman in the advanced state of pregnancy goes to work at breaking stones. The birth pangs start while she is on her way to work. She goes through the painful process of delivery with none to help, drawing courage and strength from her faith in God:

> At last after an hour of torment as she lay drenched in a pool of blood and aus, she felt a boundless surging overwhelm her.... Clutching him with eager, deft hands, she performed the services of the midwife on herself with a cool, assured touch which only the old dai, Kesari, in her native village, was known to bring to her task. And, what was most surprising, even to her, was the fact that having cut the naval strings which united her child to her with the rough end of the silver hansli round her neck, she emptied the basket in which she carried the food, donated the roti to the birds as a gift-offering, put her baby in it and strode forth towards the Ridge to go and break stones. ("Birth" 25)

In a vision, she sees Goddess Kali herself going through the travails of child-birth. Birth acquires a symbolic significance in this context. Every woman who goes through the pangs of child-birth is in a way re-enacting the creative act of Goddess Kali, the mother of mankind.

"Lullaby" shows a working mother in a crisis. The lullaby sung by the young mother Phalini, rocking her dying child to sleep is drowned in the noise of the merciless machine:

> The engine chuk-chuked; the leather belt khupp-khupped; the; the; the; the bolts jig-jigged; the plugs tik-tikked; the; the whole floor shook like hard wooden seat of a railway train. And she had to go on feeding the gaping mouth of the machine. ("Lullaby" 57)

The lullaby stops when the baby dies, but the machine goes on unmindful of the suffering of those who work it. Anand's pathetic tales of peasant women point to the gross injustices perpetuated by the patriarchal social order:

> She sang, bending over the child's head till she almost touched the feverish brow and kissed the close-fisted hands which Suraj Mukhi was rubbing on his eyes, even as he cried. And then she threw another handful of

> jute into the jaws of the monster.... She bent down to look at the child. His eyes were open, his face was still, he cried no more. That was good, she could feed the machine with more jute. ("Lullaby" 59-60)

In "The Cobbler and the Machine", the old cobbler Saudagar's problem is that he is killed by over-work. The machine which he brought took a toll on him, since the money he had to pay to the owner, Lalla Sain Das, as a debt never ceases to vanish howsoever, he was working hard to repay it. The story ends with the death of Saudagar:

> But that day never came, for worn out by the fatigue of producing many more shoes than he had ever sewn to pay off his debt, drained of his life-blood by the sweat that was always pouring off his body, he fell stone dead one evening...it was not enough for Saudagar and his pupils to love the machine and work it, but to own it. ("The Cobbler and the Machine" 113)

Mulk Raj Anand's short story, "The Gold Watch", presents an Indian clerk working in a British firm, who is forced to retire prematurely before five years of his service because a better-connected replacement has been found for the job. Mulk Raj Anand presents the agony of Srijut Sudarshan Sharma, an employee of a firm facing superannuation, in a touching manner. The General Manager of Marmalade Empire of Henry King & Co. announces the doom of a poor clerk politely in the short story entitled "The Gold Watch". The opening sentence of the short story reflects the apprehension of a middle-class employee in a remarkable manner: "There was something about the smile of Mr. Acton when he came over to Srijut Sudarshan Sharma's table, which betokened disaster" (*Greatest Short Story* 79). The panic, the fear, and the confusion that overwhelm the clerk at the possible loss of his livelihood show Anand's capacity to get beneath the skin of his characters as few writers can. Anand beautifully paints the old poor man tragedy:

> But Srijut Sharma still stood, as though he had been struck dumb. He was neither happy nor sad at this moment, only numbed by the shock of surprise. Why should he be singled out from the whole distribution

> department of Henry King & Co., for the privilege of the gift of a gold watch! He had done nothing brave that he could remember. A gold watch, with an inscription in it! Oh, he knew, now: the intuitive truth rose inside him: The Sahib wanted him to retire. ("The Gold Watch" 84)

On his retirement, he receives from his British boss a gold watch which he drops and breaks while receiving:

> Srijut Sharma put both his hands out, more steadily this time, and took the gift in the manner in which a beggar receives alms. ("The Gold Watch" 89)

This little incident is very symbolic of all that has gone wrong in the twenty-year long relationship between Sharma and his British superiors, with the Indian's pathetic inferiority complex being complemented by the white man's superiority complex. Anand's leftist leanings and his immense sympathy with the underdog have led some readers to surmise that he is less successful when dealing with the affluent-specifically the landed gentry. The mode of perception in most of these stories is symbolic. All his men and women are real figures drawn from contemporary life and represent the reality of flesh and blood. The stark realism of Anand's texts represents an emerging consciousness actively becoming aware of a sense of history and therefore resisting the mediation of myth which might make the repugnant and repulsive appear as divinely ordained.

Anand is almost all by himself not only in reflecting the situation of the sweepers, coolies, workers, and peasants in his novels, but in leaving the fictional space to groups marginalized hitherto, for the enactment of their lives at their own will. From these novels a history of the evolution of the subaltern in Indian society may meaningfully be formulated. Anand's achievement lies in the abrogation of the imperial language and appropriation of the same to tell the stories of Punjabi peasants. Unlike other post-colonial or neo-colonial writers, he is not obsessed with the project of identity—self-definitions of intellectuals, aristocratic alienations, metaphysical meanderings, transcontinental travels, but is concerned with the immediate socio-cultural issues and their impact on the private worlds of common men and women.

2.6 Women: The Marginalized Class

Anand's *Gauri* (1960) must be accorded a special place in this because the novelist focuses on a character subjected to multiple forms of marginalization—a peasant woman in a post-colonial society. Anand is simultaneously addressing two issues here—the class structure that discriminates against the poor and the gender bias that relegates women to a secondary status. Into a literary tradition (of Indian-English writing) which generally glossed over the issues of class/gender, Anand's work injects the occasional sense of the Indian working class: the labourer and the peasant, and their struggle for survival in a world dominated by the forces of colonialism and capitalism. Within that, Anand again exposes yet another form of exploitation based on gender that operates within all classes and castes reducing women to a state of glorified slavery. The novel traces the protagonist Gauri's growth from the initial powerlessness to self-confidence, passivity to activity, submissiveness to freedom from restraint, and unfolds the author's vision of female empowerment.

The novel begins with the marriage of Gauri, and her subsequent departure for her husband's village. Gauri's travails begin almost immediately after that. She is constantly bullied and ill-treated by her husband's aunt Kesari (who entertains a sort of nephew-fixation) and abused and beaten by her strong-limbed and weak-minded husband Panchi. In a quick succession of misfortunes that follows, Gauri and her husband are thrown out of their ancestral home following a family feud; they fail to make a home of their own on account of the terrible famine that breaks out in the village; and pledge all their earthly possessions to a moneylender. Their zest for life is shattered by poverty, hunger, and helplessness. Panchi begins to believe that it could all be due to the ill-luck his bride brought him. Gauri's pregnancy, ironically, comes as the last straw and Panchi, terrified by the idea of "one more mouth to feed", turns his wife out.

Back to her mother's place, Gauri soon realizes that she is an unwanted burden on the family's meagre resources. Once again poverty and hunger subsume all personal and familial relationships and Gauri is sold against her will to a rich banker in Hoshiarpur. Ironically, when Laxmi, Gauri's mother, had to choose between her cow that feeds the family and her daughter whom the family has to feed, she chooses the former. Gauri falls ill in Seth's house and is rescued by the doctor of the local hospital of Colonel Mahindra. The assistant doctor, Brata tries to molest Gauri and this incident brings about a rift between the two doctors. Yet, after all this, when she is physically and psychologically recovered under the care of Dr. Mahindra, Gauri tells him: "I am with child by my husband, and I want to go back to him.... I want to go back home..." (*Gauri* 180). In the meantime, rains come and a repentant Panchi goes to Gauri's village seeking his abandoned wife. Gauri's mother comes to Hoshiarpur, searching for her daughter, and Gauri is restored to her "rightful" place in her husband's home. The happy reunion does not last long. Enraged by the village gossip and rumours about Gauri's exile at Hoshiarpur, Panchi beats his wife and demands proof of her "chastity" ... (*Gauri* 262). Gauri once again leaves home, this time never to return but determined to bring up her child in a better environment. The mythic structure of the novel is too obvious to be missed or ignored. Anand had used material from folk and mythical tales before, but this is the first novel wherein he structures the text on the lines of a mythical tale. Anand invokes the canonical text, *The Ramayana*, early in his narrative when Gauri is told by her mother to be like "Sita". Sita has always been considered the epitome of feminine virtues such as domesticity, devotion to one's husband and children, and capacity for self-sacrifice. Like the mythical heroine, Gauri too suffers and shows a tremendous capacity for suffering. While Sita is abducted by the demon Ravana, Gauri is forcibly sold to the demon like Seth by her uncle Amru. Like her mythical counterpart, she too lives in exile, and returns to her husband chastened by the flames of suffering. But once again the male authority asserts itself when Panchi comes under the pressure of gossip-mongers and demands proof of Gauri's chastity very much like Rama who abandons his wife under the influence of public gossip. Gauri decides to leave her husband and lead an independent life. Anand's intention obviously is to subvert the canonical narrative in such a way that a totally new image of Sita-figure emerges. Anand describes Gauri's final departure from her husband's house as follows:

> For a brief moment, the thought that the earth must open up to rescue her as it had opened up to receive Sita came as an echo from some distant memory. But the ground was hard and solid under her feet and showed no sign of opening up, to prove her innocence. She waved her head to forget Sita and thought of the road to the town. (*Gauri* 264)

Another short story "The Tamarind Tree" portrays a younger mother who cannot satisfy her desire for the taste of the sharp, sweet tamarind fruit. She has to be veiled at her in-laws house with the baseless fear of possible stares at her. The image of veiled Rupa resembles the caged bird. Roopa wistfully remembers her childhood days of innocence and enjoyment. The overweight of the old age traditions has made it highly impossible for her to speak to her husband. Despite her efforts to obey and please her in-laws, she is reproached. She stands for the traditional Indian woman who tolerates the sufferings, agonies silently, giving up her desires like a caged bird with no freedom to fly free. Thus, it remains to be seen that Lajwanti, Roopa, Parvati, Gauri, Sajani and similar women of Mulk Raj Anand represent the wrenched condition of the woman in the traditional Indian society. Mulk Raj Anand in his book—*The Bride's Book of Beauty* (1949), gives a very real picture of the low status of women in India.

Urmila Pawar's *The Weave of My Life: A Dalit Woman's Memoirs* Published in 1988 in Marathi, this autobiography of her helped to bring out the experiences of Dalit women. Pawar recounts her life over several decades, as well as her childhood experience when she used to live in the rural part of Western India. She converted to Buddhism, and moved to the great city of Bombay, and involved herself in the movement for Dalit emancipation. Apart from that she is a keen observer and knitted down her own life struggle in her books, which are translated by Maya Pandit, which powerfully records the growing nature of Dalit life and government throughout the twentieth century. Written in a realistic fictional mode, it is characterized by honest, frank and bold articulation of a Dalit woman's experiences and may easily be compared with Afro-American women's narratives. There is no attempt to camouflage any bitter truth about her personal, domestic and societal life here. That is really admirable. She has shown to the world that; a subaltern woman of the lowest Mahar caste can speak and even write thereby articulating her individual and social vision. The honesty and authenticity of her experience articulated in her *Memoir* is highly appreciable. It is an odyssey of herself and shows her spiritual journey from ignorance to knowledge, from helplessness to courage; from diffidence to confidence and from multiple bondages to emancipation within the patriarchal framework.

Indian society has practiced an extreme form of patriarchy since the beginning of known history, though the relics of matriarchy were found as late as nineteenth century in certain regions. It is based on male predominance and female subordination. It praises the wife-mother role of women but treats her as no better than the legal, economic and sexual property of her husband. This is sanctified by socio-legal treatises. Thus, it is laid down in the laws of Manu that "no act is to be done according to her own will by a young girl, a young woman, though she be in her own house. In her childhood, a girl should be under the will of her father; in her youth under that of her husband; her husband being dead, under the will of her sons. A woman should never enjoy her own will. Though of corrupt behaviour or immoral, a husband should be adored alike a god by a moral mate" (Briffault 147-48).

Woman began her course of life as a member of an extended family which was a small community in itself as it spanned several generations and comprised of the patriarch and his younger brothers with their families, married sons and their families, all the unmarried sons and daughters, and widowed or deserted daughters who returned to their parental home. All the males born in the family inherited the ancestral wealth but the daughters were not entitled to a share. They were compensated at marriage with jewellery, clothes and household articles which was originally intended to be "woman's wealth" solely under their control. Eventually, however, it became transmuted into "dowry" which was demanded by husband and marital family. Thus, women lost all their assets in course of time and became economically dependent. Elders even parents, did not treat male and female children equally. The family betrayed a strong pro-son bias because the son would remain in the family, carry on the family name, care for parents in old age and perform the necessary rituals after their death. The daughter was viewed as "stranger's wealth" because she was to be given away in marriage at a great expense as dowry had to be paid for the purpose. So, a woman counted less in family and a low premium was placed on her life.

This set-up led to violence against woman almost as soon as she was born and female infanticide was prevalent in certain regions of the country. It was forbidden by law in 1877 but the woman remained unwelcome and undesirable. A daughter could not have a carefree childhood because she had to handle household duties and undergo chastisement as a preparation for married life. Education was denied to her even among the traditionally literate upper classes who deemed education a must for boys. The girls were married well before puberty and sent to their husband's house as soon as they came of age. A strong bond between wives and husbands could not develop under the extended family. Nor could there develop a female bond among the unrelated outsiders who came in as daughters-in-laws. They were all dependent persons competing for a better share in the resources of the family. With the early start of the married life came early motherhood which was physically traumatic, debilitating and injurious up to the point of death. If the wife failed to produce a child or bore female children only, she was treated as an offender of the worst kind. That could be an excuse for her being deserted by her husband. If she was not deserted, her husband would marry again and have an additional wife to ensure a male heir. Ignorant of the elementary facts of genetics, people laid the blame for barrenness or birth of female children on the wife only. If the husband died earlier, the wife had to undergo a lot of traumatic experiences. In some parts of India, like Bengal and Rajasthan, widows were immolated on the funeral pyre of their husband. The practice was legally stopped in 1829. In the regions which did not practice widow immolation, they had to live on sufferance. They had to wear drab clothes and to renounce all sort of pleasure. Sometimes they were physically disfigured, for example, by shaving off their heads. They were deemed inauspicious and kept away from all ceremonies in the family, except, of course, mourning. There were strict rules for their food. The windows, along with the deserted women, were treated as household drudges. Though widowers could and did remarry, the widows could not in case of upper castes. It must be mentioned that most of those widows lost their husband early in childhood as marriage took place early and difference in age between wife and husband was quite appalling upto the nineteenth century, which made widowhood inevitable. The Widow Remarriage Act of 1856 legalised remarriage of the widows but that brought little change in reality.

Demands for social reform were conceded from time to time. Immolation of the widows was banned legally in 1829 and remarriage of the widows was banned legally in 1829 and remarriage of the widows was legalised in 1856 thanks to the efforts of Raja Rammohun Roy and Vidyasagar respectively. Then came legislation prohibiting child marriages and giving more rights to women in respect of marriage, divorce, inheritance, etc. such measures met a lot of resistance from religious bigots. In case of the religious minorities the progress has been much slow for the same reasons. Impact of the legislation as well as of western ideas has not been even in different regions and classes. But despite all that, we have little reason to be complacent about the condition of women in India. While the universal demographic pattern shows a female deficit. The general proportion of women in the total population is not only unbalanced but also declining consistently. That is, however, a passive form of violence to women. But other forms of violence have not disappeared despite modernisation. Mostly, they are practiced in other decisive ways. Formerly, female infanticide was very common in certain regions of the country. In the Bhatti community of Jaisalmer, Rajasthan the sex ratio is 550 women to 1000 men only as against the national ratio of 929 to 1000. Marriage parties have not visited the villages of the community for decades. It was reported in 1988 by Rajendra Singh, a member of the community, that forty girls were murdered soon after their birth in the community. But the urban, educated and relatively well-off people are employing sophisticated means instead of the crude ones. Diagnostic techniques of amniocentesis, basically designed for detecting foetal abnormalities, is harnessed to determine the sex of the fetus and followed by selective abortion of female fetuses.

The constitution of India provides for compulsory education for all upto the age of fourteen, but this is generally neglected in case of girls. The percentage of girls attending school varies from state to state, sometimes it is below 20% and rarely reaches 50%. Though the educated young people in upper middle and upper classes are asserting their choice to some extent, most of the marriages are still arranged by the families. It is estimated that fourteen million child marriages take place in India every year. Early marriages, complications in child birth cause 13% of deaths before the twenty-fifth year. Maternal mortality in India is very high as compared to other nations. The average Indian woman becomes pregnant eight times, gives birth to six to seven children out of which four survive.

The entire process of arranging the marriage is humiliating to women. A girl has to show her skills and undergo a long test and interrogation by parents and guardians of the potential groom. The boy is rarely asked a question or required to prove his abilities. The traumatic experience is worsened when the girl is rejected for some reason or other and has to confront interrogation teams before selection. Even then the question of dowry remains. The girls who do not have parents or guardians to arrange and pay a dowry hardly get married. Educated people are allowing some freedom to their daughters and delaying their marriages but considerations of caste, community and religion are rarely brushed aside even there.

Demands for dowry before and after marriage do not seem to have diminished by legislation and education. Women are harassed and tortured for extorting more money and consumer goods which results sometimes in death (either through suicide or outright murder). Often such deaths are camouflaged as accidents, if not suicide due to mental derangement. Daughters are still treated as outsiders. Once married they are welcomed in the parental home on limited occasions only. They are reminded again and again: "your place is next to your husband. Your home is where he is." So, when they are abused and forced to flee, they rarely find a sympathetic response at the parental home. Attempts at "reconciliation" are made ignoring the gravity of situation which often leads to an untimely end of their lives.

Janki's pathetic account of herself in the following passage, in fact, hints at the exploitation of women in the conservative Indian society:

> I have certainly begun to think clearly of all those who deny us freedom. First of all, my parents who created me not because they loved each other but because they considered it their duty, and who regarded me, when I was born, as a curse because I was a girl. Then my husband and his relations, who were more concerned with dowry I brought than with me. Later, when the owner of my house died, society considered me as one who should be dead to all impulses and live to worship the memory of my dead lord and master. Do you (Ananta) remember the things that were said all over Punjab because I ran away with you? The followers of the Mahatma in Bombay who believed in freedom yet despised me because I was not married to you. (*The Big Heart* 174)

Divorced or separated women are deemed an unnecessary burden to the parental home and somewhat guilty rather than victims by society. Responsibility for the failure of marriage is generally laid at the door of wife ignoring the truth that husbands, in-laws too play a role. The Hindu Succession Bill of 1955-56 entitles Hindu daughters equal rights of inheritance in their father's estate. But property rights to wives are denied by religious or personal laws. Divorced wives enjoy no rights to their husband's property. Economic constraints have necessitated middle-class women to seek jobs to supplement the family income. But their choice is generally limited to nursing, teaching, etc. which are deemed suitable for women. Employment however, does not give them control over their income. They are expected to hand over their salary to their husband or in-laws and keep contented with the petty amounts granted to them for their daily expenses. Their lives are further complicated by the problems of managing both the job and the home, alcoholic husbands squandering away their earnings and the suspicions about their character.

Lower-class women have been always working. Though the principle of "equal pay for equal work" is never challenged, women are paid less than men for the same work. The other problem they face frequently is sexual harassment and abuse. In the case of the poor and illiterate victims, a class bias is often evident. The women of lower classes are supposed to have nothing like character and so charges of molestation and rape are dismissed lightly if they happen to be the victims. Often, they are alleged to be lying in order to extort some money and that is the excuse for setting at liberty the accused belonging to upper classes by judges.

As a responsible writer and thinker Anand suggests various answers to the human problems dealt with in his novels, refraining from the imposition of any kind. As said earlier, Anand is aware that man has to turn inward and find the right solution. He should develop a "big heart" that cherishes values like equality, human tenderness, religious tolerance, devotion to duty, liberty. Anand's central aim is to project his "desire image", what he would like life to be as against what it is. According to him, an artist should interpret reality and not reproduce it. His object is not merely to shock his readers by a representation of reality but to stimulate their consciousness. Anand has exposed social evils in its myriad manifestations and has evocatively presented different layers of human experience in his fiction. His wide reading and travel have enabled him to view humanity at large in a proper perspective. His close association with the underdogs and his passionate record of their woes have given his writings a rare cogency and an intimate quality of felt life.

Works Cited

Abraham, Francis and John Henry Morgan. *Sociological thought from Comte to Sorokin*. London: Wyndham Hall Press, 1989. Print.

Anand, Mulk Raj. *Coolie*. New Delhi: Penguin Books, 1993. Print.

——. *Gauri*. New Delhi: Arnold Heinemann, 1981. Print.

——. *Lajwanti and Other Stories*. New Delhi: Orient Paperbacks, 1999. Print.

——. *Mulk Raj Anand Greatest Short Stories*. Mumbai: Jaico Publishing House, 1999. Print.

——. *The Big Heart*. New Delhi: Arnold Heinemann, 1980. Print.

——. *The Bride's Book of Beauty*. Bombay: Kutub Publisher, 1949. Print.

——. *The Lost Child and Other Stories*. New Delhi: Orient Paperbacks, 2004. Print.

——. *Two Leaves and a Bud*. Bombay: Kutub Publisher, 1946. Print.

Berry, Margaret. *Mulk Raj Anand: The Man and the Novelist*. Amsterdam: Oriental Press, 1970. Print.

Bhattacharya, S.K. *Bengal Renaissance: Social and Political Thought*. New Delhi: Classical Publishing Company, 1986. Print.

Briffault, Robert. *The Mothers: A Study of the Origin of Sentiments and Institutions*. New York: Vol. I, 1952, 345; for the original text, vide, *Manusmriti* (v. 147-148). Print.

Cowasjee, Saros. "Anand's *Two Leaves and a Bud*". *Indian Literature*, Vol. xvi, Nos. 3 and 4 (July-December, 1973). Print.

——. *Coolie: An Assessment*. New Delhi: OUP, 1976. Print.

——. *So Many Freedoms: A Study of Major Fiction of M. R. Anand*. New Delhi: Oxford University Press, 1977. Print.

Desai, A.R. *Social Background of Indian Nationalism*. Bombay: Popular Prakashan, 1966. Print.

Ganguli, Dwarakanath. *Slavery in British Dominion*. Calcutta: Jijnasa, 1972. Print.

Gramsci, Antonio. *Selections from Prison Notebooks*. (trans.) Quentin Hoare and Geoffrey Nowell Smith. London: Lawrence and Wishart, 1971. Print.

Guha, Ranjit. 'Preface'. *Subaltern Studies,* Vol. i (ed.), Ranjit Guha, Delhi: Oxford University Press, 1982. Print.

Hemenway, Stephen Ignatius. *The Novel of India*, Vol. ii. Calcutta: The Writers' Workshop, 1975. Print.

https://www.researchgate.net/publication/261778600. *The Weave of My Life a Dalit Woman.* Memoirs by Urmila Pawar translated by Maya Pandit. Web. 23 May 2018.

Iyengar, K.R. Srinivas. *Indian Writing in English*. New Delhi: Sterling Publishers, 1985. Print.

Marx, Karl and Frederic Engels. *Selected Works*. Moscow: Progress Publishers, 1977. Print.

Patel, S.J. "Agricultural Labourers in Modern India and Pakistan". *Indian Journal of Economics*, Vol. XXXIII, July, 1952. *The World of the Rural Labourer in Colonial India*. Ed. Gyan Prakash, Delhi: OUP, 1992. Print.

Paul, Premila. *The Novels of Mulk Raj Anand*. New Delhi: Sterling Publishers, 1983. Print.

Robertson, R.T. "*Untouchable* as an Archetypal Novel". *Kakatiya Journal of English Studies,* 2.1, 1977. Print.

Shastri, Shakuntala Rao. *Women in The Sacred Laws*, Bombay, 1959. Print.

Social Welfare, Vol. XXXIV, Nos. 11-12, Feb.-March, 1933. Print.

3

The Indian Inferno: Caste Propagation and Consciousness

3.1 What is Caste?

Caste is known as *jati* in common parlance. Caste as a system of social relations has been assigned a central purpose in Hindu society for numerous centuries. A lot of conjectures, controversies and explanations have been derived regarding its origin, nature and role in Indian society. As said by K.L. Sharma (1998) in his book *Indian Society* the origin of the caste system dates back to the age of the *Rig Veda*. There is a reference to the word *Varna* (colour) in the *Rig Veda*. 'Arya' is mentioned to as light-skin and 'Dasa' as dark. The people of the two *varnas* (fair and dark complexioned) differed not only in their skin colour but also in their worship and speech. Thus, the difference was both racial and cultural.

The Purusha-Shukta, a part of the *Rig Veda*, states that the Brahmanas, Rajanyas, Vaishyas and Shudras sprang from the mouth, arms, thighs and feet of the Purusa (God). Later on, these became castes. However, there is no reference of castes becoming hereditary. In later Vedic civilisation which consisted of Samhitas—Atharva, Yajur and Sama and their Brahmanas and Sutras. The conception of sacrifice gained importance in this later Vedic age. The doctrines of Karma, Maya, transmigration, the identity of the individual soul with the universal soul, and Mukti as main tenants of Hinduism, find expression in the Upanishads. The recitalists of Yajnas came to be called Brahmanas. They became a distinct class. The Aryans who conquered territories they formed another group known as Kshatriyas. The remaining

Aryans grew into a distinct class and were called as Vaishyas. The non-Aryan became the fourth class and were known as Shudras. Primarily these categories remained non-rigid divisions; however, step by step restrictions were levied on modification of duties. Further subdivision occurred. Birth became the only real criterion of one's identity (caste) determination. Today caste is an endogamous group, that is, its members marry within the caste. A man is born in a caste and remains in that caste forever. Members of the caste used to have a particular occupation on a hereditary basis. A given caste occupies a particular rank in the hierarchy of castes, hence some are superior to it and some inferior. In attendance, to caste, there are strict rules concerned with fooding, drinking and social communication that stand to be followed by all castes.

Religion in India has never been static. Today it has created ruckus into the arenas of politics and economic life. Religion is a really complex phenomenon in India. For example, elements of Aryan Sanskrit and Dravidian tribal religion are found in a mixed form at various levels. So is the interaction between the 'great' and the 'little' traditions according to Milton Singer and Robert Redfield. The class and caste system of India is the direct product of religion. The *varna* system on which Indian society is based is very much correlated with religion. The Literal meaning of *varna* is 'colour'. India has always been the meeting and melting point of the world. Different races came to India and thrived. The Indus valley civilization was the first then came the Aryans. With the Aryan came the term *varna* which means colour. So, the initial difference was based on 'colour' of the skin since the native Indians were brown coloured people known as the Dravidians. The Aryans as they expanded in the great Northern Indian plains the indigenous people shifted to the southern forested areas.

3.2 Origins and History

There is a widespread belief among orthodox Hindus that *chaturvarna*, or the hierarchical four-tier social structure of ancient India, had a sacred origin. This belief is engendered by the ostensibly religious justification of *chaturvarna* in the

Rig Veda, the *Manusmriti*, and the interpolated forms of the *Ramayana* and the *Mahabharata*, where it has been declared to be of celestial origin. In reality, however, the support to *chaturvarna* given by the religious texts on the pretext of its allegedly divine origin served merely to sanctify and perpetuate an ancient form of unjust division of labour that was based on the oppression and exploitation of the entire working class, which constituted the overwhelming majority of the population in ancient India, by a small and parasitic ruling class. The 'other-worldly' spiritual injunctions were in the nature of a consciously contrived functional ideology that served to camouflage a this-worldly socio-economic edifice of exploitation. In other words, the societal roots of the metaphysics of *chaturvarna* were engrained in the relations of production in ancient India.

"In some cases, the untouchables might face criminal charges if they contaminated certain things with their touch. For example, it was a criminal offence for a member of an excluded caste knowingly to pollute a shrine by his presence" (Hampton).[1] They were also forbidden to enter the streets in which the houses of the upper castes were located, and there were many customs and laws that kept them beyond the villages and towns. "Since they were regarded exterior the caste classification, they were ordained solely to live at the borders of the village and were at no time a vital part of village life. However, their amenities were still essential to the well-being of the community and consequently still had to be part of the structure in command to oblige the superior castes" (Velassery 8).

In the age of the Dharmasutras, all peasants, except rural artisans, craftsmen, and landless labourers, were reckoned as Vaishyas. By the middle of the period of the dharmasastras, however, most of the peasants, including those who tilled their own land, were demoted to the status of Shudras. From that time onwards, the Brahmins and Kshatriyas effectively constituted the ruling class of ancient India, with the Vaishyas playing a somewhat auxiliary role. Thus, by about the 1st or 2nd century A.D. the entire working class, including all small and marginal farmers, landless labourers, artisans and craftsmen, and all manual labourers, was relegated to the status of Shudras. Since industry and trade were undeveloped in that ancient period, the Vaishyas also constituted an insignificant proportion of the population. The Shudras, therefore, constituted the overwhelming majority of the people of the country. It was this vast class of Shudras that was relegated to the bottom of the socio-economic pyramid and ruthlessly exploited by the composite ruling class of the Brahmins and Kshatriyas, using both the power of religion and the power of the state as its apparatuses of control.

The concept of swadharma was central to the injunctions of the religious texts regarding the division of labour consummated by *chaturvarna*. Manu defined swadharma as swakarma or the occupational duty as prescribed by the Dharmasastras. All major religious texts, including the *Manusmriti*, the *Bhagavad-Gita*, and the interpolated versions of the *Ramayana* and the *Mahabharata*, prescribed the unquestioning service of the three 'higher' *varnas* as the swadharma of the Shudras. The vast working class of Shudras was thus denied all social, economic and political rights, which were, of course, dominated by the Brahmins and Kshatriyas. Shudras enjoyed no civil liberties or privileges, and were not permitted to perform any sacrifices or homa, read or learn the Vedas or recite the mantras (prayer rituals). "They were similarly not permitted to come inside temples and worship and they possibly will only serve the upper three castes as a slave, barber, blacksmith or cobbler" (Gurjari). The *Manusmriti* also denied the Shudras the right to education, the right to property, the right to carry arms, and even access to religious observances. The *Manusmriti* declared that if a Shudra acquired any property, any Brahmin or Kshatriya had the right to take it away from him forcibly. It is believed that caste as it is today, is a remnant of the varnasrama dharma. A differentiation of castes made on the basis of one's occupation for the common good of a given society. However, there is another theory which maintains that the Hindu religion originated the caste system as it favoured the so-called ruling caste. According to this Hindu belief, the four different castes emanated from the Brahma but from his different parts. The Brahmins, the highest in the caste hierarchy were said to proceed from the forehead of the

Brahma, the Kshatriyas from the shoulders, the Vaishyas from the stomach and the Shudras from the foot of the Brahma. While the division based on the kind of work performed by a particular group is quite agreeable to reason, the theological explanation offered is an outrage to human dignity and become the basis for the ignominious and iniquitous social evil called "untouchability".

The grossly exploitative class structure of ancient India, which was cleverly camouflaged and sanctified by the Dharmasastras, particularly by *chaturvarna*, has remained virtually unchanged to this day. The original four *varnas* have proliferated into over a thousand castes and sub-castes due to numerous socio-religious and economic factors. These include false ideas regarding the hereditary transmission of purity and impurity, differences of rituals and ceremonies, endogamous marriage and other forms of socio-cultural intercourse, geographical location, and above all, economic status, particularly land ownership. The myriad castes and sub-castes of contemporary India cannot in all cases be classified under the original *chaturvarna* of the Dharmasastras, although they have all risen on the matrix of the ancient caste system of India. Perhaps the most important regressive development is that the entire caste system has become hereditary and transformed itself into a crystallized prejudice structure. Although it is still a superstructure of the relations of production, it has over the centuries acquired a degree of autonomy, and in some ways, behaves independently of the relations of production. This is the most distinctive characteristic of class relations in India today. The proliferations of castes, and the relative improvement of the socio-economic status of some of the 'middle' castes, have to some extent diluted the structure of the four-tier hierarchy of ancient Indian society.

3.3 British Rule and Its Impact on Indian Caste System

"The variability of the caste structure was stricken by the arrival British. The British brought with them their own traditional form of government, and as Christians, they did not have much sympathy for the Hindu institutions" (Ghurye 270). The caste structure substantially affected the economic organisation within the Indian village. The rural community was essentially a food-providing unit, where each family of the craft or service caste was linked with one or more of the property owning-farmer-caste family. This system was branded as the jajmani system, which survived in India up to the arrival of the British. Coming to the Indian society, Karl Marx was the first thinker to draw sharp attention to the extremely poisonous impact of caste on Indian society and its fundamental link with the relations of production.

In his famous essay on "The Future Results of British Rule in India" (1853) published in *New York Daily Tribune*, August, 8th, Karl Marx, characterized the Indian castes as "the greatest and critical obstruction to India's advancement and power". The industrialization and commercialization of India under British rule, facilitated by the spread of railways, would lead to the collapse of the out-of-date village communities, and with them also the caste system. But Marx wrote later on that he had overstated the possible impact of the spread of railways on the traditional relations of production characterized by the Indian village community. The important point, however, is that Marx clearly and causally connected the archaic social formation of caste in India with the relations of production. "During the preliminary days of the British East India Company's rule, caste privileges and customs were encouraged, but the British law courts began to disagree with the discrimination against the lower castes" (Alavi 5).

Britain and the Britishers not only changed the caste system into a class system but also affected the Hindu folks in indirect ways:

> A certain number of traditional caste-linked crafts were made impossible to make because of the large number of importing factory-made goods from then megapolis. Because of this, countless weavers had to work in agriculture. In different occupational areas, livelihoods that had been passed down from generation to generation had to be shut down because of newly opened factories, for example, the small-cottage textile industries prevalent that time. (Bouglé 81)

On or after these events, not only the occupations got modified, but the identical communal standing among the castes was affected. This stratified arrangement has been disturbed and a new class system has emerged because of capitalism, multiculturalism, modernism, and globalization in the post-colonial era.

3.4 Dimensions of Class and Caste Embodied in Literature

Just as the caste system has been in India since times immemorial, attempts to abolish it has also been there from that time onwards. As said and wrote by Swami Vivekananda, "The caste classification is opposite to the faith of the *Vedanta*. Caste is an evil social custom and our every eminent preacher has tried to disrupt and dissolve it down. From Buddhism downwards, every sect has preached against the caste system and every time it has only riveted the chains" (31). Thus, right from the times of *Upanishads* intellectuals have articulated against the caste classification. Buddha preached against it 2500 years ago. In the nineteenth century, there were four major movements with the main aim, among other things, to abolish the caste system. They are *Bramho Samaj, Arya Samaj, Ramakrishna Movement*, and the *Theosophical Movement*. These movements tried exhaustingly to teach the individuals with the concern of the evils of caste structure. Mulk Raj Anand also protested against this caste system through his fictional and non-fictional works. Mulk Raj Anand brought to Indo-Anglian fiction new matter, a new technique, new style, and new attitudes. In the "Preface" to the second Indian edition of *Two Leaves and a Bud* (1951) as Anand says until he began to write about the outcastes, the pariahs, the underdogs and to resurrect them from the obscure lanes and alleys of India, nothing very much had been heard or written about them in polite literature in the languages of our subcontinent:

> In spite of their nationalistic concern, Bankim Chandra's novels were but romances abstractedly imitative of Scott with a historical or mythical slant; Tagore was chiefly interested in the upper-landed gentry of Bengal and the 'bhadra-lok', the middle-class section of Calcutta city;

> and Sarat Chandra in the lower middle classes; and Munshi Premchand chose his themes from the defeated peasantry and humble folk of Uttar Pradesh. (Iyengar 333-34)

Novels writing in English in India began (in the modern sense of the term) not earlier than the later part of the nineteenth century. That was but natural because English became the official language of British India and the medium of instruction for education. English exposed Indian intellectuals to the ideas of Mill, Spencer, and Bentham and made them aware of the socio-political changes that were taking place in Italy, Germany, Russia, Japan, etc. on the other. But it also made Indians acquainted with the literary tradition of the west in general and of England in particular. As Uma Parameshwaran in *A Study of Representative Indo-English Novelists* accurately observes, the English educated in the earliest epoch "responded actively to certain kinds of English literature and philosophy, such as romantic idylls, philosophical treatises, idealistic outpourings, re-enactments of history. This accounts for their interest in Scott, Dickens, Wordsworth, Carlyle, Ruskin and Macaulay, and their imitation of them" (16). But we observe another tendency too in Indian English novels from the very beginning. That is the tendency to notice social life and to reflect upon it. That was but natural at a time when Indian society was subjected to ruthless criticism by the Christian missionaries and the western education had brought in liberal bourgeois ideas about human relations. The elite, as a result, became aware of the weaknesses of Indian society like superstitions, early marriage, polygamy, the miserable condition of the women in general and widows in particular and the most excesses of the caste system. So, the early novels are not entirely devoid of social criticism and protest such as Ramesh Chandra Dutt's *The Lake of Palms* (1909), S.K. Ghosh's *The Prince of Destiny: The New Krishna* (1909), Sir Jogendra Singh's *Nasrin* (1915). But Indian English literature witnessed an unprecedented growth of socially committed writing by the 1930s. According to William Walsh (1990), "the art of fiction was an end in itself and not just a means for communicating other kinds of truth" (63). Walsh names three of these "genuine novelists"—Mulk Raj Anand, R.K. Narayan, and Raja Rao—and strangely enough, the first one of them turns out to be a socially committed novelist by faith. His novels appeared "like so many packets of explosives" (63) to the régime.

Around the 1930s when the freedom movement picked up momentum and united the whole nation into a great force, the Gandhian protest against the caste system became an equally powerful force. The famous fast undertaken by Gandhi in 1932 to prevent the establishment of a separate electorate for the untouchables was the climax of protest against the caste system in India. In many universities, the students took a vow not to observe the hierarchy of castes in their social dealings with others. The Angry young man in Mulk Raj Anand found the time perfectly ripe to present his long-preserved feeling of protest against the caste system. His technique of protest was quite totally diverse from that of others. Instead of writing a tract against untouchability as recommended to him by Mahatma Gandhi, he wrote a novel, as "novel was more human and could reproduce contrary emotions and shades of feeling" (Naik 11).

This thesis presents the class and caste consciousness in Indian society that was beautifully portrayed by Mulk Raj Anand in many of his novels starting from *Untouchable* (1935), *Coolie* (1936), *Two Leaves and a Bud* (1937) and *The Village* (1939), *Across the Black Waters* (1940), *The Sword and the Sickle* (1942), *The Big Heart* (1945), and *The Road* (1960), etc. Anand exposes the unpalatable aspects of the ritual fanatical Indian social life, especially from the viewpoint of those at the receiving end. In the record of Indian writing, the most outstanding writer that contributed very significantly to Indo-Anglian literature is Mulk Raj Anand. Anand has established the basic form and themes of Indian literature that is written in English. The simple fact that his novels *Untouchable* and *Coolie* are available in thirty-eight (38) languages of the world substantiates the point we have tried to focus so far that Mulk Raj Anand is an artist of universal recognition and greatness. For him Literature is life and the large majority of questions raised by him are social questions, questions of tradition and convention, norms, symbols, and myth.

3.5 Detailed Analysis of *Untouchable*

Since the publication of his first novel *Untouchable* in 1935, Anand's literary career has been amazingly diverse. This study, however, limits itself to his fictional writings: novels and short stories. In his long and fruitful life, Anand has shown a serious engagement with the socio-political progress of the time and this political awareness directly informs his artistic vision. His anxiety with the structure of power and how it touches the individual and society has a direct bearing not only on his fictional themes and characters but also on the formulation of his literary doctrine which anticipates all the vital concerns of what far ahead came to be called post-colonial theory. The narrative form of Mulk Raj Anand's novel *Untouchable* shows a skillful organisation of the various tools of narration i.e., point of view, focus, atmosphere, characterization, etc. The novel shows how the untouchable at the time when the novel was written lived in inhuman conditions and were subjected to worst kinds of humiliation, sometimes on trifles and sometimes without any cause whatsoever. We would do well to begin, with what Mulk Raj Anand said about what he wanted to show in the novel:

> I wanted to bring to light the ghosts of the "dead souls" murdered without a rite by the Dharam bugs. I wanted to beckon all the phantoms, so that they should haunt the dreams of the half dead, and awaken them, may be, to the lingering sparks of life.... I wanted to burn and shine like.
>
> Tiger, Tiger, burning bright.... (18)

Anand so detested the caste system, particularly its inhumane treatment of the untouchable caste, that he made it his mission to educate the universal public with the hope of eliminating this appallingly painful custom. His first attempt to bring into worldly light this hard-hearted practice was in his 1935 novel *Untouchable*. Untouchability, caste discrimination, and exploitation were where Anand put his greatest efforts in trying to expose, overcome and eliminate their roles in Indian culture. Nevertheless, it was stated that there were only four castes in the Hindu practice, there was a lower sub-caste of the Shudras. This deprived and poor group was called the Chandalas and they were believed to be impure.

Due to their congenital occupations—human waste transporters, butchers, hunters and graveyard workers—in conjunction with their magical religious practices and their basic lack of hygiene, these uneducated people were not even believed to be human. They were deemed to be untouchable and polluted. Because they were not permitted to interact with any other castes other than to perform their everyday menial and unhygienic jobs, they lived basically on the fringes of society. The term used to identify a person of the lowest possible stature in the Hindustani culture was untouchable. It was held that if an individual of a higher-ranking caste came into physical contact with a person of the untouchable class, the higher-caste Hindu would be dishonored, tainted, tarnished and desecrated. His Bakha of *Untouchable* is but a fictional recreation of Bakha, his childhood friend. His experience in Gandhi's ashram had instilled into him an abomination of this social taboo which has been contributory for so much of exploitation in India and to a lesser extent in some other countries.

For Anand casteism and untouchability are two great wounds in the Indian psyche that need to be healed or two cancers in the body politic of our society burrowing its very vitality. In this Anand is an ardent disciple of Gandhi. Anand had the first-hand experience of this insidious practice of untouchability as his childhood was spent in the midst of children of all castes. Hence Anand took it as a challenge to portray the lowly and colourless lives of the untouchables in his novels. In *Untouchable* obviously and in *The Road,* Anand has created two immortal heroes drawn from the crust of the so-called casteist society. Bakha of *Untouchable* has a perennial appeal as a child hero who grows from innocence to maturity and as a fete in the fiction of a sweeper boy, the likes of whom never entered the realms of literature before Anand's bold venture. The sweepers cluster is described at substantial length by Anand, thus underlining the fact that they have an existence of their own, if it may be called an existence, about which the caste people, whose dirty jobs these untouchables do, have no concern or knowledge. It is a symbol of the filth and grime that mark their persons and their lives. This is the paradox that the individuals who are responsible for maintaining the hygiene and sanitation of the high caste people are methodically deprived of their elementary rights to hygiene or cleanliness.

But this is just one level or kind of discrimination. But the credence that their proximity or their touch or contact can pollute and contaminate a high caste person is a shameful denial of the basic humanness of these men and women. It is a contradiction in terms as those who practise it takes it as a religious decree and the untouchables themselves have assimilated it into their mindset and being, as their fate and as designed by God Almighty. The privileged caste Hindus proclaim in all sneer and insensitivity: "They ought to be wiped off the surface of the earth" (Anand 41). To believe that a human being was so repulsive, filthy and sickening was an inhuman, brutally cruel and mercilessly callous concept. According to Anand to actually practice this principle was immoral and morally undesirable. His first novel *Untouchable* is brief. The action takes place on a single day and the novel centres on one character. It presents, like Ferdinand Oyono's *Houseboy* or Abubakar Tafawa Balewa's Hausa novel *Shaihu Umar*, a totally unsentimental account of a young person placed in a position of social subservience, the society to which he belongs insisting almost ritualistically on the enforcement of this servitude. Saros Cowasjee (1970) in his introduction to *Private Life of an Indian Prince* has asserted that before *Untouchable* there were no Indian novels prepared to plead on behalf of the low castes. The novel describes the outcaste's colony consisting of scavengers, the leather-workers, the washermen, the barbers, the water carriers, the grass-cutters and other outcastes from Hindu society. The place where these people reside is the most unhygienic one. A brook soiled by dirt and filth of the public latrines ran near the lane. The odour of the dead animals left to dry on its banks is suffocating. The absence of a drainage system gave out the most offensive smell. The writer observes that "the ugliness, the squalor and the misery which lay within it, made it an 'uncongenial' place to live in, that is to say it's a place where animals could stay better, the place is not hygienic for a human being to live" (Anand 1). Bakha, a young boy of eighteen, son of Lakha, the Jemadar of all the sweepers in the town. After a short introduction of the protagonist, Anand describes his friends, Chota, the leather worker's son, and Ram Charan, the washerman's son as they share the same lot with Bakha. The houses of untouchables are also painted by Anand. The uncongeniality of his home, twelve feet by five, dank, dingy, one-roomed mud house. The organising principle of the novel is to present a day in the life of Bakha. It could be an ordinary day like the other day that he has already spent or like the days which he is going to spend. E.M. Forster (1935), who wrote the preface of the book, makes an illuminating comment:

> Bakha is a real individual, lovable, thwarted, sometimes grand, sometimes weak, and thoroughly Indian. Even his physique is distinctive; we can recognise his broad intelligent face, graceful torso and heavy buttocks, as he does his nasty jobs, ... (7)

Bakha has a high sense of duty. To him work is worship. He values cleanliness as he "worked away earnestly, quickly without loss of effort. Work, to Bakha, is a sort of intoxication that gave him good health and sound sleep. Even Havildar Charat Singh is also amazed by his work, though cleaning the latrines yet he remained clean. He praises Bakha "You are becoming a gentreman, ohe Bakhya! Where did you get that uniform?" (*Untouchable* 8). Charat Singh to show his kindness asked Bakha to come to the cantonment area and take a hockey stick from him. Bakha is moved beyond words for such a kind gesture:

> Bakha stretched himself up; he was astonished yet grateful at Charat Singh's offer. It was a godsend to him, this spontaneous gesture on the part of one of the best hockey players of the regiment. 'A hockey stick! I wonder if it will be a new one!' he thought to himself,

> and he stood smiling with queer humility, overcome with gratitude. (*Untouchable* 9)

And he continued his exhausting work of cleaning the latrines as men came after another. Labour, as defined by Marx, is an essential condition of human life. It provides man self-realization. It is an act of real freedom and Anand's protagonists never shirked from the labour they are entrusted with. Man, in society and man at work are the central elaboration of Anand's major novels. Labour, on one hand, distinguishes human beings from even most highly developed animals. On the other, it confirms them as a member of society. Labour, in fact, is a necessary social activity which attaches a man to his product. Any kind of disharmony arises when the product of man becomes his master and begins to exploit him. It first happens when an individual pass to the group and ultimately polarizes the society itself. This we clearly see in Anand's successive novels from *Coolie* onwards. In *Untouchable,* it also gains ground but it is implicit in the theme. What the novelist strikes more is not economic forces as under capitalist in *Coolie* and *Two Leaves and a Bud* but non-economic forces, i.e. feudalism in *Untouchable.*

Anand gives a heart rendering description of the ways Bakha is treated by caste Hindus. It was a custom at that time that when sweepers entered the town, they had to beat a drum hung around their waist to announce their approach so that those who did not want to get touched by them would be on guard. But one day Bakha Walking along with thoughts of joy, sometimes of his hockey match and sometimes of his becoming 'sahibs' walks into the town. He buys some jalebis to eat. But as soon as he wants to eat them, a Lalaji, that is a man of upper caste, gets touched by him as Bakha has forgotten to announce his approach. This creates an ugly scene. Bakha is abruptly disturbed. The novelist frequently reminds the reader of one-day incidents in the life of Bakha and leaves us to think that it could be any ordinary day in the life of the untouchable. Bakha is both an individual as well as a type, representing the lot of untouchables at the same time. He is slapped, Bakha feels first all the fiery, anguished and an outrage evokes but secondly, something stops him. Bakha was surrounded by a barrier, not a physical barrier but a moral barrier.

After finishing his job of cleaning the latrines Bakha goes to his home for tea but there is no water in the house. Anand paints a very real picture of the society where he shows to the readers that for the basic amenities or needs of the life that is water, the untouchables have to depend on others. The issue is very grave in nature.

The daily struggle for untouchables continues. The two episodes, i.e., the well and the temple ones, are presented to expose the society that Bakha belongs to. Sohini, Bakha's sister goes to fetch water as her brother is thirsty after a long labour and toil. She waits in a long queue near the well. She expects some caste Hindus to pour down water in her pitcher. When Pundit Kali Nath calls Sohini first to fill the pitcher, Gulabo, the washerman's wife is jealous of Sohini's beauty. Pandit Kali Nath has been described with a suggestive irony. He slowly moves onto the brick platform of the well. He seems thoughtful as he feels his stomach jammed due to over-eating. Pandit Kali Nath is a glutton. He reminds the reader of John de la Havre's notes in *Two Leaves and a Bud* which he had prepared to defend the Indian coolies in the tea plantations of Assam. He writes:

> 75% of the coolies on the Assam plantations suffer from keratomalacia (bad eyesight) for lack of proper nourishment fats and greases. 50% of the population of India suffers from dental diseases for lack of any milk in the diet. Two million women die in childbirth in India as a result of malnutrition. 20% Anglo-Indians and members of the upper classes of India die of gluttony, overeating, another form of malnutrition. (106)

Kali Nath is one such man. He abuses food while the majority of the outcastes remain starved. Not only this he is a sex-incarnate. Though his whole life revolves around endless recitation of sacred verses, he hates the men who serve him most faithfully. Pandit Kali Nath is shrewd, schemy and selfish. He sees what he means. Among the crowd waiting for the mercy of the caste Hindu, he favours Sohini by seeing her innocent beauty. The holy priest does not forget to say Sohini that he will like to see her cleaning the courtyard of his house at the temple. Bakha after having his tea goes again to sweep the roads of the town. In his way, he meets his friends and gets the information that in the afternoon a hockey match is going to take place between the 31st Punjabis boys comprising of the babu's sons and 38th Dogras boys eleven most of the poor untouchables. Bakha in his way also meets the two babu's boys and request the elder one to teach him. Bakha is a young boy having a dream of becoming Sahib. Since the age of six, he wanted to study. But he has reconciled to his hereditary craft since he knew nobody would teach an untouchable. Still, the light of being educated flickered inside him and he tried to educate himself by buying the first primer of English but he couldn't read it. Again, getting a chance to be taught he was willing to pay the elder Babu's son an anna per lesson. Bakha's dedication and urge to study are evident in these words:

> The anxiety of going to school! How beautiful it felt! How nice it must be to be able to read and write! One could read the papers after having been to school. One could talk to the sahibs.... And he had felt a burning desire, while he was in the British barracks, to speak the tish-mish, tish-mish which the Tommies spoke. (*Untouchable* 30)

Moving forward he buys cigarettes from the shopkeeper who throws him the packet as a butcher might throw a bone to an insistent dog sniffing around the corner of his shop. But he couldn't complain. Now Bakha wanted to have some sweets from his hard-earned money, so he went to the confectioner shop and bought *jalebis*. He caught the *jalebis* which the shopkeeper again threw towards him as a cricket ball since his touch could defile him. The money which Bakha paid to the shopkeeper was splashed with water and then accepted by him. Bakha was enjoying his walk into the street relishing his *jalebis* but suddenly was given a tight slap and his *jalebis* flung far from his hands on the ground. Bakha accidentally touched a high caste man.

After being abused and humiliated by Lalaji Bakha stood in the crowd and tears rolled from his eyes. Luckily for Bakha a Tonga-Walla appeared and dispersed the crowd to go their own way and clear the street. Bakha when left alone again thought about what all happened to him this hour. A certain realisation of his position in society came to him as he says:

> The cruel crowd! All of them abused, abused, abused. Why are we always abused? The santry inspictor and the sahib that day abused my father. They always abuse us. Because we are sweepers. Because we touch dung. They hate dung. I hate it too. That's why I came here. I was tired of working on the latrines every day. That's why they don't touch us, the high castes.... For them I am a sweeper, sweeper—untouchable! Untouchable! Untouchable! That's the word! Untouchable! I am an untouchable! (*Untouchable* 43)

With this realisation and becoming aware of his position, he began pronouncing his approach '*Posh posh,* sweeper coming' with a loud sound. Bakha's unimportant daily life is occupied with abuses and mortification. The climax occurs when he is said to have unintentionally touched a caste Hindu and is slapped by him. Being a sensitive and smart lad Bakha could not stream the injustice and shame of it. Anand makes this the moment of truth in Bakha's life as he has an unparalleled illumination and clarity as to why he is being hated, and maltreated. He realizes painfully that his status of being an untouchable makes him a sucker, a pushover, a good for nothing in a caste-ridden society. The loud noise speaking for his anguished self. He began to move ghastly to clean the compound of the temple. He was occupied with the terror which had a mysterious and enigmatic effect on him as he passed in the adjoining area of the temple. Bakha surveyed the heap of dust and leaves which he had come to clean. He threw the basket and the broom on the ground and was ready to begin his job. He saw a miniature temple with a beautifully polished image of a snake enclosed. He was slightly afraid of the snake but his fear ceased when he saw the devotees worshipping it. He shouted his call of caution to avoid the repetition of the morning disaster. People were chanting the names of different Gods. Bakha had a faint idea about some of them and did not know anything about the rest. He wanted to know but untouchables were never allowed to enter the temples. As his curiosity became more and more acute, he dismissed his conflicting thoughts and moved towards the stairs. Looking here and there he climbed up a few stairs but soon fear returned and he came back to the place from which he started. But as we have seen previously that Pandit Kali Nath had already called Sohini for cleaning his courtyard. So, when Bakha rushes there he hears an uproar at the temple premises. The hypocrisy of the affluent class comes into clear vision when Anand talks about Pandit Kali Nath and his likes in the society.

Pandit Kali Nath heads the society which is orthodox, obnoxious and hypocrate. The 'touch-me-not' priest who worships a bull emitting foul smell and keeps distance from a human being. In this regard Saros Cowasjee (1977) has observed the ironical situations Bakha undergoes:

> As irony is implicit in the theme, one finds it everywhere and even more pervasively than in any other Anand novel. The novel unfolds with a child of modern India shackled by age-old traditions; the Hindus who pride themselves on their cleanliness gargle and spit in the stream and pollute the water while a person incomparably cleaner than themselves is treated like a dirt.... There are orthodox Hindus who worship a bull emitting foul smells but will not touch human being; there are temples whose doors are closed to those who keep its ground clean; we see the queer Hindu notion of 'pollution by touch' and 'pollution from distance'; and the hypocrisy of Hindu women who treat the sweepers as pariahs but want to be called 'mother' by them. (55)

After decades of the independence Indian Government is still running the "Swachha Bharat Abhiyan". This only indicates the poor level of personal hygiene and cleanliness among Indians. In the same book, Cowasjee says: "The Hindu religion is responsible for this fiendish segregation of humanity" (51). This is not acceptable. This reveals rather an insufficient understanding of what Hindu religion means or stands for. Casteism is a social practice and no Hindu religious leader of any merit and significance would admit it as a part of his religion. Giving a place to casteism in Hindu religion is done by certain wolves in sheep's skin for certain privileges and advantages. As Gandhi says at the end of the novel, if the Hindus oppress the untouchables, "they should understand that the fault does not lie in the Hindu religion, but in those who profess it" (Anand 139). As the action in the novel develops, we see him standing in front of the temple and shouting, "polluted! Polluted!" with the accusing finger on poor Sohini. The great pandit's misbehaviour with Sohini and his shameless accusation that she made physical contact with him and defiled him is a typical illustration of the general hypocritical behaviour of the white-washed guardians of religion. It also shows that lust knows no untouchability. Pandit Kali Nath's lustful behaviour with Sohini is only a human frailty whereas his accusation that she polluted him with her touch is beyond doubt diabolic. Bakha wants to teach the pandit a lesson but he couldn't retaliate:

> ...there was futility written on his face. He could not overstep the barriers which the conventions of his superiors had built up to protect their weakness against him. He could not invade the magic circle which protects a priest from attack by anybody, especially by a low-caste man. So in the highest moment of his strength, the slave in him asserted itself, and he lapsed back, wild with torture, biting his lips, ruminating his grievances. (*Untouchable* 56)

After his own humiliation in the market and his sister's humiliation at the hand of the pandit tore him apart. He was beaten but he couldn't show it. He led Sohini go home and himself went to collect the food from the quarters. When he came back his soul was tormented with the height of abuses he incurred today. When his father consoled him, his dejected heart found some peace but still restless. After the consoling words of his father, he went to Ram Charan's sister wedding. There the three friends enjoyed themselves with sweets. As there was a hockey match planned today so, Bakha went to Charat Singh for his hockey stick as promised by him. Charat Singh gave Bakha a new stick and it was beyond the reality that a sweeper like him will be treated by a caste Hindu with such a favour. His happiness knows no boundary. He imagined himself scoring goals after goal with the hockey stick. As the match proceeded between 38th Dogra boys and 31st Punjabis boy it turned into fighting, scratching, hitting, kicking and yelling. A small boy got injured by a stone thrown by the boys. Bakha carried that boy to his home to save his life but for saving his life he got abuses again. Because by touching the boy he polluted him. The mother of this boy shouted at Bakha for defiling her house and her religion. Since Bakha all the afternoon was not found working at the latrines his father was very angry with him. When he returned home tired and dejected his father abused him for not working and spending his time wondering here and there and turned him away from the house. While he is sitting lost in his own thoughts, he is greeted by Colonel Hutchinson, chief of the local salvation army. He lived nearby the outcaste colony. Colonel Hutchinson wants to win the confidence of the boy so that he can take him to the church and talk about Jesus Christ. He tries to explain Christianity and Jesus Christ to Bakha but he is not able to comprehend it: "Who is *Yessuh Messih*, Sahib? Bakha asked, eager to allay his curiosity. 'Come, I shall tell you,' said Colonel Hutchinson. Come to the church" (*Untouchable* 116).

Though Colonel Hutchinson is very honest in his work but Bakha when hears the shrieking and hoarse voice of Mrs. Mary Hutchinson, he run away from his clutches. Roaming around he reaches to the Bulashah station. To his surprise masses of people are flocking and proceeding to Golbagh where Mahatma Gandhi is going to arrive. Bakha became conscious since in the crowd he actually touched many people. He remembered the day happening. So, he stopped at one side of the pavilion end of the ground. He leant by a tree. He wanted to be detached because he was conscious that he was a sweeper. The same image of futility recurs:

> There was an inseparable barrier between himself and the crowd, the barrier of caste. He was part

> of consciousness which he could share and yet not understand. He had been lifted from the gutter, through the barrier of space, to partake of a life which was his and yet not his. (*Untouchable* 128)

Bakha had heard about Gandhiji and the people poured all the information about him being an incarnation of God. This only increased the curiosity of Bakha. He climbed the tree and sat like an ape to see what was going on. Gandhi arrived with his followers. He started his speech by addressing the depressed classes of society. Bakha was thrilled to the very marrow of his bones. He was amazed by the thoughts of Mahatma. He thought of giving his life for him. Again, when Mahatma Gandhi spoke Bakha was puzzled and confused:

> They (untouchables) have, therefore to purify their lives. They should cultivate the habits of cleanliness, so that no one shall point his finger at them. Some of them are addicted to habits of drinking and gambling of which they must get rid. (*Untouchable* 138)

But as we have already seen in the 'well scene' that for the basic need of life that is water the untouchables were not allowed to touch its main source and water is needed for every human activity whether it is cleaning, bathing, cooking, sweeping, etc. so if there is scarcity of water how they are to clean themselves. So Bakha is confused at what Mahatma is talking about. As Mahatma proceeds in his speech, he says that "all public wells, temples, roads, schools, sanatoriums, must be declared open to the untouchables" (139). As Mahatma's speech ended Bakha started to make his way in the crowd and in the crowd, he heard two persons talking to each other about Mahatma and the untouchables. A young poet, Iqbal Nath Sarshar and his companion Mr. R.N. Bashir, Barrister-at-Law were debating about Mahatma. The poet was advocating the concept of a machine. A machine that could clean the latrines. As we see the young poet advocates his concept:

> ...caste is now mainly governed by profession. When the sweepers change their profession, they will no longer remain untouchables. And they can do that soon, for

> the first thing we will do when we accept the machine, will be to introduce the machine which clears dung without anyone having to handle it—the flush system. (*Untouchable* 146)

Bakha goes back to his house dreaming about the machine and the Mahatma. But after decades of Independence, manual scavenging is still rampant, and the greatest violator of this is our Indian Railways. As being the largest government sector employing manual scavengers to clean the railway tracks and toilets which discharge the human waste directly under the tracks. Apart from exposing the absurdity and stupidity of caste consciousness Anand also probes the different levels of casteism practised. In this novel, he is able to point out the degree of caste among the low caste groups. There are castes and sub-castes. Bakha is a sweeper or scavenger belonging to the lowest sub-caste. It is this that makes Gulabo a washerwoman look down upon Sohini who is a sweeper girl. This is untouchability within untouchability, if one may say so. K.R. Srinivasa Iyengar observes: "...there are degrees of caste among the low-caste people, there being none low without one being lower still" (337).

Anand also has a cool dig as it were the practice of touching a Mohammedan to neutralise the pollution caused by an unholy touch of an untouchable. The irony is that the high caste Hindus ordinarily regard the Muslims as outcastes. Anand takes pains to uncover the ridiculousness of this system while at the same time castigating the high caste people and the Hindu religion which are responsible for the perpetuation of this unholy practice. He points out the several myths that have grown up around this system. He reproaches the untouchables for their sense of inferiority and self-effacing, of course, a patrimony of thousands of years of serfdom and servility. He ridicules the high caste superciliousness that thinks that it is presumption on the part of the plebeians to smoke like the rich. He is angry with the high caste housewives who favour the lazy sadhus with hot vegetable curry and rice while they fling stale bread at the untouchable. He is irritated by the segregation of the untouchables in hotels by allotting separate tumblers. Bakha is created by Anand as a sweeper with a difference. He is endowed with a keen sense of his own lowliness, and the possibility of his escape from this sordid reality into a world of the Tommies. This opportunity is provided him by some of the babus and sahibs who are more friendly towards him. His make-believe world consists of his occasional puff at a cigarette thrown by the high caste people, his sporting the clothes of the white man and his fondness for hockey. These are little details that work up to give a credible and authentic picture of Bakha's genuine aspiration to transcend his own limitations. Anand after providing three different alternatives for Bakha's liberation leaves it to him to choose one. But Bakha doesn't find any of the three solutions too enchanting. He is nevertheless fascinated by Gandhi's suggestion of liberation from their inferior status by their refusal to accept the 'leavings' from the plates of high caste Hindus and by seeking free access to wells and temples. He is moreover attracted by the poet's proposal to end their drudgery by adopting a flush out system and mechanization. Anand suggests three solutions to the age-old problem of untouchability: Jesus Christ or conversion to Christianity, Mahatma Gandhi or his approach to the class of social outcaste for the abolition of untouchability, the Machine or the introduction of the flush system. These alternatives are posed in the conclusion of the novel. But these three solutions have not yielded any result since we all know that still untouchability is practised in different parts of India. It is deeply rooted in Indian psyche.

Anand's approach to this problem as manifested in the novel is one of the actions done for the amelioration of the untouchables, and a corresponding distrust of abstract propositions and solutions. He steers clear of any intellectual or philosophical approach to this problem so entrenched in the culture and psyche of our people; Anand finds it a moral obligation to respond to this human problem not only on the part of individuals but society as a whole. In this, it is not so much Anand the Marxist, as Anand the Humanist what is grappling with this ancient problem that has defied solution till today. His socialism is not revolutionary or violent but well-grounded in ethical principles and rooted in India's cultural values. His approach is existential, viewing the pernicious practice of untouchability from the victim's situations and perspective. The perspective of the subaltern is a necessary pre-condition for any objective analysis of their situation. Anand moreover brings to his job an artist's detachment as he by caste is a Kshatriya and not an untouchable. However, he is able to strike a sympathetic chord as his heart vibrates with the untouchable's abject state, and his artistic genius finds the fictional correlative to make the story and plot convincing.

3.6 Detailed Analysis of *The Road*

There are several authors in India as well as abroad writing on the theme of untouchability and segregation. However, no one has been gifted enough to come near Mulk Raj Anand as we have already seen his works. He handles the theme with great penetration and affinity. He pierces into their hearts and operates as an expert physician, repudiating the maltreatment imparted to this erroneously supposed squalor and filth in the Indian society. The age-old problem of untouchability and casteism has really been insurmountable. Anand's novels do not carry any grudge against any individual. Rather, his grievance is against society at large. Continuing his journey Anand once again wrote another novel on untouchability in free independent India. His novel, *The Road* published in 1961, is again a reaffirmation of Anand's emotional involvement in the problem of untouchability, Anand created this 'enchanted mirror' primarily to illustrate to Nehru that untouchability is still a reality all the government's protestations to the contrary notwithstanding.

In *The Road* (1961), Anand returns to the theme of untouchability once again, though the temporal locale of the text is now shifted to post-independence India. This insistent return to a theme which he has already fictionalized with phenomenal success earlier, is meant to make an important point: political autonomy has not brought liberation to all the sections of society; one-third of Indian citizens, namely *Harijans*, still remain enslaved in India even after more than decades of independence. Anand felt the need to make this point urgently, being a personal witness to the discrimination and humiliation to which *Harijans* were subjected in a remote village of Haryana. As Anand himself explains to Saros Cowasjee (1971):

> Well, it was a kind of shock to me when I went to live in Haryana, twenty miles from Delhi, in the human empire of Jawaharlal Nehru, to find that the outcastes not only in south India, but also in the mixed north were still consigned to the limbo of oblivion. There was something tragi-comic to me in the fact that the caste Hindus would not touch the stones quarried by the untouchables to make the road, because the stones had been touched by the untouchables. I mentioned this to the great Nehru. He did not believe me. He was quite annoyed at my citing this difficult fact. I said I would prove it to him by showing it to him in the 'enchanted mirror'. (124)

Anand's novel *The Road* is a fictional representation of this unpalatable reality. In the course of the narrative, *The Road,* however, acquires a symbolic connotation. It comes to signify a journey, progress, and development. In a broader social context, it connects the village to Delhi; the epicenter of power. The outline of the story of the novel is that the people in the village of Govardhan produce plenty of cattle milk and a large amount of vegetables. But selling them to their city, Gurgaon, is a big problem as there is no transportation facility. The government is aware of this problem faced by the villagers, decides to fulfill their aspiration by building a road connecting the city to Govardhan. The work is started. The villagers are very happy that soon vehicles would be able to reach their village and they would have an era of economic prosperity. Bhikhu and other untouchables also get the chance to work in the road construction. The landlord Thakur Singh who has become rich by exploiting the untouchables cannot tolerate the idea of Bhikhu and other untouchables drawing wages just like the caste Hindus for taking part in the road construction. They can work and earn money as their wages. Thus, the control hitherto exercised by the upper caste Hindus over the life of the untouchables is slowly disappearing. Hence, they are stricken with fear coupled with jealousy that a progressively liberated and independent untouchable community may attain to the status of the 'twice-born', a sense of insecurity has been generated in the high caste Hindus as the outcastes are climbing up the social ladder helped by the government's economic and poverty alleviation programmes. The point is well made by philanthropist Dhooli Singh: "They wanted to build it also, but they do not want you to work and earn money and all other things are lies" (*The Road* 57).

The caste feeling soars up. The upper-caste Hindus refuse even to touch the stones quarried by the untouchables. But the village headman Dhooli Singh, inspired by the teachings of Gandhiji decides to treat the untouchables as children of God or Harijans. He courageously joins hands with the untouchables in the road construction. The landlord Thakur Singh becomes furious. By his instigation, the village priest excommunicates Dhooli Singh. Soon the landlord's son, Sanju, a merciless goon, translates into action his father's fury with the untouchables, by burning their huts. Dhooli Singh's son Lachman, who is in love with Thakur Singh's daughter Rukmani, also joins hand in the arson organised by Sanju against the untouchables, in hope that it would please Thakur Singh and one day he will be able to marry Rukmani. On the other hand, the contra-temps lacerate the magnanimous heart of Dhooli Singh with sorrow, and he decides to help the untouchables to build their huts. He generously permits them to occupy his own house till their huts are rebuilt. Dhooli Singh's wife becomes angry at his behaviour of freely mixing with the untouchables and getting polluted, and she leaves him. But Dhooli Singh stands all these ordeals with fortitude.

When the government authorities come to know that the road, instead of uniting people, divides families, threatens friendships, spoils marriages and is responsible for the burning of the huts of untouchables, they send an official to instruct the people that untouchability has been legally abolished and anyone perpetuating it can be punished under the law. Soon reason prevails over emotion in Dhooli Singh's son Lachman and he joins the untouchables in the road construction. Sanju, also behaves with repentance for some time, but soon the feudal blood he has acquired wings him to pursue his crusade against the untouchables. Meanwhile, the construction of the road continues. Finally, when the road is ready, Bhikhu "did not go towards home. Instinctively he went in the direction of the road he had helped to build. And in his soul, he took the direction out of the village, towards Gurgaon, which was the way to Delhi town, capital of Hindustan, where no one knew who he was and where there would be no caste or outcaste..." (*The Road* 110). The evil untouchability has continuously motivated Mulk Raj Anand to transform his words into action. He finds that legislation as a method of social transformation does not add up in the instances of untouchability since untouchability is intensely entrenched in the Indian inner identity. He realises that this social evil can be removed only by appealing to the hearts of the privileged people who unscrupulously perpetuate it. He comprehends that untouchability can be eliminated solely through learning of feelings or empathy.

Hence, Anand, the angry young writer who protested against it in 1930s again tries his hand in the post-independence era with the problem of untouchability. The era is not very different from the social milieu of *Untouchable*. The law of the land has not influenced the attitude of society. As in *Untouchable*, so in this novel too, we find the caste Hindus ill-treating their outcaste brethren. They are not permitted to come into bodily communication with the twice-born, or allowable to go inside the temple or for coming or worshipping the God. The priest, Suraj Mani, at the temple in Govardhan village, exploits the myth of law of karma to satisfy his priestly greed. He combines with Thakur Singh, the landlord, in inciting the Kshatriya caste against the Dalits over the issue of building the village road. He tries to convince Thakur Singh that purificatory ceremony will undo the defilement caused by the touch of the untouchables while handling the stone. He further appeases the landlord by telling him that untouchables are poor because of their sins rather than because of their exploitation by him. His own words reveal how behind the facade of the purificatory ceremony his greed operates:

> Those people are condemned by their karma to work out their doom among the flies and the dust of their huts. The reek of their thatched roofs, and the stifling heat is punishment enough for them.... And, our people were wrong in openly refusing to break the stones touched by the Harijans. It is easier for you to flee out of fire than for them to escape from their past deeds. Always they will remain tainted by their past deeds, but you are twice born.... Now, a purificatory ceremony is necessary. And the shadow of the evil stars that is on your family can only be cured by a special puja.... (*The Road* 40)

In both these novels, we come across the "slapping scene." In *Untouchable*, it is highly dramatic and creates resonance, but in *The Road*, it is a mere contrivance. Taking place in the closing pages of the novel we come across the smacking incident. The thirsty Bhikhu accepts a brass tumbler of water from Rukmani, the beautiful daughter of Thakur Singh. Her brother Sanju, who hates the untouchables sees this and rushes towards Bhikhu and slaps him for defiling the tumbler. Like his prototype Bakha, Bhikhu for a moment thinks of retaliating but common sense warns him of the perilous sea in which he and the other untouchables struggle even after fourteen years of Indian Independence. The upper caste's intransigent attitude to the changed social situation is evident in their refusing to touch the stones carried by the untouchables while enjoying the yield of the fields tilled by them. Pandit Suraj Mani in this novel reminds us of Pandit Kali Nath of untouchable. Pandit Kali Nath and Pandit Suraj Mani are black-marketeers of their religion for selfish ends. As they have not received the divine light, they are incapable of the Gandhian realisation that untouchables are children of God.

In their shallowness, they mix up religion, politics, and social life and vehemently preach on pollution by touch, pollution from distance or on the *karma* theory which says that the sufferings of the untouchables is only a punishment divinely ordained for their bad deeds in their previous births, and that they should submit themselves to every blow and kick the upper castes give them at every step of their lives with humility for the sake of caste-promotion in the next birth. Like Lakha, in *Untouchable*, Laxmi also wishes her son Bhikhu to internalise the caste rules in his person. Believing the caste order to be a divine dispensation. She feels that every member of the low castes is working out the consequences of his misdeeds of the previous birth or births. The religious merit, accruing from obedience to laws of caste, Laxmi firmly believes, would liberate the outcastes from such sins. She like Lakha, persuades her son to give the attitude of defiance towards the caste Hindus and earn religious merit by abiding by their will. See how naively she, like Lakha, tries to convince her son of the efficacy of caste system, "Then through our good deeds shall we rise from our low castes and be born into high caste" (*The Road* 1). Mulk Raj Anand's anger with such guardians of religions seems to echo the fiercy words spoken by Swami Vivekanand:

> Priesthood is the bane of India.... Do you ponder our religious conviction is well worth the name? ours is 'Don't touchism', only 'Touch me not'. Good heavens! A country, the big leaders of which have for the last two thousand years been only discussing whether to take food with right hand or the left, whether to take water from the right-hand-side or the left...if such a country does not go to ruin what other will? A country where millions of people, live on the flowers of the *Mohua* plant, and a million or two of Sadhus (monks) and a hundred million or so of Brahmanas suck the blood of these poor people, without even the least effort for their amelioration—is that a country or hell? Is that a religion or the devil's dance? (40-41)

The Road portrays not only the suffering of the untouchables but also of the magnanimous caste Hindus who try to awaken the conscience of the members of their community against the evils of untouchability. Dhooli Singh, in *The Road* is a social reformer and a staunch disciple of the Mahatma. His following of his master's footsteps was a hard task. His single-handed fight against untouchability in a society where casteism is interpreted in terms of religion and is considered as a challenge to the religion itself. But he represents the true religion; he personifies the author's vision of an ideal Hindu.

The ending of the novel has captured the attention of many reviewers. According to Premila Paul the ending "makes Anand's view quite ambiguous" (24). After the construction of the road, instead of celebrating it, the hero makes an escape. He coolly disappears through the road and heads towards Delhi, the capital of the nation. The action is confusing. If the rulers are not concerned about the welfare of the untouchables, then, the 'road to Delhi town, capital of Hindustan' remains a path offering no solution and so the hero's action hardly has any symbolic significance. Perhaps Bhikhu must have reached the conclusion that even if prosperity and modernity embrace the village, the attitude of the villagers will not change and untouchability is bound to haunt and harass him and therefore, the solution to his problem may be found in his anonymous mingling with the multitudes in Delhi. However, his decision is not in conformity with his character. He is defiant by nature. This is indicated at the very beginning of the novel. In his reply to his mother who pleads with him not to fight against the upper-caste youths who block their entry into the temple:

> Son, we are at fault, Laxmi said.
>
> 'Join hands to them all and obey them. Don't fight....!' And she turned to the superior ones, saying: 'Have pity on Bhikhu. He is a hot headed boy!' .... And we will not go to the temple if you think we will pollute it....!
>
> 'Ma—what are you saying?' Bhikhu protested.
>
> 'Son, we are Chamars', she tried to persuade him.
>
> 'And they are twice-born!'
>
> 'One is a leather worker by profession and not by birth!'
>
> Bhikhu shouted and he proceeded. (*The Road* 4)

Bhikhu is portrayed throughout the novel as a defiant person who faced the realities of life boldly and with determinism. Hence, his escapist action at the end of the novel is not in conformity with his character. But we have to understand that there is a strong commitment of his village to a fatalistic view of life in which human nature cannot operate separately from the malicious intervention of the gods which means that Bhikhu will not really affect any change. Battles may be won, but not campaigns. This may be the case for at least his generation, though Anand prognosticates, in every novel, the ultimate triumph of decency over antiquated prejudice.

Like Bakha, Bhikhu, in *The Road*, suffers because of unjust social order. Like Bakha, he is both sturdy in body and a bard. Like Bakha, he possesses quick intelligence. He, however, is more daring and radical in thinking than Bakha, because Bakha represents the agonies, frustrations and the resultant resentment of outcastes of the 1930s, Bhikhu voices their protest against their oppression in the post-independence India, that is to say, the 1960s. He does not believe that good actions by any outcaste will undo the bad deeds of the previous births. Whereas his mother, Laxmi, since she is orthodox, believes that the outcastes will rise from their low status through good deeds. Bhikhu protests against the principle of rebirth: "I will see you to the door of the temple, but don't talk of good and bad deeds...we have done plenty of good deeds in our life, but no merit has accrued" (*The Road* 1).

Bhikhu, the protagonist here, is a new avatar of Bakha of the earlier novel. He is strong and able-bodied with a strong faith in the gospel of work. Unlike Bakha he is literate; he can read, write, sing and even compose verses. In brief, he is the child of independent India. He has found new cultural models in Sant Kabir and Jawaharlal Nehru. The tragedy is, the society in which he lives has not changed correspondingly to accommodate the likes of Bhikhu or let them live with dignity and self-esteem. This, in turn, must be viewed as a part of the feudal politics that continue to dominate life in villages. In *The Road*, Anand brings home the fact that social distinctions—both economic and caste-based—which were the order of the day in the pre-independence India, continued to prevail after independence. Thakur Singh who belongs to the caste of Kshatriya is not only the headman of the village but also owns a hundred bigha land. He thus is both the moral and material prop in society. If power corrupts, the concentration of material and social power in him has corrupted him absolutely. His own son Sanju indulges in arson by setting afire the thatched huts of the outcastes. Anand puts the glaring injustice in the mouth of his protagonist "Their fault may pass 'said Bhikhu', Ours seem hereditary" (*The Road* 57).

The high-caste Hindus are unwilling to let go of the ossified caste-structures since they enjoy a privileged position in this orthodox dispensation. This section is represented by the landlord—Thakur Singh, and the priest—Suraj Mani in the novel. It is important for them to keep the untouchables poor because it is wealth and not caste that determines the social status in the changing world of materialistic values. If the road brings prosperity to men of lower castes, it must be resisted. However, there are also men like Dhooli Singh who believe in work and progress for all. It is important that even liberal humanists like Dhooli Singh too would go only up to a point, and not beyond, in their penchant for reform. He would happily let the Chamar boys work, earn and make a better future, but he wouldn't even consider the possibility of letting his daughter marry an untouchable.

Some critics found this straightforward account of real-life incidents too documentary to be serious literary work. However, as Alastair Niven (1978) rightly describes it, Anand's *The Road* is "a fable". The prime objective of the narrative is to give a moral: liberty without equality is incomplete and devoid of substance. Anand clearly suggests that constitutional legislation alone does not eradicate social evils. On the other hand, an attitudinal change is imperative to bring about real social change. One should not look at this departure as 'defeat' or 'flight' of the protagonist. Even as violence becomes an increasingly important factor in Anand's texts, his revolutionaries opt for alternate modes of retaliation. They choose to wait but do not take to violent action hastily. Apart from the disappointing ending of *The Road*, Anand overlooked some thematic facts. In spite of the fact that the public works department has been beset with corruption, Anand has not exposed the corrupt practices either of Diwan Roop Krishan, the B.D.O. or of Tulsi Das, the Engineer. Nor does he expose the hollowness of political promises made for protecting the weaker sections during the elections by the Congress under the leadership of Nehru. On the other hand,

Anand exudes a lot of optimism that the government would be able to instill confidence among the tottering outcastes and would thus enable them to stand on their own. Anand's faith in the policies of the Congress Government may be seen in Dhooli Singh's comments after the huts of the Dalits are burnt down by the landlord's son, "And tomorrow I will go to Gurgaon and get enough money from the Sarkar for building huts there" (*The Road* 52).

In fact, *The Road* would have been a more powerful novel if Anand had dealt with the above political questions in the novel. As a stark realist Anand unravels how the low castes with thousands of years of slavish existence have accounted for ingraining a sense of inferiority in them. The feeling that their birth as an outcaste is the result of their sins in past life; a belief enunciated, propagated and enforced by the high castes on the low ones have caused such as incapacitating sense that they have always docilely resigned to the authority of the caste Hindus. Quietly groaning under the heavy weight of conventions, and holding their actions or Karma of the previous birth responsible for them to be born in low castes. Bakha's father Lakha in *Untouchable* and Bhikhu's mother, Laxmi in *The Road* represents the fatalist outlook, common to low caste persons of the old generation. Their notion of the inherent weakness of outcastes, which is deep-rooted in their being, has emanated from their unquestioned respect to the stringent laws of caste order as well as their belief in the law of karma. The belief in the inferiority of outcastes, and that of the superiority of high castes forms an integral part of their existence.

Anand in these novels has mounted a bitter but ironic attack on the contradictions and hypocrisy that mark the attitudes and behaviour of the ostensibly superior castes. He lashes at their complacency and issues a stern warning that this caste system will not stand the test of time. As the so-called low caste people, thanks to the widespread availability of education and opportunities for employment, are slowly shedding their complexes and are becoming aware of their inhuman situation and their responsibility to pull themselves out of this pathetic situation. Anand also talks about sub-caste within the caste hierarchy in *Untouchable* as well as *The Big Heart*. A member of the particular sub-caste behaves with another member of sub-caste in accordance with social gradation and receives respect or suffers indignity corresponding to the place of the caste in the system. Since a particular sub-caste is considered superior to another sub-caste, people hailing from the former look down upon the people belonging to the later. Illustrations will make the point clear. Ram Charan, the son of a washer-woman and Bakha, the son of a sweeper, belong to the caste of outcastes. Since the caste of washermen ranks higher than that of a sweeper, Bakha understands the distinction. Similarly, in *The Big Heart*, Anand emphasises how the distinctions in the same caste cause social waste and unnecessary furor. Both the Kaseras and the Thathiars belong to the caste of Kshatriya, the second highest in caste order. The caste of Kaseras ranks higher than that of the Thathiar. Hence, Murli Dhar, the head of the Thathiar brotherhood, feels that he would go up in social esteem if Seth Gokul Chand, who belongs to the Kasera caste, joins the marriage celebrations of his grandson. He does not bother about the members of his own sub-caste like Ananta, the protagonist, and his friends. Ananta, cutting across the considerations of caste and community, tries to organise all workers in a union to fight against the capitalists like Murli Dhar and Gokul Chand. Similarly, Puran Singh Bhagat rejects the caste taboos and gradations based on caste snobbery. His own words expose the caste snobbery of high caste towards the lower ones: "Our merchants are descended from a caste ridden society with an utter contempt for the lower orders ingrained in them as a part of their Dharma" (*The Big Heart* 144).

In *The Big Heart*, how caste snobbery has been an unnecessary evil in caste divided society is dealt with by the novelist. When, after great pressure and persuasion, Seth Gokul Chand attends the wedding ceremony, it creates a lot of trouble among the people of his own caste. Seth Ghanshyam Das, an old dealer, believes that their religion was contaminated after Seth Gokul Chand had eaten with Murli Dhar, "Live not in the city ruled by those who betray religion! Ishwar! Hey Parmatma! Hey Swami! After spoiling our caste too" (*The Big Heart* 186).

3.7 Anand's Short-Stories on the Theme of Caste System

One of the social evils that Anand continually returns to his creative works, is the caste system. In "Silver Bangles", a sweeper girl is accused of theft for wearing a pair of silver bangles given to her by her prospective mother-in-law. The high caste lady, Shrimati Gopi Goel, of the house, conjures up false charges since she feels insecure in the presence of the pretty sweeper girl as her husband is attracted towards Sajani:

> She had seen, passing on his face, the ghost of a smile every time he had seen Sajani arrive. Sometimes, there had been a light in his eyes which she could not help mistaking for a mischievous twinkle. And, once or twice, she felt, she had caught him 'red-handed' or rather 'red-headed' because he had looked up to the untouchable girl with the segment of his lascivious lips slavering and wet.... ("Silver Bangles" 110)

Shrimati Gopi Goel is so jealous of this sweeper girl that she lights up false charges of theft and stealing of her own silver bangles and throws the girl outside with these words:

> Get up and go out and don't you come into this house again. You have raised your head to the sky-low people, wearing silver bangles!!! Don't you know that Untouchables in the south are not supposed to wear silver at all.... And you go posing like cheap film star.... Go die! ("Silver Bangles" 118)

"The Barber's Trade Union" is though written in an exceedingly light-weight manner, the issue it raises is grave in nature. Since, in light vein Anand again questions the caste system in our society. When the story starts the narrator describes Chandu being an intelligent boy but being poor he is taken out of the school to learn the caste profession.

Chandu left his schooling after his father died of the plague. Chandu started his profession of shaving and hair-cutting at the house of the high caste notables and then to the town. In the town, he saw people wearing professional dress. So, he also plans to change his attire. Chandu, the barber boy, is tormented and ill-treated by the caste Hindus for dressing up as the city doctor:

> Ram! Ram! Ram! said Bijay Chand, the burly landlord, touching the scared thread which hung over his ear since he had been to the lavatory. The son of a pig! He is bringing a leather bag of cow-hide into our house and a coat of the marrow of, I don't know, some other animal, and those evil black Angrezi shoes. Get out! Get out! You son of a devil! You will defile my religion. I suppose you have no fear of anyone now that your father is dead! ("The Barber's Trade Union" 32)

Chandu finds this humiliating and collects his fellow working class as a mark of protest and organizes the fellow barbers into a sort of non-cooperation movement:

> The rumour about the barber boy's strike spread, and jokes about the unkempt beards of the elders of the village became current in every home. Even those who were of high castes, even the members of the families of the elders, began to giggle with laughter at the shabby appearance of the great ones and made rude remarks about their persons. And it was said that at least the landlord's wife threatened to run away with somebody, ... ("The Barber's Trade Union" 38)

Chandu was doing good business in the town and even bought new clothes and tools. The village elders decided to call another barber from other villages. But Chandu had a different plan. He had conceived the notion of opening up a joint shop with the other barbers in the city area. So, he invited the barbers of Verka, Dhunoo, and others, within the range of seven miles from his village to open up a shop in partnership. 'Rajkot District Barber Brothers' Hairdressing and Shaving Salon' is the name of the shop opened by Chandu and his idea is actively pursued by other men too. The village elders are made to realize the importance of barber's trade, and the barbers form a guild, thus heralding a new era of labour-fraternity and comradeship. Anand probes the social maladies of contemporary times with rare insight. These tales are social products shaped by their times.

He analyses the impact of industrialization and urbanization in a number of stories. "Old Bapu" demonstrates how poverty makes man age faster. The protagonist here is the victim to an unjust social system which discriminates on the basis of caste and class:

> I am old, he said to himself in the silent colloquy of his soul with his body. The boys call me old Bapu because I am older than them.... The caste Hindu urchins have no respect for the untouchable elders anyhow. And their fathers want to throw everyone of us into the garbage pit to use as manure for better harvests.... But I do not want to die.... Hey Ishwar. (93)

3.8 Comparison of *Akkarmashi* with *Untouchable*

This chapter also seeks to compare Mulk Raj Anand's *Untouchable*, a fiction to Sharankumar Limbale's "Akkarmashi" a fact (an autobiography), which narrates the plight and sufferings of a large segment of the Hindu society which acquired different names in different periods of Indian history—Antyaj or Chandalas (exterior castes), Achoot (untouchable), Harijan (children of God), scheduled castes (a constitutional name), and now Dalit (depressed, a self-assumed socio-historical name). Anand's depiction of an untouchable in his *Untouchable* and the three solutions offered by him regarding the removal of untouchability, it seems to be just touching the tip of an iceberg of the complex 'chronic' and perhaps racial disease of Hindu collective consciousness, if it is compared with Limbale's *Akkarmashi*.

The *Akkarmashi* originally written in Marathi and later on translated into Hindi by Dr. Surya Narayan Ransubhe in 1991 depicts the agony and sufferings of Sharankumar Limbale in particular, and the Hindu untouchables in general. Limbale's description is so truthful and revealing that it belittles E.M. Forster's tall claim regarding Anand's *Untouchable*. Akkarmashi a word of Marathi means in the words of Dr. Ransubhe, "Akkarmashi ka arth hai jarajputra, Avaidh santan, samaj dwara amanya samandho se janmi santati, istri ki majboori ko dekhar, use rakhail bananewale sampann aur amanviya purush sambandho se janami santati, aisi santati ko Marathi mein Akkarmashi kahte hain" (Limbale 5) [Meaning of Akkarmashi is love-child, illicit-child, offspring born out of socially unacceptable relationship, offspring born out of a relationship in which a woman has been made a mistress by a well-to-do and inhuman person, by exploiting her helplessness].

In the *Akkarmashi*, Sharan's story runs like this: Sharan, not only an untouchable, but an akkarmashi also, belongs to Hannur village somewhere on the boundary of Maharashtra and Karnataka. His story begins from his maternal grandmother, Santamai, of Mahar caste, a deserted woman, having only one daughter—the mother of Sharan Kumar, who lives with a Muslim Mahmud Dastgir, referred as Dada by Sharan, within the framework of the modern institution of 'live-in-relationship'. Dada himself a 'deserted' husband without any issue, lives with Santamai, as a committed partner, Masa Mai only daughter of Santamai from her first husband and mother of Sharan Kumar, marries Vithal Kamble of Baslegaon and gives birth to three sons. The eldest son dies very early. Hanmanta Limbale, as Patel of Baslegaon, under whose suzerainty Vithal Kamble works as an annual contract labour and receives ₹ 800, exploits the helplessness (due to acute poverty) of Vithal Kamble by making his wife his (Limbale's) mistress. In turn, he supports them in the rainy season. But it does not work for a longer time and eventually, Kamble deserts Masamai and deprives her of two sons. Masamai does not marry again. Hanmanta Limbale likes her decision and makes a separate arrangement of her at Akkalkot, where Sharan appears on this earth as an 'Akkarmashi'.

Later on, disenchantment grows in Limbale, and he starts levelling accusations of being faithless against Masamai, so that paternity claim of Sharan Kumar can be disowned. Being mentally agonised of his accusations and tortured of atrocities, she returns to her mother Santamai along with Sharan. Here Sharan grows under the live-in-partner Dada, Mahmud Dastgir, and also collects his experiences as an untouchable as well as an 'Akkarmashi'. Masamai, here again becomes mistress of another 'touchable' Yashwant Sidramappa Patel, a prominent person of Hannur village, where they live, and gives birth of eight more 'Akkarmashi'—Six females and two males. Sharan obtains his Bachelor Degree in 1978 and gets appointment for the post of Telephone operator. Sharan writes in the preface of *The Akkarmashi*—his autobiography Sharan writes "Mere saale Subhash ki Atmakatha bhi isi prakar ki hai. Uski Maa Achoot, Pita Berar samaj ka. Pita amir, Mahanagarpalika ka sadasya; Aur Maa? Mahanagarpalika ki majdoor aurat" (Limbale 9) [Biography of my brother-in-law is the same. His mother, an untouchable, father from Berar society. The father-rich, a member of Metropolitan council, and the mother? Fourth grade woman labour of Metropolitan council]. This is not the story of Sharan; it is only his genealogy and chronology. As a matter of fact, his story of sufferings and miseries is the story of an untouchable of post-independent, democratic republic, secular and socialistic India. Despite several constitutional, and legal measures initiated by the state still we have a number of 'Sharan' and 'Subhash'.

The story of Bakha in *Untouchable*, it seems to me, is just a struggle for emancipation from the sufferings of untouchability while the *Akkarmashi* apart from being a struggle for emancipation from the human bondage, it is also a craving quest for identity. Mathematically, we can say that if the *Akkarmashi* is almost universe set of miseries, the *Untouchable* just its subset. In the description of every incident, Sharan shows the injuries and scars caused by glaring discriminations and atrocities perpetuated by caste Hindus. Space limitation doesn't permit to narrate all the painful experiences of Sharan's life here, but few incidents need to be described. In the very beginning, we find how the students of untouchable community enjoy the left-over, remnants and droppings of the 'touchable' at the end of the picnic. When Sharan describes this incident of the picnic, his mother, Masamai, complains "Ghar ke logo ke liye usme se thoda le aata to kya bigarta? Bacha hua anna amrit hota hai" (Limbale 14). [It wouldn't have caused you any harm if you would have brought some of that droppings for, we people. The droppings are like nectar].

Another event also clearly shows the prevalence of acute poverty prevalent among untouchables. Sharan narrates:

> fasal ke dino mein janwar jyada kha lete. Jwar ke bhutte khane ke bad unke gobar mein phule huae dane dikhte, dano mein bhare huae aise gobar ko Santamai alag se rakhati. Ghar lautate samay raaste mein nadi ke pani mein us gobar ko Santamai dhoti. Gobar nikal jata, dane alag ho jate. Maa un dano ko sukhati. Sukhane ke bad woh kam ho jate. Mujhe lagta, unhe sukhana hi nahi chahiye, sukhane ke bad to we kam ho jate. Dane sukhane ke bad hum ghar lautate. Un dano ko woh chakki mein khud peesti, gati hui. (Limbale 23)

[In the harvesting season, cattle would eat more than they could digest. The undigested grains were visible in the dung. Santamai would keep such dung separately, while returning home, Santamai would clear the dung in the river water. Thus, grains and dungs would get separated. Maa would dry the grains. The amount of grains would get lessened after being dried. It seems to me, that must not be dried as it would get lessened. We would return home after having dried the grains. She would grind the grains herself while singing in the grinding stones]. Here we find even animals are more fortunate than the untouchables who get more fodder than they needed. Sharan narrates further that Santamai would never give the bread of those grains to him, and his brothers and sisters. She would alone consume those pieces of bread.

They would eat "Chani"—dried pieces of carrion when they would have scarcity of food. Stones would serve the purpose of bath-soap and alkaline soil as detergent. Sharan would use the soap-lather floating in the river, but only on the condition that he would help the person from whose clothes soap-lather floats.

Sharan's story impels one to analyse the reasons responsible for the sub-animal status of untouchables in our society. Sharan, even, cannot claim his lineage among untouchables as his biological father is a Patel, a Savarna. Savarna calls him an untouchable and the untouchable calls him an "akkarmashi". We come across a situation when the two Patels—the father of Sharan and the father of other brothers and sisters Limbale and Sidramappa visit Masamai together. She is unwilling, but Sidramappa wants that she should share bed with Limbale for the night. Is Masamai not more than an animal?

The revelation of facts regarding the conditions of untouchables in the *Akkarmashi* questions the efficacy of the three solutions to the problem of untouchability offered by Anand—change of faith, Gandhi's approach and Machine. As a matter of fact, Anand himself rejects the first option as it is evident when Bakha recalls his father's reaction regarding the change of faith. Regarding the other two solutions, "Bakha is duly impressed, feels more hopeful of the future than at any time since the day dawned, and returns to his house to tell his father about Mahatma and about the machine that will clear dung without anyone having to handle it" (Anand 146-48).

The *Akkarmashi* appears in the nineties, and cries loudly where is the change. Gandhi fails to understand the problem. Gandhi tries to see the problem of casteism and untouchability as an unrelated issue, and according to him, certainly not rooted in the Varnashram as it is not found in Hindu's original scriptures. He assumes untouchability just a deviance so its eradication is sufficient enough to ensure all sorts of justice to the untouchables. Probably, he could not see that the caste names of untouchables are the words of abuse for the 'touchables'.

Arundhati Roy underlines this agony of untouchables in her masterpiece, "They were also demanding that untouchables no longer be addressed as Achoo Paravan or Kelan Paravan, or Kuttan Pulayan, but just as Achoo, or Kelan, or Kuttan" (Roy 69). If 'untouchability' has its physical dimension only, then how does 'Gulabo' and 'Masamai' become the mothers of the touchables. And being a confirmed believer of his own assumption, his "Harijan campaign included a programme of internal reform by Harijan, promotion of education, cleanliness, and hygiene, giving up the eating of carrion and beef, giving up liquor, and the abolition of untouchability among themselves" (Anand 294). Even Anand differs from Gandhi although very mildly. When Bakha hears Gandhi saying, "In order to emancipate themselves they have to purify themselves. They have to free themselves of evil habits, like drinking alcohol and consuming carrion" (Anand 138). He felt, "That is not fair" (Anand 139). Gandhi does not see that, in fact, Sanskritisation depends upon resources and the power to buy them.

The third solution—Machine certainly brings a change in the physical dimension of untouchability but what about its psychological dimension. According to the Manual Scavenging report 2017, available on "Wikipedia Manual Scavenging" "is a caste-based livelihood involving the elimination of crude human excreta from bucket toilets or pit latrines, that has been formally stopped by law in India as a debasing practice. The workforces, called scavengers, rarely have any special protecting apparatus. The biggest violator of this law in our country is the Indian Railways where countless train carriages have lavatories dropping the human dung from trains on the tracks and manual scavengers are employed to clean the tracks by hand" ("Manual Scavenging", *Wikipedia* 2017). And these jobs are on a larger level done by people belonging to the lower caste. Why still after decades of independence the mechanization of toilets in India not done? A comrade in the novel *The God of Small Things*, speaks, "But frankly speaking comrade, change is one thing, Acceptance is another" (Roy 279).

Sharan Kumar goes to another village for hair-cutting where his identity as an untouchable is not known to the barber. Bakha is a fictional character while Sharan, a living individual. Sexual exploitation of the untouchable woman by the touchable man has been prevalent in every part of India. Sexual exploitation of tenant of womenfolk was rampant to such an extent particularly in the zamindari system, that the foremost peasant leader of Bihar in the zamindari period, Swami Sahajanand Saraswati notes in his autobiography *Mere Jeevan Sangarsh* (My Life Struggle) about this rampant sexual exploitation.

Comparing the intensity and density of sufferings of untouchables described in the *Untouchable* and "*Akkarmashi*", the latter seems to be the story of modern India. *Untouchable* has earned worldwide publicity and evoked sympathy for untouchables, but still couldn't change the hearts of the caste Hindus which is very much evident in "*Akkarmashi*". *Untouchable* ends with some solutions, as Anand perceives the whole things only externally and mechanically as an observer, but "*Akkarmashi*" ends with the baptism of Sharan's son. Sharan gives a name 'Anarya' as he perceives the whole things 'culturally and psychologically' as a 'sufferer' hence wishes to return to his 'historical' or 'mythical' root as even after many millenniums, his integration could not get completed into the Aryan's fold despite centuries have passed.

Conclusion

Taking into account the narratives in various novels we conclude that caste is one of the themes on which different writers of different ages have written down. Starting from Mulk Raj Anand to the contemporary names and their works. Anand shows his righteous and human indignation and..."disgust for the cruelty and hypocrisy of Indian feudal life, with its castes, creeds, dead habits, and customs and its religious rites and practices" (Anand 86). His protest against the inhuman institution of caste, which he has attacked in *Untouchable, The Big Heart* and *The Road* emanated from his empathy for Bakha and Bhikhu, the protagonists of *Untouchable* and *The Road* respectively. His indignation against the caste system also springs from how it has existed for over two thousand years, despite the fact that it was non-existent in society in ancient times. In view of its absence in Vedic age, Indologists believe that it was later invented by self-seeking interests. Hence, it must be an enlightening study to look into its genesis, evolution and how it was sanctified by religion.

A study of the cultural life of Indian people would reveal that the institution of caste did not exist in the earliest society, a fact extolled in his writings by Anand himself. The literary accounts of the Vedic age, which are the only source and guide for the study of the epoch, bear it out. The *Rig Veda,* which represents the cultural ethos of the earliest Indians, evidences how the society functioned in accordance with the principle of varna-vyavastha. The hymns of the *Rig Veda* unequivocally speak of the existence of the enlightened social institutions: neither the professions were determined by heredity; nor the law of endogamy governed a group. Nor was there any taboo on common get-togetherness; with the people hailing from the various groups dining together. A poet in the *Rig Veda* refers to the social mobility of the age:

> A bard I am, my Father a leech,
> And my mother is a grinder of corn,
> Diverse in means, but all striving,
> Equally we strive for cattle. (*Rig Veda*)

As is clear from the hymn cited above, people of the same family followed various occupations. The gamut of social relations was not contaminated by the concept of high and low. The society, being rationally divided among the classes, the early Aryans carried on social obligations that were commensurate with their abilities and aptitude. Hence, there was nothing divine, sacred and mythical in the origin of the Brahmins and Kshatriyas.

If Aryans opened the factions of warriors to able-bodied people and relatives of tribal chieftains, who constituted the class of the Kshatriyas, the profession of priests did not require any specific versality. The ritual being very simple, all people could offer their prayers themselves. Further, those who settled down to such vocations as agriculture, cattle rearing, trade, and commerce were known as Vaishyas. As regarding to the fourth class, what to speak of the class as a whole, the term Shudra is mentioned for the first time in Purus Shukta (the concluding Mandala of the *Rig Veda*). Reasonably, the Das and Dasyus formed the menial workers.

The simple life of the Rig Vedic Aryans became complicated in the later Vedic period. Though there is a great deal of ambivalence in the later Vedic literature with regard to status and privileges of various class groups, it is not uncertain that priesthood came to attain prominence and arbitrary laws, if not practised, came to be laid down for menial workers during the period. The compilation of the *Sam Veda* and the *Yajur Veda*, *Samahitas* and the Brahmans solely for the recitations at the grand sacrifices unambiguously points out that the sacrificial cult dominated the religious life of the Aryans. Therefore, a class of people, which claimed to be well versed in the priest craft, that often performed the sacrificial rites at different occasions came into being. The evolution of sacrificial cult delivered a blow to the simple mode of worship practised in the early Vedic society.

The growth in the power of the Brahmins was correspondent to the decline in the status of the Shudras. The Brahman texts lay down the most reactionary and anti-human norms for the treatment of the low class of people. They theorise the superiority of the Brahmins over the low castes even in legal matters:

The grasping greed of the Brahmins, so much in evidence clearly in the *Atharva Veda* has passed all the bounds in the Brahmans. Here the Brahmin coolly claims that in every dispute between a Brahmin and a non-Brahmin the judgement should be given in the favour of the Brahmin. With cheerful disregard of other people's interest a Brahmana author declared that murder is no murder if the victim is not a Brahmin. And another declares with the same cool confidence that a Shudra is Yatha-Kamvadhya i.e. one who can be killed at will (Ghosh 422).

The rigidity of caste system set in an indignant revolt against it. Dr. Radha Krishnan comments on the state of caste system in the age of Buddha is quite pertinent: "In the time of Buddha the caste system was in the confused condition where distinctions were based on birth rather than on qualities" (437).

The people's urged for a change. Rigidity in religion is reflected in the rise of reformatory movements like Buddhism, Jainism and the rationalist school of philosophy as that of carvaka in the sixth century B.C. Buddha's emphasis in his teachings on the goodness of action rather than on chance of birth attracted the depressed classes to Buddhist fold. The social and spiritual equalities promise in Buddhist fold endeared Buddha to the masses because the authors of Dharma-Sutras had condemned the outcastes to deplorable existence. So much so, that they had evolved the theory of untouchability. The belief that mere touch of a Shudra may result in high caste being contaminated was given formal sanction in Dharma-Sutras. In the words of Apte:

> We see in the Dharma-Sutras the beginning of the formal theory of defilement resulting in the taboo of all contact on the part of pure men of the upper castes with an impure man, namely, a member of the lowest caste. (516)

Not only was the theory of segregation of the outcastes from the caste Hindus invented but the caste order was made more complicated as society moved ahead. Society was thus moving in a retrograde direction. The writers of the *Smritis* wove myths and legends around even such selar institutions as state, Kingship and caste. Manu, for example authoritatively declares that the Brahmins, the Kshatriyas, the Vaishyas, and the Shudras issued forth from the mouth, arms, thigh, and foot respectively of the Brahma. According to Manu: "Now, for the sake of preserving all this creation, the most glorious (Being) ordained separate duties for those sprang from (his) mouth, arm, thigh (and) feet" (Hopkins 12).

Manu, in concocting the theory of Divine Origin of caste order, has laid emphasis on two points. First, the Shudra sprang from the most impure part of the legendary Purush and hence they were the lowest beings. Secondly, the members of every caste must obey the laws of caste, since by doing so they obey the divine dispensation. Under such dispensation, since the twice-born castes would perform important functions as those of warriors, military and civil officers, priests, teachers, and traders, they felt no constraint in carrying out these duties. But the duties of the Shudras were altogether different. Menial service to the caste Hindu, particularly to the Brahmins became the eternal lot of the Shudras. Manu emphatically states: "But a cudra, whether bought or not bought, (the Brahman) may compel to practise servitude, for that (cudra) was created by the self-existent merely for the service of the Brahman" (Hopkins 243).

Further, if the ordinance of Manu bears testimony to the state of the caste order, the lot of the low castes people was worse than that of a slave. A slave can dream of better days after his release from the captivity of his master. But the laws of caste under Hindu social order chained the Shudras in such iron chains from which one could never aspire for freedom. No matter, howsoever, talented a low caste person could be, he was denied the opportunities to develop his talent since caste laws forced servitude on him. He was believed to be born with innate instincts to serve, hence was chained in steel shackles of slavery. Manu again authoritatively declares: "Even if freed by his master, the Cudra is not released from servitude: for this is innate in him: who then can take it from him?" (Hopkins 243).

However, the serious blow to the status of the Shudra was yet to come. After the theory of karma was concocted, the birth in a family of Shudra was looked upon as retribution of the sins of the previous birth or births. However, a Shudra could avoid being born in a low caste and be entitled to be born in high caste, if he meekly performed the caste-duties, rendering service to high caste, without grumbling and complaining. Manu elaborates the theory of karma: "If he be pure, obedient to the higher castes, mild in speech, without conceit and always submissive to the Brahmans, he attains (in the next trans-migration) a high birth" (Hopkins 303).

The *Gita* also upholds the same obscurantist belief in karma. It, too, enunciates the theory of the law of karma by emphasizing the performance of duties (Varnashram dharma) by low castes, as it alone qualifies a Shudra to be born in higher order, because merits accruing from the fulfilment of such duties go on accumulating in the other world. If one contrasts the history of the origin of caste; where the classes were functional groups, with a rigid caste system, one would say that other-worldly beliefs were forced on a purely social and secular institution. As a result of the concoction of such theories, the status of the Shudras sank down to the lowest level in the social scale. Hence, the Shudras received treatment no better than meted out to animals. In social life, they suffered from numerous disabilities. In matter of residence, they were forced to live on outskirts of village or town. R.K. Mookerjee, quoting *Jataka* stories, points out: "how the Chandalas were treated as despised out-castes doomed to live outside the city or village and their very sight was regarded as impure" (544).

Thus, the dehumanizing laws of caste sanctioned by Hinduism condemned a teeming millions of Hindu families to a hellish existence. They were completely cut off from the social main stream; untouchability came to be practiced with great rigidity. In order to ensure the segregation of low caste from high ones the former was not only doomed to live outside a village but while moving about a street, they had to strike sticks to warn the high castes to avoid their touch. They had no share in the management of economic forces as they were obliged to follow such low occupations, as handling dirt, scavenging, fish selling, shoe making and repairing, and removing the hides of the dead animals.

If Anand's novels, particularly *Untouchable* and *The Road* are perused, keeping the above background in mind, one wouldn't fail to note two fundamental points raised by Anand in exposing the Hindu obscurantist ideology of casteism in India. One, the principle of karma has been the main cause of over-whelming self-pity among the low castes about their poor lot. They have inherited the spirit of resignation down through their countless ancestors. Also, the same belief has armed the twice-born castes with cruelty, aggressiveness and they have, therefore, used it to stifle every voice of protest of low ones emanating from the former's high handedness, branding the latter as wrong-doers. Secondly, with hereditary determining occupations, the low castes have no option but must solely depend upon the low jobs, thus being excluded from sharing power in power structure. According to Mulk Raj Anand:

> Someone in the great *Mahabharata* had cried, "caste, caste—There is no caste!" And I wanted to repeat this truth to the "dead souls" from the compassion of my self-explanation in the various Hindu hells, in the hope that I would, myself come clean after I had been through sewer, as it were. (16)

To Mulk Raj Anand, casteism is a hoary lie furnished by the influential and wicked in the world to maintain discrimination.

His prime concern as a social critic is to remove the caste system as it damages social cohesion by giving certain sections of society an unfair advantage over others permanently. It is a heinous crime. It poisons and destroys the dignity of man. Hence, it must be rejected. Anand is right in the beginning of his career as a novelist by presenting the evils of the caste system through his novels and short stories. We see that man is the chief exponent of humanism. As a matter of fact, the man in Anand may be a humanist, a Marxist or a Gandhist but the writer in him always on the side of Bakha, Bhikhu struggling, toiling and suffering in the rigid caste society which he is unable to defy. He is faithful to all the ideologies which lead the untouchables to a respectable and happy life. Anand voices his resolve in *Morning Face* (1968):

> I could sense that though I had grown up to be unconventional and accepted the low caste and outcaste people as my equals, our elders still kept the untouchable at a distance for the fear of pollution of their person and spoliation of their status. The anger against the snobbery of the twice-born in despising the good Bakha had already gone deep into my elusive spirit and got buried in my being as a kind of resentment against all those who stop the human flow, erupting at any manifestation of the old Hindu prejudice. At any rate, I vowed in myself, never to accept in my life, and go wherever the slaves were cleaning, washing and scrubbing, to become poor for Bakha's sake, to mix with the perfumes with bad smells melt all my senses into diffused personality. (325)

In fact, by projecting the social oppression, moral degradation and economic agonies of the outcastes in his creative works, Anand has advanced their cause. How close Anand is to the outcastes in artistically rendering their suffering is indicative by the fact his friends of childhood Bakha, the sweeper's son, Ram Charan, the washerman's son and Chota, the leather worker's son, figure in his first novel *Untouchable*. By selecting Bakha, Bhikhu, Ananta as protagonists in his novels articulated to the international audience the voice of dumb millions who had never before figured in the world of Indian writing in English.

Endnote

1. Deshpande, Manali S. *History of The Indian Caste System and Its Impact on India Today*. California Polytechnic State University, San Luis Obispo Fall, 2010. Web 3rd April 2016.

Works Cited

Alavi, Seema. *Sepoys and The Company Tradition and Transition in Northern India 1770-1830*. India: Oxford University Press India, 1998. Print.

Anand, Mulk Raj. *Apology for Heroism*. New Delhi: Arnold Heinemann, 1986. Print.

——. *Author to Critic: The Letters of Mulk Raj Anand to Saros Cowasjee*, ed. Saros Cowasjee, Calcutta: Writers' Workshop, 1973. Print.

——. *Lajwanti and Other Stories*. New Delhi: Orient Paperbacks, 1999. Print.

——. *Morning Face*. Bombay: Kutub Popular, 1968. Print.

——. *Mulk Raj Anand Greatest Short Stories*. Mumbai: Jaico Publishing House, 1999. Print.

——. *The Big Heart*. New Delhi: Arnold Heinemann, 1980. Print.

——. *The Road*. Bombay: Kutub Popular, 1961. Print.

——. *The Story of My Experience with a White Lie*. Indian Literature vol. 10, no. 3, 1967. Reprinted in *Critical Essays on Indian Writing in English*. Macmillan, Silver Jubilee Students Edition, 1977. Print.

——. *Two Leaves and a Bud*. Bombay: Kutub Publishers, 1946. Print.

——. *Untouchable* (Preface by E.M. Forster). Gurgaon: Penguin Books India Ltd, 2001. Print.

Apte, V.M. "Social and Economic Conditions". *The History and Culture of the Indian People*, vol. 1, Ed. R.C. Majumdar. Bombay: Bharatiya Vidya Bhavan, 1965. Print.

Balewa, Alhaji Sir Abubakar Tafawa. *Shaihu Umar*. Translated from the Hausa by Mervyn Hiskett. London: Longmans, 1967. Print.

Bouglé, Célestin. *Essays on the Caste System*. London: Cambridge University Press, 1971. Print.

Chandra, Bipin. *India's Struggle for Independence*. New Delhi: Penguin India, 1992. Print.

Cowasjee, Saros. *So Many Freedoms: A Study of the Major Fiction of Mulk Raj Anand*. New Delhi: OUP, 1977. Print.

Das, A.N. *The Republic of Bihar*. New Delhi: Penguin India, 1992. Print.

Deshpande, Manali S. *History of The Indian Caste System and Its Impact on India Today*. California Polytechnic State University, San Luis Obispo Fall, 2010. Web. 3 April 2016.

Ghosh, B.K. "Language and Literature". *The History and Culture of the Indian People*, vol. 1, Ed. R.C. Majumdar. Bombay: Bhartiya Vidya Bhawan, 1965. Print.

Ghurye, G.S. *Caste and Race in India*. Bombay: Popular Prakashan, 1969. Print.

Hopkins, Edward W. *The Ordinances of Manu*. New Delhi: Oriental Books Reprint Corporation Book Publishers, 1971. Print.

Iyengar, K.R. Srinivasa. *Indian Writing in English*. New Delhi: Sterling Publishers, 1985. Print.

Krishnan, Dr. Radha. *Indian Philosophy*, volume I. London: George Allen and Unwin Ltd., Humanities Press Inc. New York, 1920. Print.

Limbale, Sharankumar. "Akkarmashi". Translated edition (Hindi). New Delhi: Granth Akademi, 1991. Print.

Mookerjee, R.K. "Social Condition". *The History and Culture of the Indian People*. ed. R.C. Majumdar. Bombay: Bharatiya Vidya Bhawan, 1968. Print.

Niven, Alastair. *The Yoke of Pity*. London: Arnold Heinemann, 1978. Print.

Oyono, Ferdinand. *Houseboy*. Translated from the French by John Reed. London: Heinemann, 1966. Print.

Parameshwaran, Uma. *A Study of Representative Indo-English Novelists*. New Delhi: Vikas Publishing House, 1976. Print.

Paul, Premila. *The Novels of Mulk Raj Anand: A Thematic Study*. New Delhi: Sterling Publishers Pvt. Ltd., 1983. Print.

Prabhu, P.H. *Hindu Social Organisation*. Bombay: Popular Prakashan, 1962. Print.

Roy, Arundhati. *The God of Small Things*. New Delhi: India Ink, 1998. Print.

Sharma, K.L. *Indian Society*. New Delhi: NCERT, 1998. Print.

Vaishyas. *Gurjari.net*. Web. 23 April 2016.

Vivekananda, Swami. *Caste, Culture and Socialism* (Published by Swami Ananyananda). Calcutta: Ashutosh Lithographic Co., 1983. Print.

Walsh, William. *Indian Literature in English*. London: Longman Group, 1990. Print.

Wikipedia Contributors. "Manual Scavenging." *Wikipedia, The Free Encyclopedia*. Wikipedia, The Free Encyclopedia, 20th April 2017. Web. 20 April 2017.

Yadav, Shiv Kumar. "A Comparative Study of Mulk Raj Anand's *Untouchable* and Sharan Kumar Limbale's "Akkarmashi"". Ed. T.M.J. Indra Mohan. *The Novels of Mulk Raj Anand*. New Delhi: Atlantic Publishers, 2005. Print.

4
Literature of Dissent: Breaking Hegemony

4.1 Social Remonstration throughout the World

Since ancient times, society's alleged rebels and activists have looked for ways to loan their voices in defense of freedom, equality, justice, and dignity, and aligned with unjust conditions. Literature is one such instrument for initiating positive action. Literature contributes much to the social order if it is critical enough to kindle deliberate and debate on developmental issues. Society can only flourish dynamically and attain mature culmination with the aid of criticism. Since art is always confronted with complex social, political and cultural contradictions, there is a need for art to be a foremost force in responding to these contradictions and challenges. A reading of the societal protest is a part of the progression showing the ability of literature to resolve society's challenges through protest.

The chapter shows how the different forms of writing can be a contributing factor towards socio-political and cultural development in this world. Charles Dickens wrote about child labour, Frances Trollope about illegitimacy, Thomas Hardy about seduction, and class segregation. The Literature of the nineteenth century was a product of the rapid urbanization and manufacturing of Western countries, end to end through the intensification of communist thought. It may be divided into twofold broad categories: literature that focuses on enlightening society's ills and literature that either advocates or opposes firm forms of public or partisan reform. These broad categories encompass a wide variety of works that treat a range of subjects, including slavery, women's rights, minority rights, poverty, nobility, racial discrimination, ethnocentrism, and the immigrant experience.

4.2 European Protest Literature

According to Lynn M. Zott, (www.enotes.com/topics/nineteenth-century-social-protest-literature, 2019) German author Ludolf Weinberg, feasibly best encapsulated in what way nineteenth-century protest writers projected their role and also the purpose of their works. Despite the fact, Western countries are widely known by all means the epicenter of nineteenth-century social dissent, with such well-known writers as Charles Dickens, George Eliot, and Elizabeth Gaskell permeating social criticism into their works, authors from further nations correspondingly fashioned fictitious works that enthusiastically replicated the radical and social controversies of the day. In France, Victor Hugo's Les *Misérables* (1862) (www.enotes.com/topics/nineteenth-century-social-protest-literature, 2019) remained one of the most authoritative depictions of corruption and immorality in literature. Hugo's reputation and influence eventually came under mockery by the French Realists, however, who spurned what they perceived as Hugo's propensity to idealize life and sought in their own works to depict an objective and "scientific" view of society's ills. The best known of the Realists, Émile Zola, wrote profusely, most notably *Germinal* (1885), a condemnation of industrialization and the political structures that foster social inequality. Gustavo Flaubert's *Madame Bovary* (1857) and Guy de Maupassant's *Une Vie* (1883) were other important contributions to the Realist movement. In Russia, where the tyrannical tsarist state tolerated little or no open dissent, a tradition of progressive liberalism nevertheless survived. In the nineteenth century a newfangled, extremely radicalized cluster, the *Raznochintsy* arose out. Among the older generation of liberals, Fyodor Dostoevsky and Ivan Turgenev produced novels of public protest. While Dostoevsky, in his depiction of the character Raskolnikov, showed radicalism to be misguided as well as dangerous, Turgenev presented a much more sympathetic picture of a radical in his central figure Bazarov. Turgenev's use of the term "nihilist" to typify Bazarov brought it into wide use in political discussion throughout Europe and America to describe revolutionaries who advocate the absolute destruction of the way things are now.

While European protest writers usually centered on philosophical queries of eccentricity, and therefore, the dynamics of social structures, American reformist literature usually stressed political problems. The most outstanding of those problems were slavery, women's equality, corruption within the government, and the distribution of wealth. Mark Twain is considered to be one of the key American promulgators of literary societal protest, largely due to his novel *Huckleberry Finn* (1885). In it, he achieves a skillful blend of dissent and fictional craftsmanship by highlighting the detracting features, and hypocrisies of American society. Edward Bellamy used a unique technique to advocate social modification in *Looking Backward* (1888), a utopian novel symbolically portraying a socialistic form of government. While scorning the gung-ho social and economic system developing in America, the novel depicts a society in which citizens are equal on all levels. In his works, George Washington Cable, prominent Black writer fortified classlessness through civil rights, an assessment most powerfully specified in his novel *The Grandissimes* (1880), within which he portrays South a part of America still suffering from the inheritance of slavery. *Uncle Tom's Cabin* rejuvenated the abolition movement. Later, Upton Sinclair's *The Jungle* had a serious influence on reform within the meatpacking business. During the hopelessness, John Steinbeck's *The Grapes of Wrath* had a comparable impact, educating the American public regarding the plight of migrant employees and manufacturing support for new pact agreement legislation.

Social Protest literature has existed in various forms throughout literary history, awakening people to the injustice around them. The voice of protest should be directed towards changing an erroneous system, not individuals, and should point to areas of growth and renewal. Protest literature is not propaganda for war, provocation for looming violence or advocacy of hatred based on ethnicity, gender or religion. It should offer positive and remedial criticism since no literature of note would just stop at cultivating skepticism, helplessness, disappointment and estrangement to its readers. Protest literature shows a wide range of dissenting voices from a placid complain to fundamental criticism.

4.3 African Protest Literature

The chapter discusses selected Shona novels' (Mazuruse 2010) portrayal of the theme of protest in the post-independence era in Zimbabwe. The ideas that these novels cause on protest are examined in the context of socio-political and socio-cultural issues in post-independent Zimbabwe. The study is an exploration of the extent to which protest literature is vital in the struggle of African people to liberate themselves from imperialist servitude. Novels on socio-political protest show how the government has failed to deliver on most of its promises because of neocolonialism and fraudulence. Novels on socio-cultural protest show how cultural innovations in post-independence Zimbabwe brought troubles. The reading comes to the conclusion that for literature to be reliable and useful to society it is not sufficient to highlight weaknesses in criticizing, but it should go beyond that and offer productive and corrective criticism. This shows that protest literature is a vital tool for social change in Zimbabwe. This study, therefore, aims to show that it is possible to move out of the at hand predicament if novelists move away from intense cynicism and give insights of positive ways out. At independence, the injustices of colonialism were expected to be eliminated to usher in a new ideology which would create an egalitarian society. Thus, the immediate post-independence period was characterized by slogans castigating imperialism and hailing socialist transformation. The Failure of the socialist ideology marked the beginning of post-independence problems.

People soon discovered that independence had brought no end to political oppression and certainly no alleviation to their problems because of the perpetuation of imperialist interests by the ruling class. The wealthy got richer and therefore, the poor got poorer. Those few with economic power are also the same people with political power. The get-rich-quick middle class cannot be taken as a replica of whites but just a caricature. The irony is that, for some members of the ruling class, commitment to socialism never goes beyond the level of rhetoric. This shows that post-independence problems have their roots in the colonial structures continued in the post-colonial period. Nyawaranda's *Barika Ramashefu* (1991), Chimhundu's *Chakwesha* (1991), Mahanya's *Matsvamoyo* (1992) and Mabasa's *Mapenzi* (1999) all criticise the neocolonial state of post-independence Zimbabwe. The novels portray the hypocrisy and self-fulfilling attitude of the ruling elite. Neocolonialism is simply the continuation of social and economic legacies of colonialism in the post-colonial era of formerly colonized countries. The term neocolonialism was popularized in the wake of decolonization. According to Ngugi (1986):

> Neocolonialism is a situation in which a country is nominally independent but its economy is still in the hands of the imperialist bourgeoise. Nothing has in substance changed. The only change is that where before the imperialist bourgeoise used to exploit the masses through its settler or feudal representatives, now it does so through a native bourgeoise who takes the flag at independence. (95-96)

This perpetuation of colonial values and practices has given rise to several contradictions in the post-independence period resulting in the failure of independence to fulfil the expectations of the majority in Zimbabwe. The ongoing nature of imperialism is multifaceted and can be manifested in different forms. In the post-independence Zimbabwe situation, neocolonialism is manifested in the social, economic and cultural spheres through which manipulation and underdevelopment of the country by imperial powers is evident. The adoption of colonial values in post-independent Zimbabwe has led to most post-colonial problems that have proved detrimental in the construction of a new political order. The struggle for women emancipation in Zimbabwe predates colonialism, continued throughout the colonial era and after independence (Gaidzanwa 8). Most post-independence problems affecting women are as a result of the continued subordination and discrimination of women, both in 'traditional' society and revolutionary politics. Mutasa, in *Sekai: Minda Tave Nayo* and Nyawaranda, in *Barika Ramashefu* protest against the failure of independence to bring change to the perception of gender relationships as promised during the liberation war. With independence, it became necessary to move beyond sexual discrimination by redressing the legacy of historic imbalances through legislation that outlaws' discrimination. Women of all ethnic orientations share the unfortunate commonality of being subjugated, excluded, marginalized and rendered invisible in language and public life. Black women have been confronted with injustices like deprivations of liberty, adequate food, shelter, and medical care. Women experience oppression like sexual abuse, domestic violence, and emotional harassment. African women have historically demonstrated that sexist socialization is the chief cause of their oppression. Historically, African woman has fought against sexual discrimination as well as race and class discrimination.

According to Elizabeth Lockwood the genus of protest literature arose out of South Africa's black anti-apartheid movement during the 1980s. By examining three novels, Mongane Wally Serote's *To Every Birth It's Blood* (1981), Miriam Tlali's *Amandla* (1980), and Njabulo Ndebele's *Fools and Other Stories* (1983), as well as Oliver Schmitz and Thomas Mogotlane's film, *Mapantsula* (1988). Protest literature in South Africa functioned to inspire the fight against the apartheid government. It appeared in various forms between the National Party's execution of apartheid in 1948 and Nelson Mandela's release from Robben Island in 1990. One of the crusades against apartheid begins with Nadine Gordimer's essays on protest and writing. Gordimer, a white liberal South African novelist, and political activist, explores the effects apartheid has on South African society in her novels, short stories and essays:

> In other words, Gordimer argues that the South African culture of protest arose precisely because of the apartheid government's enforced repression of ideas. In a country where people may not express political opinions, they

> are forced to give voice to their opinions in other forms. Two such powerful substitute forms are literature and film. As Gordimer asserts, "Protest is not a revolutionary means but a reforming one.... Protest is the need to speak out in a silenced society." (Lockwood 93)

Andre Brink, writing five years later, also saw the significance of protest literature as an apparatus of transformation. This investigation of the "human condition" is precisely how protest literature gains its authenticity. Protest literature reveals, explores, and ultimately relies on a form of being the "everyday" beneath apartheid which black South Africans know and relate to. To interpret this birth of consciousness, it is vital to understand the history of the political movement that gave rise to protest literature. Protest literature is founded in the theory of Black Consciousness, which was created by Steve Biko, a medical student at the University of Natal. Influenced undoubtedly by the black political thought flowing out of America at the time, Biko broke from the National Union of South African Students (NUSAS). He established the South African Students' Organization (SASO) in 1969 (Arnold 19), extending membership only to people of colour. SASO and its theory of Black Consciousness quickly spread throughout South Africa, influencing the actions and convictions of students of all ages. Biko later wrote that the key to Black Consciousness is "mental emancipation as a precondition to political emancipation" (Biko, quoted by Arnold 20).

The idea that blacks must first liberate their minds is a fundamental concept of Black Consciousness; they must become conscious of their own worth, even in the face of continued white oppression. The second vital aspect behind Black Consciousness centers on Biko's assertion that as long as blacks allow whites to speak for them, blacks will never learn to speak for themselves. Without learning to rely on their own voices for protest, they will never gain a political voice. This aspect of Black Consciousness allowed Biko to justify opening SASO membership only to people of colour. Protest literature arises from the vision of political unity borne of Black Consciousness. Books of the black South African anti-apartheid canon are steeped in pro-Movement sentiments (Gordimer's discussion of Black Consciousness in South African art is a key voice in understanding how the political movement impacted the contemporary literary scene. Consequently, the white liberal artist who understands that "a purely white-based culture is as meaningless for white as for black, in the future South Africa" (139) is left alone:

> the rejection of whites—only values by no means implies a concomitant opting in [to] the black culture. The white artist, who sees or feels instinctively that exclusively white-based values are in an unrecognized state of alienation, knows that he will not be accepted, cannot be accepted by a black culture seeking to define itself without the reference to those values that his very presence among blacks represents. (Gordimer 138)

He is thus trapped in a "double alienation" (Gordimer 138). How white South African protest literature reflects this "double alienation" is a subject worthy of another thesis; the relevance of black protest literature, however, is affirmed by Gordimer's assertion that black art and culture did indeed seek to locate itself in a new sphere that was created and defined by blacks themselves. Some authors particularly advocate Black Consciousness, while others simply encourage participation in the growing protest against apartheid. Despite these differences in the authors perspectives, my own use of the term "Movement" universally applies to the fight against apartheid, regardless of whether particular authors specifically promote Black Consciousness.

According to Femi Folorunso Nigerian literature in English has witnessed extraordinary growth in the past decade and a half. The award of the Nobel Prize for Literature to Wole Soyinka (arguably black Africa's chief literary artist) in 1986 long-established the eminence of this literature. Of late, Ben Okri and Niyi Osundare have helped to strengthen this distinction. The practice of protest poetry in Nigeria began with Okigbo's *Path of Thunder*. This poem was a premonition of the catastrophe that was to envelop Nigeria in the mid-1960s, culminating in the civil war that unfortunately claimed the life of Okigbo's himself.

In the text, Chinua Achebe's *Anthills of the Savannah* and Kole Omotoso's *Just Before Dawn* are in the front position of unsophisticated experimental novels by Nigerians in the preceding two decades. Achebe's narrative contends with the collapse of humanism caused by several years of armed intervention in the nation's politics. One of the legendary phenomena of the past two decades is the rise of female writers. Achebe evidently has not touched on caste as it is not to be found in his country in the form in which we find it in India. While class plays a rather serious role in the action of Achebe's novels caste is not mentioned at all. However, if caste has to be broadly defined it could include distinctions of groups of people as undesirable or outcaste or ostracised, it could be by extension applied to a category of people referred to as "Osu" specifically mentioned in *No Longer at Ease* where the protagonist Obi Okonkwo is in love with Clara who is an 'Osu'. In fact, the conflict in Obi's life commences when this truth is revealed to his Christian parents who vehemently oppose this move. His whole village is against his marrying an "Osu" girl. Osu is an outcaste traditionally treated so by the Igbo tribes. Probably the real reason for this is hidden in the misty past or shrouded in mystery just as their many other beliefs were.

It is undoubtedly a clear case of social ostracism which brands a whole section of people, generations of a family as an outcaste, Although the concept of caste cannot be applied here as it is, it can be extended to it. Achebe disapproves of this 'caste' division within the same tribe. The fact is that such a distinction, however, limited it may be, exists among the tribes in Nigeria. Anand and Achebe are equally aware of the overwhelming power that class system can command, given the capitalist mode of production, distribution and consumption, the class division which is inevitable will spawn conflicts and struggles. The real problem of the third world is that of the gap between the rich and the poor. And the gap has been widening over the years as the inherent logic of capitalism dictates. The continued pauperization of the poor will escalate the conflict between the rich and the poor classes. Achebe proposes struggle as the only way out of the present political and social muddle. He assigns a specific and important role to the new elite of Nigeria in this process of liberation. They need to be reeducated and regenerated.

4.4 Afro-American Literature

The initial script by blacks in America was autobiographical and became known as the Slave Narrative. Olaudah Equiano (1745-97) was the first black in America to write an autobiography. Three themes developed in early African-American writings about were the issue of slavery, space, protest, and escape. She is one of the first writers to use an epistolary style (in the form of letters). The work of Afro-American authors forms an integral part of the literature of the United States and has endowed it with a distinctive richness and sense of multiculturalism. The writings of the most Black authors living in the United States fall in the category of Afro-American literature the earliest beginnings of which can be traced back to the slave literature of Philips Wheatly (1753-84) and Frederick Douglass (1818-95), as well as the politically and socially relevant writings of Booker T. Washington and W.E.B. Du Bois (1868-1963). One of the founders of the NAACP, Du Bois published the highly influential *The Souls of Black Folk* (1903) which created a black intellectual and artistic consciousness.

Some of the other notable Afro-American writers whose prose and poetry continue to receive critical acclaim are Langston Hughes (1902-94), Richard Wright (1909-60), Ralph Ellison (1914-94), Amiri Baraka (1934-). The 1940s-1960s was an epoch of social alteration for African Americans. Influences incorporated the Second World War, the Second Great Migration, world-wide social movements such as communism and Marxism, and early civil rights legislation which opened up schools and jobs for many African Americans. Metropolitan realism—city sensibility defines much of the literature of this era. *The Invisible Man* is part of the cannon of 20th century American literature, though Ellison's only major published work.

Toni Morrison wrote richly wicker stories often with sturdy female characters. *The Bluest Eye* (1970), *Sula* (1973), *Song of Solomon* (1977), *Tar Baby* (1981) are some of her immense novels. She is the first Afro-American female to win the highest honour, i.e. Nobel Prize for Literature. Alice Walker best known work, *The Color Purple* (1982) won the Pulitzer Prize in 1982. It's the story of two sisters who through severance and trials continue to support and fortify each other. Though all these writers have highlighted in one way or another, the black experience in white America, Toni Morrison's work stands out because of its comprehensive and multidimensional approach to the Afro-American experience. She invents universally identifiable characters, recreates their tragic past, highlights their traumatic present and envisions a better future for them—in an extraordinary prose style that has power, beauty, and richness all its own. Though all her characters try to find meaning in their lives as individuals, she attributes success to those who put the community first and who turn to African mythology and culture to enrich their original assets with a view to cultivate the sense of fraternity and mutual racial relationships.

Maya Angelou's, *I Know Why the Caged Bird Sings* (1970) her serial memoir is a pantheon of modern American literature. African-American writers have entered the usual American readership. While issues of identity and race are still prominent, the varieties of human issues are also topics of present-day African-American literature. With the publication of *The Souls of Black Folks* in 1903, W.E.B. Du Bois emerged as the national leader of a new generation of African American activists who broke with the leadership and views of Booker T. Washington. Declaring that blacks ought to not settle for inferior citizenship and will in its place fight for the right to vote, civil equality, and also the right to education, Du Bois sent out what at the time was an avant-garde call for change in the racial conditions. In doing, therefore, he became at the same time one among the foremost authoritative and controversial black individuals in America.

4.5 Dalit Literature: The Contemporary Writers

As said by Dr. Jugal Kishore Mishra in India, the writings that are about Dalits are the most prevailing protest literature.

Dalit (subjugated or conked out) is not a novel word. It seems that it was used in the 1930s as a Hindi and Marathi translation of 'depressed classes', a term the British used for what are now called the Scheduled Castes. In recent times the term is expanded to include scheduled tribes, poor peasants, women and all those being exploited politically, economically and in the name of religion. So, Dalit is not a caste. It is a symbol of resistance and uprising. The principal motive of Dalit literature is the liberation of Dalits. Dalit struggle against casteist tradition features a long history. In modern times, because of the legacy of Mahatma Phule and Baba Bhimrao Ambedkar, Dalit literature got thrust in Maharashtra. He encouraged Dalit women to write forcefully about the discrimination and humiliation meted out to them (Mishra).

Dr. B.R. Ambedkar, a pioneering Dalit voice believed that only education could bring about a change in the lives of the Dalit which reels under oppression and atrocity. He opened many schools and hundreds of Dalits sent their children to Dalit run institutions. These institutions produced the first generation of Dalit literates in large numbers who took to writing and started publishing newspapers and magazines. But prior to the name came into being in the 1960s, such people as Baburao Bagul, Bandhu Madhav, and Shankarao Kharat were already creating Dalit literature. Arun Kamble, Shantabai Kamble, Krushna Kamble, Raja Dhale, Namdev Dhasal, Bandhu Madhav, Laxman Mane, Laxman Gaikwad, Hari Narake, Sharankumar Limbale, Waman Nibalkar, Bhimsen Dethe, and Bhau Panchbhai are noteworthy Dalit writers. Namdev Dhasal's works specify the anguish and aspirations of Dalits in our country. The Dalit litterateurs think that so long as the discriminative caste system exists there can never be complete freedom, brotherly feeling, and justice established in the nation. In its official form, it sprouted out of a progressive movement called Little Magazine which was a kind of disobedient demonstration of the educated youth of those days against the institution.

Verses, short stories, work of fiction and memoirs inscribed by Dalit authors provided beneficial perceptions on the interrogation of Dalit uniqueness. These are Mahasweta Devi, Namdeo Dhasal, Daya Pawar, Arjun Dangle, etc. While dealing with the trends of Dalit literature, the writer will make a modest effort to point out the central issues of its philosophy. In this context, it can be said that Dalit literature questioned the conventional literary theories and upper-caste ideologies and explored the neglected aspects of life. Dalit literature is know-how-based. That is why authenticity and vivacity have become hallmarks of Dalit literature. These writers make use of the idiom of the out-castes and under-privileged in Indian society. Humiliation, rage, distress and unconquerable hope are the themes of Dalit literature. In their quest for changes, Dalit writers have rediscovered the low caste saint poets of the Bhakti movement. Even they found relevance in Buddhism. These writers make an ardent plea for a complete revamp of society. As Arjun Dangle, the Marathi Dalit writer put it, "Even the Sun needs to be changed." Thus, the input of Dalit literature has been immense.

4.6 Select Critical Study: *The God of Small Things*

The year 1997 was an eventful one in the history of Indo-English literature. An innovative author appeared together with her initial novel and attained the Booker beforehand the culmination of the day. Set within the southern Indian state of Kerala and divided chronologically, between the twilight nineteen-sixties and the initial nineteen-nineties, the design of Arundhati Roy's *The God of Small Things* pivots around a destined, prohibited relationship between a Syrian-Christian adult female, Ammu, and a low-slung status 'untouchable' carpenter, Velutha. Much of the narrative of the novel is accessible from the viewpoint of Roy's paired, child protagonists, Ammu's children Estha and Rahel, and the critical events of the novel—the cross-caste affair, the consequent beating and killing of Velutha by the police, and the death by sinking of the children's cousin, Sophie Mol—are exposed progressively as the adult twins see each other more than twenty years later. Untouchability was practised more rigorously in south India than elsewhere. Brahmanas and the other higher castes believed themselves to become polluted if Kammalan (Blacksmiths, carpenters, etc.) approached within sixteen hands, toddy trappers within twenty-four, Pollaya or Cheruma (peasants) within thirty-two and Paria within forty hands. Nayadi were kept at a distance of more than two hundred hands. Tanks of higher castes became unworthy of use if the untouchables passed by them. Untouchables could not wear gold ornaments, nor use umbrellas and foot-wear. They could not attend schools where children of other castes were enrolled. In Kerala untouchability assumed its most appalling features. "It is no wonder that the land looked like a lunatic asylum to Vivekanand when he first visited Kerala" (Chaitanya 50).

Arundhati Roy's presentation of the dalits has provoked a lot of controversy. She is often accused of drawing a gloomy picture of dalits which are related to their past rather than present Kerala. It is also said that she underplayed the role of the communists for the uplift of the Dalits in Kerala. We come across three characters in the novel which belong to the category of the downtrodden. They are Vellya Paapen and his two sons Kuttapen and Velutha. They are toddy trappers according to the tradition. The novelist gives a lot of information about the untouchables of Kerala in this connection. She also gives a generally perfect picture of the Dalits with their varying responses to the caste oppression through the device of the trio which depicts the three types of the dalits in Indian society, namely, the docile conformist, the discontented paralytic and the rebel who moves for equality and stakes his life. The novel mentions only the names of three untouchable castes, namely Paravans, Palayas and Pulayas. They were not allowed to enter the house of touchables.

Conditions have changed since then. They do not have to carry brooms during the childhood of Estha and Rahel. They use public roads. They are also learning skills other than their traditional occupations. Though that does not bring as much monetary gain to them as to the touchables folk. Neither the orthodox Mammachi nor the progressive Pillai permits them to step inside their houses. They are introduced to the idea of equal rights but we are also informed that touchable workers grudge their equal rights.

It is remarkable to note that the institution of untouchability has not left Christianity unaffected. Even the communists in the pursuit of immediate electoral gains submit to it. So far as Christians in India are concerned, they are but the converts from Hindu society. They have replaced their faith with the Bible and Christ but remained the mores of their Hindu past. An upper caste Christian is no better than an upper caste Hindu in his social attitude. The prejudices are particularly strong in South India where we find separate cemeteries for untouchables and others. Christianity did not prove a boon to the untouchables. When the Britishers came to Malabar, some of them converted to Christianity and joined the Anglican church. Velutha's grandfather, Kelan was one among them. Velutha's grandfather, as well as other untouchables, hoped to escape the scourge of untouchability. But it didn't do any good for them. They were given their separate churches, separate services, separate priests and even their separate pariah Bishop. Moreover, they got no benefits in jobs reservation or bank loans since Christianity is a casteless religion. To say so, Christianity has not removed the prejudices and arrogance of the converts from the upper castes, nor ameliorated a lot of the converts from the untouchable communities. It has kept the caste hierarchy inherited from the past intact.

Coming to Velutha, he is about three years younger than Ammu. He is not illiterate like his father and elder brother because when he was about eleven, Mammachi noticed his natural skills and persuaded him to send him to the untouchable's school. Besides he has got natural skills to prepare intricate toys with dried palm reeds, tapioca stems, and cashew nuts. He has learned carpentry from a German carpenter, Johann Klein and knows a lot about machines. Ammu knows Velutha from his boyhood days when he used to come with his father to the back entrance of the Ayemenem House and delivered coconuts. He made intricate toys for Ammu and brought them to her.

One day Velutha is taking part in the procession when Rahel recognises him and shouts for him but Ammu rebukes her as she knows that if Baby Kochamma or Chacko come to know about his political activities he would land into trouble. Ammu is attracted to Velutha since he has a kindred spirit, Velutha loves her children very much. Of course, there are physical aspects of attraction too. This is how the love affair started between them. The rendezvous continues for thirteen nights and then it takes an unexpected turn. Velutha's father finds out their meeting and goes to inform Mammachi as he is a docile servant. That provides a golden opportunity to Baby Kochamma to settle her account with Ammu. She goes to the Kottayam police station and cooks up a case of attempted rape of Ammu and kidnapping of three children, one of them found dead. Velutha goes to comrade Pillai for help but he is unaware of the politics. So, when naïve Velutha goes to Pillai he is dismissed by the excuse that the party is not constituted to support workers in their undisciplined private life.

Ammu is locked inside the house. Velutha is mercilessly beaten in the police station where he died. The novelist takes digs on people with power by saying that they were defending social norms, the traditional caste rules, the "love-laws" which did not permit a Paravan to love a Syrian Christian. In *The God of Small Things*, Arundhati Roy also questions patriarchy where women are no less considered as slave, no freedom from the clutches of patriarchy as we see in the case of Ammu. Ammu is the daughter of Benaan John Ipe. Her father is a male chauvinist who makes a lot of distinction between his son and daughter. He sends his son, Chacko to Oxford but deems college education unnecessary for girls. So, Ammu has no choice but to wait for marriage. Thus, denied higher education, she remains handicapped in future but shows a lot of independence of mind, courage, and moral strength as well as the ability to judge people correctly to a certain extent. At Ayemenem, she helps her mother with house work and waits for marriage proposals. As her father cannot afford a suitable dowry, marriage proposals do not come. At the same time, she finds living with her parents simply unbearable because her father is an ill-tempered bully who pretends to be an ideal husband and ideal father before outsiders but makes the life of his family miserable.

So, Ammu wants to escape from this miserable life and when she goes to spend summer at a distant aunt, ends up marrying a Bengali Hindu there. Her marriage is not based on love, even though the choice is hers. She is daring as she goes against the custom by marrying a person who is neither Christian nor belongs to Kerala. Ammu shows her strength of mind not only in marrying the man of her choice but also in divorcing him when the choice proves wrong. Her husband is an alcoholic, and he proposes to get a promotion in his job by agreeing to the manager Mr. Hollick to send his wife to his bungalow to look after him. Ammu learns about it and she is stunned but when her husband starts beating her, she takes the heaviest book from the shelf and hits him on the head. She is far from the traditional idea of an ideal woman who worships her husband like a god and obeys him blindly. The divorce leaves her no option but to return to Ayemenem with her two children, Estha and Rahel. Her father doesn't believe her story and blames her for the divorce. Ammu challenges the androcentric notions of society when she avoids surname after divorce. Though she works as much as Chacko, the latter feels free to declare the factory as his own as the law does not give a daughter any claim to the property. She is bitterly aware of the hypocrisy around her. During the first few months of her stay at the parental home, old female relations pay overnight trips to Ayemenem pretending to show sympathy for her about her divorce. But actually, it was their way of tormenting her. The rebel in Ammu does not permit her to remain contended with motherhood and divorceehood there is an unsafe edge an unmixable mix. So, she proceeds to reclaim her body. Her walk changes, she wears flowers in her hair, she spends hours on the riverbanks listening to radio, smokes cigarettes and swims in midnight.

Tired of the propriety handling her, she examines her body in the bathroom mirror which shows her worry about her passing youthfulness. The secret love affair with Velutha germinates but a short time lived. What seems an illicit relationship between a divorcee, a touchable woman, and an untouchable Paravan is actually a union of two rebels protesting against hypocritical laws of society not in word, but in deed. When the relationship is revealed, Mammachi and Baby Kochamma who have not only tolerated but assisted Chacko in his licentious affairs with working women, become highly indignant. Velutha is implicated in false cases of attempted rape, kidnapping, and murder. He is killed by police. When Ammu goes to the police station she is dismissed by the police with the remark that the Kottayam police does not take statement from veshyas (prostitutes) and their illegitimate children. He stares at her breasts while speaking and ask her to leave. Ammu is thrown out of the house separated from her children. Desperately she tries to get a job and living so that she could keep her children but at last she dies alone.

4.7 Select Critical Study: Samskara

Another novel which talks about the decaying caste system is *Samskara* written by U.R. Anantha Murthy and translated by A.K. Ramanujan. As A.K. Ramanujan says in the afterword chapter of the text. The opening event is a death, an anti-Brahmanical brahmin's death—and it brings in its wake a plague, many deaths, questions without answers, old answers that do not fit the new questions. The main event which unfolds the novel is the death of Naranappa, who also a brahmin by caste lives in the agrahara with the other brahmins but he had defied the codes and conduct of the village and lived a life of a libertine. He broke every taboo; drank alcohol, ate flesh, caught fish with his muslim friends in the holy temple tank, lived with a low-caste woman, chandri. He left his lawfully wedded wife and lived with defiance among them.

As Naranappa was their mocking anti-self and now he was dead. So, the question arises who will perform his last rite, since he defiled all the brahmanical convention so his own kinsmen started asking question whether he was brahmin enough in life to be treated as one in death? Did he have the necessary preparation to deserve a proper ceremony (samskara). The question was left to be solved by Praneshacharya as he is known all over the village as the crest-jewel of Vedic learning. Nobody in the village is ready to perform the last rites of Naranappa. The situation gets complicated when Chandri offers all her gold ornaments to perform the last rites of Naranappa. The person who will now perform his last ceremony would get the gold ornaments. Now greediness takes the place of contempt for Naranappa. But Praneshacharya handles the situation and ask everyone that he would go the temple of Maruti and will ask him what to do. Praneshacharya is amazed to see the generosity of Chandri and tells her to keep the gold with her since she has nothing left with her after the death of Naranappa. In the morning, he goes to the temple of Maruti. All day and evening he sit for a sign of yes and no without food and water. He exhausted with the heat.

Meanwhile, Chandri was also wandering around the forests. When Praneshacharya started to move without any answer famished, distressed he heard the foot steps of Chandri. When Chandri stumbled to touch his feet, the buttons on her blouse caught and tore open. She was filled with compassion for the poor Acharya. As exhausted and famished he started crying like a child in distress. Chandri loved him and peeled bananas to feed him like a mother. Acharya sleeps with Chandri, Naranappa's low-caste mistress. By what authority now can he judge Naranappa or advise his brahmin followers? His sudden sexual experience with the forbidden Chandri becomes an unorthodox rite of initiation. So, the question is, who is a brahmin, how is he made? All the battles of tradition and defiance, asceticism and sensuality, the meaning and meaninglessness of ritual, dharma as nature and law, desire (*kama*) and salvation (*moksha)*, have now become internal to Praneshacharya:

What happened at that turning? Dualities, conflict, rushed into my life. I hung suspended between two truths, like Trishanku. How did the ancient sages face such experiences? Without dualities, conflict? One wonders. The great sage who impregnated Matsyagandhi the fisherwoman in the boat and fathered Vyasa—did he agonise over it like me? Did Vishvamitra suffer, when he lost all the merits of penance for a woman? (Anantha Murthy 98).

Meanwhile, the physical problem of disposing of the body of Naranappa is solved by Chandri, the body is unceremoniously carried in a cart and burned in a field by Chandri and her muslim friends, though the Acharya does not know it.

4.8 Select Critical Study: *A Fine Balance*

Yet is it really possible for the subaltern to speak? Can men and women of the lowest socio-economic, caste strata articulate their own conditions? Set in mid-1970s India, Rohinton Mistry's *A Fine Balance* contains a multi-layered plot and complex characters that are simultaneously locally embedded and globally imaginable. While the novel's plot includes incidents that are decidedly Indian, such as experiences with the country's forced sterilization programme and caste-based conflicts, its themes are globally relevant and observable.

Rohinton Mistry's *A Fine Balance* (1996) records the dark and shameful episode of Emergency in 1975 with unrelenting honesty. *A Fine Balance* is also a text in which Mistry has made a conscious effort to 'embrace more of the social reality of India', so although the novel opens up with a Parsi woman Dena Dalal's story in Bombay, it soon enlarges its scope to include her lodger Maneck Kohlah from a hill station in north India and her tailors, Ishvar and Omprakash, who come to her from a village. The living condition of the untouchables depicted by Mulk Raj Anand in his *Untouchable* and Mistry in his *A Fine Balance* has not much changed after so many years. As Mistry describes the living condition in his novel:

> The village was by a small river, and the Chamars were permitted to live in a section downstream from the Brahamins and landowners. In the evening, Dukhi's father sat with the other Chamar men under a tree in their part of the settlement, smoking, talking about the day that was ending and the new one that would dawn tomorrow. Bird cries fluttered around their chitchat. Beyond the bank, cooking smoke signaled hungry messages while upper-caste waste floated past on the sluggish river. (96)

Mistry is also concerned about the atrocities that are committed on women as a class. When a girl was born whether in upper caste or lower caste it was considered an unfortunate event. Mistry in these lines states the conditions most poignantly:

> ... The birth of daughters often brought them beatings from their husbands and their husband's families. Sometimes they were ordered to discreetly get rid of the newborn. Then they had no choice but to strangle the infant with her swaddling clothes, poison her, or let her starve to death. (99-100)

The narrative also encompasses what Walter Benjamin has called the city poet's special concern with the ragpickers, beggars and suicide victims/heroes. As their tragic tales unfold, one gets the impression that Mistry's text is attempting to articulate the silences of centuries of exploitation, domination, and oppression of the poorest of the poor of India. The design of the novel is quite simple. Within 614 pages lies an account of social and historical developments of a country. With an unnamed city (Mumbai) at the Centre, Mistry weaves together a subtle and compelling narrative about four unlikely characters who come together soon after the government declares a 'state of internal emergency'. In the tiny flat of Dina Dalal, Ishvar and Omprakash Darji and Maneck Kohlah are painfully constructing new lives that become entwined in circumstances no one could have foreseen. The novel opens with the prologue set in 1975 which marks the coming together of the Chamar-turned tailors, Om, and Ishvar with Maneck Kolah in a commuter train in Bombay, the city by the sea. All three are then in a common quest of Dina Dalal, whom they seek as a refuge in different ways. For the tailors, she symbolises employment—an opportunity to earn a living in the indifference and the hugeness of Bombay. For Maneck she promises shelter from the horrors of the college hostel. This refuge motif, however, becomes ironical as the narrative progresses and Dina is revealed to be in as much need of succor as the three men who seek her.

Dina Dalal, also has her own share of journeying to accomplish in the text. She moves from the protected girlhood under the care of her doctor father, to the harsh reality of reductive femaleness under the protection of her brother Nusswan. Her awareness of her autonomous existence does not allow her to bow down to the patriarchy that Nusswan seeks to impose on her. Patriarchy in the form of Nusswan tries to crush all that is bright and fine in young Dina. He and his wife withdraw Dina from school and turns her into a household servant. She tries to educate herself by visiting libraries and there she meets her future husband. She moves away from the economic well-being and social security that marriage to one of Nusswan's friends would have offered her. She chooses to marry an economically unsuccessful Rustom Shroff, whom she meets. Dina's happiness is short-lived as Rustom dies in an accident. For time being she comes back to live with her brother but the sympathy wears off into invectives and insults. She comes back to her husband's flat, tries to set up her own business so that she doesn't have to beg for rent from Nusswan. She with the help of Ishvar and Omprakash manages the business. With their help, she has to also sew the Quilt—each square of which tells its own story. Dina's journey back to her husband's flat and her work for the Au Revoir fashion house brings Ishvar and Omprakash Darji into her life. After initial suspicions, the tailors become part of her family and along with Maneck Kohlah, whom she takes in as a lodger, succeed in bringing some joy to her. Mistry deftly handles the growing intimacy between Dina Dalal, Maneck and the Chamar-turned tailors, Ishvar and Om. When tailors and Maneck arrive together at Dina Dalal's "dingy little flat", she is relieved since "her fragile independence was preserved". She is at first was quite disgusted by their disordered work and unpunctuality.

The various stages in their relationship as seen in the text, her initial resistance to any kind of intimacy with the tailor, to the longing for their company, given her own loneliness, and the quick development of concern for them, as once she learns the enormity of their misery, is delineated meticulously in detail by the author. It is the mutual dependence between them that finally forces Dina Dalal to agree to let the tailors sleep in her verandah, for she could not afford to lose their service. All the sides of the dining table in her house are fully occupied for the first time after eighteen long years. Once she even tells Ibrahim, the rent collector that Ishvar is her husband and Maneck and Om are her sons. When Ishvar and Om go to their village to celebrate Om's marriage, and Maneck returns home to leave for Dubai, solitude returns to the house of Dina Dalal after one year of their lives together.

In later part of the novel, Ishvar and Om are forcibly taken to a family planning clinic and sterilized. Om, in fact, is castrated. Ishvar loses his legs due to infection and now back once again in Bombay, but now as beggars. In the meanwhile, Maneck returns from Dubai after eight years to attend his father's funeral and is shattered by his friend Avinash death. Moreover, he hears the news that Ishvar and Om have become beggars. Though he sees them, he refuses to recognize them and kills himself walking into a moving train. The novel ends up with the old Dina Dalal feeding Ishvar and Om without the knowledge of her brother Nusswan and his wife with whom she now stays. And we are told that "those two made her laugh every day" and this extraordinary relationship, it is implied, will continue. This indeed is the secret of survival as Mistry magnificently demonstrates in *A Fine Balance*. He has given the subalterns a voice and visibility in his novel. This soon comes to an end when Maneck leaves for a job in the Gulf and the tailors on a visit to their village are mutilated by their old high caste enemy the Thakur. Bereft of her tailors and without the rent that Maneck paid her, Dina is forced to go back to Nusswan's home and her circle of the journey is thus completed.

Dukhi Mochi journeys from his village to the nearby town where he is befriended by the Muslim tailor, Ashraf, who by virtue of his religion is outside the caste system. Dukhi, however, moves back to his village, but when his sons are beaten for polluting the village school by their presence, he sends them off to Ashraf to be apprenticed to him as tailors but at the end he has to suffer for his rebellion.

The Indian constitution adopted in 1950 had declared that all Indians would be equal under the law and no discrimination be made on grounds of caste, creed or gender. A constitution that was drafted under the leadership of an untouchable, Dr. Ambedkar, who was a Mahar and thus belonged to an even lower caste than the chamars-tailors in Mistry's narrative. Even Dukhi's village news of the parliamentary elections and social reforms seeps through. However, the promises of equality and justice offered by the new system is subverted by casteist politics and things carry on much as before. Narayan, however, rebels against the elision of his vote at the elections and this puts him in direct conflict with the village thakurs. Retribution is swift and a fiery death claims all the family except Ishvar and Narayan's young son Om, who were in town with Ashraf.

Ishvar and Omprakash Darji journey in this novel too. Their journey from their village by the river to the city by the sea, is foreshadowed by the journey Ishvar's father Dukhi Mochi makes his sons Narayan (Omprakash's father) and Ishvar undertake from the Chamar caste to being Darjis. Thereby changing their profession-defining surnames from Mochi-shoemaker to Darji-tailor. This is the most daring journey in the entire text as it involves moving away from being the lowest of the low, the most despised caste, which flayed dead cattle for the upper castes, tanned its hide and fashioned it into footwear. This daring gesture is noted by the village upper castes—the Thakurs—and punished twice over at intervals of several years. The entire family was mercilessly killed by Thakur Dharamsi to teach them all a lesson never to cross the caste line. Only Ishvar and Omprakash were alive because they were in town at that time.

The whole family of Dukhi Mochi is brutally killed and the hut is put on fire as we see in the novel. Thereby suggesting that caste memories are very long indeed. Ishvar and Om have to balance between their low-caste origins and their new Darji status. Their origins ultimately destroy this delicate balance and hurl them down into an abyss of abject bodily and spiritual horrors. Parsis in *Such a Long Journey* and Chamars in *A Fine Balance* offers a social articulation of difference, from the minority perspective. As Mistry boldly speaks about this class and caste system in his novel:

> What is this disease? You may ask. This disease, brothers and sisters, is the notion of untouchability, ravaging us for centuries, denying dignity to our fellow human beings. This disease must be purged from our society, from our hearts, and from our minds. No one is untouchable, for we are all children of the same God. Remember what Gandhiji says, that untouchability poisons Hinduism as a drop of arsenic poisons milk. (107)

4.9 Select Critical Study: *The White Tiger*

Moving forward in this list Arvind Adiga's *The White Tiger* (2008) needs to be looked as novel defining the class system prevalent in modern contemporary India. Balram Halwai stands as a difficult man, servant, philosopher, businessperson, and murderer. Over the course of seven nights, by the scattered light of a preposterous chandelier, Balram tells us the terrible and transfixing story of in what way he arose to be a success in life—having zero assets of his own but how so ever with wits to aid him end to end. Born within the dark heart of The Republic of India, Balram gets a break when he is hired as a driver for his village's wealthiest man. Balram Halwai, who never had an identity of his own, uses any means necessary to fulfill his dream of making money. He becomes a megalomaniac who murders his boss and confesses his rising to be an entrepreneur in the call centre hub of Bangalore.

He calls his life's history as 'The Autobiography of a half-baked Indian'. The novel may be a public observation and a study of injustice and power trendy within the system of a class scuffle in Indian society that depicts the anti-hero Balram representing the downtrodden sections of the Indian society put side by side against the wealthy. *The White Tiger's* protagonist exposes the rot in the three pillars of modern India—democracy, enterprise, and justice—reducing them to the tired clichés of a faltering nation. It is telling us that "India is not shining and, despite its claims of a booming economy, it is still "a heart of darkness which it has been since time immemorial" (Adiga 9).

As Adiga speaks out his mind why he wrote the novel he says that "he wanted to challenge this idea that India is the world's greatest democracy. It might be therefore in a detached logic, however on the bottom ground, the poor have very minuscule power..." (Sawhney). The story unfolds the way Balram breaks out to his new-found freedom from a caged life of misery through crime and cunning. This is a reflection of contemporary India, calling attention to social justice in the wake of economic prosperity. It is a novel about the merging new India which is pivoted on the great divide between the haves and have-nots with moral implications. Inequality and discrimination have continuously stayed everywhere and we become used to it. How long it can go on? Social discontent and vehemence have been on rise. What Adiga highlights is the ever-widening gap between the rich and the poor and the financial system that lets small minority to prosper at the cost of the common.

Dalit novelist Akhila Naik's *Bheda* (Odia, 2010; English, 2017) also talks about the caste question. *Bheda* addresses issues related to education, environment, gender, local history, the media, police and Hindu fundamentalism. Odia society has witnessed several social protest movements against caste at different periods in time. Bheda takes those debates further. Akhila Naik uses the word 'bheda' with multiple meaning. The primary meaning is 'a sense of difference'. If 'bheda' is used with the word 'bhaba' it implies the differences that exist among people in terms of caste, class or race. 'Bheda' also means 'target'. In the novel, Dalits are targeted by the upper castes because, after availing themselves of modern education, Dalits are now mobilizing to protest against the monopolies of upper castes. 'Bheda' also has another meaning: to properly understand the intricacies of an incident or event. Thus, all the different meanings of the word are in some or the other way is connected to the idea of caste and its corollary, caste discrimination and caste atrocities. By giving this powerful and multi-layered title to his novel, Naik wants to draw our attention to how complex the caste situation is in Indian society. He openly condemns the caste system; and by writing this novel, he is able to initiate a dialogue on the question of human rights and social justice in the backward state like Odisha, where such issues are rarely raised in the public domain. The novel is based in the region of Kalahandi, Naik himself living there. The novel is social document how once a rich land of natural resources belonging to the Dalits and Adivasis was left a barren land. Apart from frequent droughts and famines, Kalahandi has massive structural inequalities that directly affect the Dalits and Adivasis, who together constitute about fifty percent of the population in the region.

Out of the many Dalit texts that perform such functions, special reference must be made here to Omprakash Valmiki's *Joothan* (Hindi, 1997; English, 2003), Sharankumar Limbale's *Akkarmashi* (Marathi, 1984; *The Outcaste*, 2003) and Baby Kamble's *Jina Amucha* (Marathi, 1986; *The Prisons We Broke*, 2009) where the idea of social justice and Dalit empowerment come together forcefully. For example, while Valmiki and Limbale, in their respective autobiographies, expose the hypocrisies of upper-caste custom and tradition, Baby Kamble delves deep into the details of the gender inequality mahar Dalit women had to live with in a patriarchal set-up. It is only through such Dalit texts that we are able to publicly debate and discuss themes such as tradition, culture, language, gender, class and religion, apart from caste.

4.10 Women Protest Literature

Women writers of the last quarter of the twentieth century have come a long way from the time Mary Wollstonecraft uttered a need for recognition in *A Vindication of the Rights of Women* (1792) more than two hundred years ago. In postmodern literature images of women have been destabilized, deconstructed and reconstructed. No longer does the writing of women concern itself with the search for individuality alone. Increasingly, women's literature has striven to ascertain a separate ethos, an exclusive feminine myth as a counterpoint to the existent myth of male standards. Women writers of fiction, Kate Millet, Erica Jong, Diane Johnson, and Marilyn French interrogated and rejected conventional images of women. Even before the Movement, however, Margaret Fuller, Virginia Woolf, Sylvia Plath, Doris Lessing, and Simone Beauvoir among others registered their sense of indignation in their texts in no vague terms. In the novels and the short stories of Joyce Johnson, Marilyn French, Fay Weldon, Margaret Atwood, Angela Carter, Amy Tan, Bharti Mukherjee, and Alice Walker among others, feminist issues are prioritized and problematised. So, in Toni Morrison's novel *Sula* (1974) racist and sexist issues are represented with forthright realism. The quoted exchange below between Sula and her grandmother reveals the new power that black female speech has acquired:

> "...when you gone to get married? You need to have some babies. It'll settle you."
>
> "I don't want to make somebody else. I want to make myself."
>
> "Selfish. Ain't no women got no business floatin' around without no men." (*Sula* 78)

In her second novel *Sula,* Morrison has presented the black family life, showing another dimension of modes and manners prevalent in contemporary society. Before Sula is introduced to the reader, Morrison gives a life-throbbing picture of the community in which her drama of defiance takes place. It is connected to the valley by one road only, which is shaded by beeches, oaks, and chestnuts. Strangely this community, in the hills is called 'the Bottoms'. The condition of the place and the lifestyle of the community there play a significant role in the credibility of the characters and the realism of the plot. Although the entire story runs around Sula yet the family factors are equally important to shape a girl like Sula. She is fascinatingly unique in semi-rural town during the thirties, forties, and fifties when the nation's conscience did not bear the imprint of women's struggle for wider options in their lives. Sula is presented in various stages as she grows from childhood to adulthood.

As Morrison analyses Sula in this growth process, she analyses the other family members who shape her personality, values and defiant posture towards life. Significantly all those family members are women—three individuals who offer Sula different responses to womanhood. The most influential and intriguing of the three women is Sula's grandmother, Eva Peace, who has a mysterious past. All we know about her is that she comes from Virginia with a husband named BoyBoy deserts her and the three children, Eva Peace disappears for eighteen months and then returns with enough money to build a house—but minus one leg. Rumor has it that she stuck her leg under a train and collected damage money, but no one knows for sure. When Sula is introduced in the novel, she is a child of three, who has moved with his mother into the home of her grandmother. There is something about Eva's ability to control, to dominate, to command attention that makes her disability glamorous. It is a strange house of strange boarders lorded over by a strange and domineering woman where Sula with her mother and grandmother lives.

Family love is essential for healthy socialization, which Sula fails to sustain, for Eva Peace, despite all her gestures of magnanimity towards, strangers, is unable to embrace her granddaughter with warmth and affection. Hannah, Sula's mother is guilty of indifference to her relationship with her daughter. In the house of many rooms, Sula learns about women's roles and women's sexuality. This black family observes no civilized norms based on morality. They live in their community with ease and independence. To them, life means sexual enjoyment without any inhibition or remorse. Morrison boldly reveals the realistic traits of Hannah's character, a widowed mother, but a woman of insatiable sexual appetite. The story of Eva's family converges with the story of Helene Wright on the meeting point of Sula and Nel. At the age of twelve, Sula begins an intense friendship with Nel, the third woman in her life. The friendship between Nel and Sula is an example of a necessary bonding that always takes place between black women for the barest survival.

Sula and Nel both become unique individuals, denigrating and traditional stereotypes of black women. Nel seems to become a conventional, good, self-righteous, middle-class black housewife, and Sula seems to become a bad black woman. The strength of Morrison's novel lies in the fact that Nel really does become good in a conventional sense, but cannot forgive Sula for having taken her husband, and Sula who has become a pariah in the community for sleeping nonchalantly with any and all men, for sending her grandmother to the old folks home and for watching her mother burn to death, dies free of pain and guilt, of fear and judgment, her mind proudly her own. Sula's activities are fully supported by her own discretion; she does not imitate any of her kith or kin. She moves in an orbit, which she chooses by herself. Her relational connection with her family is no more than a biological necessity because Sula hates to entertain any such fragile as well as firm bonds of relationship. She grows rebel in the eyes of her family, society, and community, but herself remains free from the fetters of all familial bonds and relational obligations and with no possibility of reconciliation.

Women's literature commencing in India was not given due acknowledgment in the literary scenario during the period of colonization. The writings by women author like Urvashi Butalia, Anita Nair, Anita Desai, Kiran Desai, Shobha De, Suniti Namjoshi, Kamla Markandaya, Sulekh Sanyal, Bharti Mukherjee, Manju Kapoor, Mahasweta Devi, Shama Zaidi and Jhumpa Lahiri are a detonation of censored desires and pent up feelings that find irresistible long been gathered. Women writers have proved that their writings are grave and entail attention. Women writers have moved away from traditional portrays enduring self-sacrifice forwards conflict.

A major obsession in recent Indian women's writing has been the demarcation of internal life and restrained interpersonal relationships. Women's writing in India has been multi-faceted but often persisting secretly, sometimes in pain and in disobedience but the sanctified status is reserved for men as if they are the heir apparent to the literary throne though women may excel in literary domain. Women writers have to face Censorship—social, professional and personal, challenges that are sexist and misogynist in nature. The most unacceptable women writers are those who question social order. The Pillar of community—Marriage, Motherhood, control of sexuality and traditions must be potted for the interests of preserving the culture.

Coming to marginalized caste, Dalit women are subjected to extreme forms of social, economic, physical and mental torture and exploitation. According to the official figures, three Dalit women are raped every day most recently shown the movie "Article 15" (2019). They are casually stripped and molested and even invite death if they dare to quench their thirst from a common well. The writings of Dalits women writers are based on the lives, experiences, and consciousness of the community and assert the need for justice. Their life-cycle is fairly comparable to their higher caste counterparts nevertheless the very fact is that Dalit womenfolk have remained victims of male-controlled society for ages and still have very little claim to human rights. Their attempts to affirm their rights are often met with strong resistance from the higher castes, resulting in inhuman torture, rapes, massacres, and other atrocities. The images of savage reality that emerge through Dalit stories; the level of violence against Dalit women is quite parallel to the tribulation and sufferings of black womenfolk within the American nation.

In the case of double marginalization, they are victims of caste and gender oppression together. While on the one hand, on account of being a Dalit, they are coerced into a life of poverty and economic exploitation resulting in abject denials and discrimination, on the other hand, being women, they are forced to lead a completely dehumanized existence having little or no control over their bodies. Dalit Feminism voices their agony and articulates their oppression. The writings of Baby Kamble and Urmila Pawar emphatically express the anguish of Dalit women in Marathi Dalit literature. Baby Kamble's *The Prisons We Broke* is the first work that comes in Dalit Literature which is written by a woman. The book deals with the two major problems of society: first, the oppression and exploitation of the Dalit by the upper class, and second, the discrimination towards women in a patriarchal society.

Faustina Mary Fatima Rani Bama is a famous Dalit activist, writer, and teacher. She writes under the pen name of Bama. She is a Tamil Dalit woman who hails from a Roman Catholic family. Bama belongs to the group of those writers who propound the idea of social realism in literature. As a propounder of

Dalit feminism, she believes in portraying "challenging forms of oppression" which are both overt and covert in their own ways. She describes the common experiences of exploitation, of her own Paraiya community. Through her autobiography, "Karrukku", Bama projects the suffering of Dalit women. Her novel *Sangati* translated into English by Lakshmi Holmstrom, is an autobiography of her community which highlights the struggle of the Paraiya women. *Sangati* contributes both to the Dalit women and to the women's movement in India, especially in Tamil Nadu. The text deals with variegated experiences and stories of the Dalit women strung together.

The anecdotes which end up being testimonies of the injustice faced by them highlights the different lives led by men and women of the same community. While men do get the opportunity for recreation, women toil under the pressure of professional and domestic life. Without remorse, the women tired after a day's work have to attend to the household chores also. Bama realistically portrays the physical violence that outlines their lives. She explores the psychological stress and trauma that Dalit women go through. Her language is very different from other Indian women writers as she generously incorporates the Dalit slogans and phrases, proverbs, folklore, and folk songs. She does not flinch from criticizing the Church also. Bama as a feminist writer protests against all forms of oppression and suffering faced by the Dalit women in the first half of *Sangati*. But the later part of *Sangati* moves away from depression and presents a positive identity of Dalit women.

By presenting a positive identity of Dalit women Bama focuses on their inner strength and vigour. Bama is convinced that no one is going to help the women in her community, it is up to the women themselves to bring about the change required. The novel makes a clarion call for action and transformation. Viramma is a Tamil illiterate agricultural labourer and midwife from a Pondicherry village. Her autobiography is titled after her and is co-authored by Josaine Racine and Jean-Luc Racine, who are Tamil born ethnomusicologists educated in France to whom Viramma narrates her story in the first person. This affords an 'unusual' character to the autobiography, highlighting the evolving character of the Dalit women. Viramma like all Dalit women is doubly marginalized, firstly as a Dalit and secondly as a woman. In her autobiography, she does not only bewail and cry over her Dalit identity but also celebrates it. Dalit songs, rituals, festivals, and other community-centric ceremonies are narrated with intimacy and speak of a rejection of the Brahmanical order.

There have been many dissimilar meanings assigned to social protest literature by different people. All novels could be considered to be a form of protest in Ralph Ellison's opinion. Others consider that literature is to be set aside separate from politics and that protest literature does not exist. Even though protest literature does not directly lead to social change, it can eternally change society during an awakening, a period of the cultural renaissance that occurs during times of social stress and confusion. Because there have been so few awakenings, protest literature has a modest effect on moving people in a certain direction. For this explanation, during times of slavery and civil discrimination, many African Americans believed that there was no point to attempt creating protest literature if the protest is ineffective or does not have a reasonable chance of victory. W.E.B. Du Bois, however, thought that even if the protest was unsuccessful, it at least lets the opposition know where you stand. It also gives the creator a sense of empowerment. Though many public protests have failed, many have also prevailed and led to huge social change. This chapter sheds light upon the literature that led to these changes. In my opinion, protest literature must not necessarily bring about social change. Protest literature is a type of dissent that finds itself in the work of novels and other types of written work. To be considered social protest literature, a book does not have to essentially change a problem but offer society with reasons why something is a problem and possibly give feasible solutions.

4.11 The Novelists of Social Commitment

Anand firmly believes that a writer in an emerging society has multiple roles to play. A writer should become a teacher, guide, mentor, reformer and conscience keeper of the race. Anand, like Achebe the African novelist, considers the pedagogic function of literature the most important. The most urgent task a writer in colonial society must address is the restoration of human dignity. As an imaginative author, Anand holds, ought to infuse confidence into his fellowmen, and aid them to hold their heads tall. He clearly states the social responsibilities of an artist in the present age. According to Anand One of the primary things to be completed in the contemporary world is to instruct the public to place the enormous gathering of knowledge collected in the explorations of the former at the disposal of every person so that man can by these means learn to recognize the essential principle of human living and exercise vigilance with respect to the actual adversaries of liberty, equality, and socialism.

Dr. Bhabani Bhattacharya is another novelist who deserves mention as a socially committed novelist. A much-translated novelist, he got the Sahitya Akademi Award in 1967 in recognition of his outstanding achievement in the field of Indian fiction in English. His novels in the chronological order are *So Many Hungers* (1947), *Music for Mohini* (1952), *He Who Rides a Tiger* (1954), *A Goddess Named Gold* (1960), *Shadows from Ladakh* (1966) and *A Dream in Hawaii* (1978). He does not seem to have any political ideological affiliations but the first three of his novels show a deep concern for the suffering humanity and keen eye for social problems.

The first novel, *So Many Hungers* narrates the woeful story of the famine of 1942-43, a man-made disaster that took a toll of two million people in Bengal. Unscrupulous people like Samarendra Basu and sir Lakshminath of Bengal Rice limited store foodgrains and make money, common people are forced to starve. The conditions worsen after the mass arrest of political leaders following the 'Quit India' resolution. Ruthless suppression and atrocities, indiscreet firing and victimization of the masses bring in a reign of terror. A man lighting the street lamps in Calcutta is mistaken for a political activist and shot dead. Kajoli's husband is shot dead for no reason while hurrying to the railway station. In the name of security measures, more than forty thousand boats are snatched away from the fishermen and burned. Thus, the fishermen are deprived of their living. Coastal villages are evacuated under the same pretence. The victims know the falsity of the government's excuse but they are helpless. Then hoarders, profiteers and black-marketeers are let loose by the authority. The unholy alliance of the government and traders compels the peasants to sell all their rice at a nominal price. Later, the peasants have to buy it in the black market at a ten times price.

The rice hunger begins as a thin stream but swells soon into a mighty flood. Rice, the common staple food, becomes a rare luxury to them and they have to sell their belongings for a handful of rice. They sell their land, cottages and cattle, and become uprooted. Inflation has reduced the worth of their money to nothing, so they get little even by selling all their belongings. The flow of destitute then rushes to Calcutta which has its own limitations. Counterpoised to the hunger for food on the part of the poor is the wealthy men's hunger for sex. So, brothels prosper and peasant girls are forced to prostitution. Even Kajoli, the daughter of freedom-fighter peasant finds no alternative to save her mother and younger brother. A fisherman, unable to bear the sight of her child's hungry, blank stare and having no milk to feed the child, buries the baby alive. Then there are pathetic scenes like one eating bits of food from garbage and a baby suckling the breast of its dead mother. Kajoli's mother commits suicide as she does not like to be a burden on her already starving children. Such things happen despite fair harvest and during a war that was supposed to be fought for democratic and human values.

As Iyengar remarks: "*So Many Hungers* is no doubt an impeachment of man's inhumanity to man, but it is also a dramatic study of a set of human beings trapped in a unique tragic predicament" (414). There may be people who think that the novel has become outdated now as the British have left and famine seems to have become a thing of the past. Unfortunately, hoarders, profiteers and black marketeers have not disappeared. Attempts to create false scarcity of salt, sugar, onion, pulses and mustard oil are not unknown to us. The roots of the tragic predicament narrated in the *So Many Hungers* are still there in our society and we have to beware of them. This is the relevance of the novel to our own times.

His novel, *He Who Rides a Tiger* takes us back to the days of Bengal famine. "Less somber in its hues than *So Many Hungers*, the indictment it carries is delivered with more deftness, and satire and entertainment are mixed in almost equal proportion" (Iyengar 416). Kalo, an honest blacksmith contented with his profession, is uprooted from his town and moves to Calcutta. He feels hungry and attempts to steal a banana from a first-class compartment. He has eaten nothing for days and so he cannot help it. But the magistrate does not care and punishes him with three months of rigorous imprisonment. This happens at a time when despicable crimes of jute merchants, rich merchants and other rich people involved in immoral traffic go unnoticed and unpunished. In prison, he experiences the tyranny of the warden and comes out an embittered man. Released from jail, he joins the flux of hungry men in Calcutta. But his efforts to survive honourably bear no fruit. He helps the corporation gang in removing dead bodies from streets and gets just one rupee a day which cannot keep him alive. Then he becomes a pimp. To his great shock, one night he finds his only daughter brought to one of the harlot-houses. He rescues her just in time but she carries a stigma which is difficult to forget.

So, Kalo resolves to avenge the injustice done to him by the alliance of 'caste and cash'. So Kalo the blacksmith becomes Mangal Adhikari the Brahmin overnight and a 'miracle' takes place. A stone Shiva rises from the ground and a temple is built around it. Fraud pays rich dividends where honesty had made even survival difficult. Both riches and honour are now showered upon him and he receives them jubilantly. The novelist explains his psychology behind the behaviour as follows in the words of the protagonist since it was not just a question of living. It was a question of revenge. We've got to hit back. Through what better means than the temple? And let their proud women, limbs draped in jewels and chastity, bow down to a girl who has almost fallen.

Even amid this drama of lies and deception, Kalo shows his best human qualities. Instead of casting into the Ganga the buckets of milk donated by the devotees for the idol's bath, he manages to divert the same after bath for feeding hungry children. His devotees include all the rich of Calcutta and even the magistrate who had sentenced him for a petty crime, comes to him and touches his feet humbly. But his satisfaction is not everlasting. Prosperity does not pacify his conscience. He feels alienated from his former self. His daughter, Chandralekha too longs for the former days to return as their new life is simply suffocating. Her role as the Mother of seven-fold Bliss, an object of adoration, brings no pleasure to her.

So, both father and daughter are increasingly ill at ease. Kalo buys a blowpipe, and tools and runs a smithy in the upper chamber of the temple secretly, but as the smoke leads to suspicion, he has to give up the attempt. Various complications arise in his life and he feels like a man riding a tiger who does not know when to stop and how. At last, Kalo gathers courage and reveals the whole truth before a big assembly. That shocks and enrages the audience but brings the utmost solace to Kalo and his daughter. Purged of lies and deceptions of the past fully, they feel contented to begin a new, modest and truthful life.

Thus, *He Who Rides a Tiger* is a powerful indictment of the society that perpetuates superstitions, corruption, injustice, and degradation of the human race. It shows that a system that makes life unbearable to the poor and honest and rewards the rich and dishonest cannot but breed charlatans and cheats. It also demonstrates that human beings are not basically mean, unkind and deceitful. Only a section of them is led by baser instincts, the majority of them are compelled to do things which are unbecoming to them simply for the sake of survival. The latter cannot resist the pricking of their conscience which compels them to return to the path of virtue sooner than later. That is why the novel remains relevant to us even after the disappearance of the British and the famine.

It is not possible to discuss in detail all the earlier authors with social commitments. I have only mentioned the most important figures in this tradition, and I think Shashi Deshpande deserves a discussion. It is further important to notice that she brings the topic of women's social problems into sharp focus. Her commitment consists of concentrating on the theme of meaninglessness and sexual confusion suffered by women inside a patriarchal culture. She seeks to assert thereby that the inequality of sexes is neither a biological imperative nor a divine mandate but a construct. As the principal and seminal concern of feminism are to assert the beingness of women and her novels are concerned with women's quest for self, we cannot but call her a committed feminist even though she does not feel enthusiastic about the label.

Women in her novels liberate themselves from external restrictions (imposed by society, culture or nature) and internal inhibitions (their own fear and guilt feelings) and establish themselves as autonomous beings. They also come to realise the fundamental truth that a person has to discover one's self oneself. Her first novel is *The Dark Holds No Terrors* (1980). It is the story of a defiant woman Sarita (Saru for short). She develops a strong dislike for her mother who treats her son Dhruva and her daughter Sarita differently. In one of her recapitulations, Saru records her conversation with her mother:

> Don't go out in the sun. You'll get darker.
>
> "Who cares?"
>
> "We have to care if you don't. We have to get you married."
>
> "I don't want to get married."
>
> "Will you live with us all your life?"
>
> "Why not?"
>
> "You can't."
>
> "And Dhruva?"
>
> "He is different. He is a boy." (Deshpande 40)

The situation worsens when her brother dies and failing to save him from drowning, she is held responsible for his death. The boy is six then and she is eleven: "you killed your brother... why didn't you die?" are the words of her mother and they drive her to show that she has every right to live. She, therefore, defies her mother and goes to Bombay to study Medicine. Then she falls in love with Manohar who does not belong to her caste or class. Saru takes one more step in defiance of her mother by marrying Manohar much against her mother's wishes. Marriage, which is the promised end in a traditional society seems to Saru as the way out of her mother and her home, the first step towards autonomy. But soon she realizes that marriage is no alternative to the bondage of the parental home that her new role as a wife is no better than the role of a daughter she resented. The new situation is expressed as follows:

> I had come away from my parents in a fever of excitement after the last battle. The die was cast, the decisions taken, my boats burnt. There could be no turning back. Then, this ridiculous anti-climax. (Deshpande 31-32)

While Sarita succeeds in her career as a doctor, her husband Manohar (Manu) grows jealous of her. Domestic discord sets in as the husband who promised to become a Shelley proves a Sadist. Thus, she concludes that she has exchanged "one pair of pinching, torturing shoes for another," that marriage like the parental home means "the chalked lines drawn by others," that there is "no such thing between man and woman" like love and women are mere "prisoners of sex". Marriage too, like parental home, appears as an enclosure. She visualizes it in terms of the dark rooms where terror awaits her. She leaves her husband and goes to live with her father. Her mother is dead now but the escape lands her in an "atmosphere of brooding stillness" only. The neighbourhood is curious about her past and she feels guilty for leaving her children behind and coming to the house where her mother had died without forgiving her.

At the end of the process, she learns to free herself of guilt, shame, and humiliation. She realizes the mystery of human existence. In a world where human beings fail, neither her father nor her husband can be her refuge. She has to find her own way to salvation because her life is her own. She needs no longer to be a puppet of others. She has to look after her children and she has to attend her patients. She hates Manohar for his brutality but also pities him. As everybody is lonely in the world, she need not despair. Ultimately, Sarita's fear of losing herself in the dark mysterious universe is dispelled. She becomes aware of the fact that the dark holds no terrors if you believe in yourself and accept your responsibility. That you believe in your strength to face her 'home' and return to the profession she belongs, the proud profession of a doctor.

That Long Silence (1988) takes its title from a statement by Elizabeth Robins which forms the epigraph of the novel. As Elizabeth Robins stated that if she were a man and cared to know the world I lived in, I almost think it would make me a shade uneasy—the weight of the long silence of one-half of the world. The novel seeks to remove the weight by breaking the long silence that has surrounded the world of women. It traces a woman's passage through difference, guilt, fear, smothered anger and silence towards articulation and affirmation. It sums up the evolution of women through four generations the protagonist has known and looks forward to a better prospect for them. Mohan, a middle-class man indulges in some malpractices as he seeks prestige and security. Then he faces an inquiry and the possibility of losing his job. His accomplice Agarwal advises him to stay away from his office and his Churchgate flat till the dust settles. That presents no problem as the children are away on tour with the friends of the family. So, he goes to his flat at Dadar. His wife Jaya accompanies him in silent resentment. An intolerable period of anxious waiting follows which triggers off a process of self-examination and self-criticism in Jaya's mind. She is haunted and tormented by the memories of the past. She recollects her early life as well as the seventeen years of her married life. She remembers her failures and frustrations. That emotional upheaval ultimately ends giving her guidance for the future.

The novel pinpoints how our culture keeps silent about women. At one point in the novel Jaya discovers that her name is missing in the family tree, her uncle, Ramukaka, has prepared meticulously. That is explained with the excuse that as a married woman she belongs to her husband's family. That does not satisfy her because the names of her mother, her aunts, and her grandmother do not figure either. Their names are blotted out of the family history despite all they did for the family. Thus, it is a man's version of history that prevails.

Social institutions and their norms in the male-dominated society stifles the growth and free expression of the individual. They suppress normal human feelings and go to the extent of making cynics of the individuals. For example, when Jaya finds her upstairs neighbour Kamat lying dead on the floor of his flat, she leaves the place in panic and silence. Kamat, a widower, and lonely man, was her best friend but she cannot pay homage to him for the fear of running her marriage. Jaya's self-realization strikes a new note that deserves mention:

> But what was that 'myself?' 'Trying to find oneself'—what a cliché that has become. As if there is such a thing as oneself, intact and whole, waiting to be discovered. On the contrary, there are so many, each self, attached like a Siamese twin to a self of another person, neither able to exist without the other. (Deshpande 69)

Many people (including her mother and two grandmothers) have become part of Jaya's personality and her unconscious. That is why attempts to recall them are so much evident in the novel. To conclude, the heroines of Shashi Deshpande strive for self-realization, and self-assertion and they succeed in it. Equality between sexes is the dream they cherish. But they seek their solutions always within the range of family. This phenomenon seems to be rooted in the very nature of feminism in India which respects the institution of the family. Then, there is the psychological phenomenon called symbiosis. Eric Fromm uses this term in his book *Escape from Freedom* for the union of individuals in such a way that they lose the integrity of their self. Victimization is not only the way a victimizer controls or manipulates others, but it is also a means of controlling himself. So, the victimizer needs the victim. Manohar, Jayant and Mohan need their wives desperately. As for the victim, she too needs the victimizer because it is not easy to be free. Symbiosis, thus, forms the basis of both sadism and masochism and Shashi Deshpande's novels illustrate it well. So, the novels of Shashi Deshpande are significant both socially and psychologically.

Arundhati Roy as a woman writer reflects the social, economic, political and religious aspects of Indian society specially in

Kerala in her masterpiece. The biased treatment of Hindu family between their sons and the daughter, the dual standards of quasi communists, caste discrimination in Christianity, wife thrashing, rejection of girls education and other significant issues, like Industrial development, Gulf money, indifferent behaviour of police with the women and the helpless people are ingrained issues in the novel. *The God of Small Things* depicts the socio-political milieu of Kerala during the sixties. Nevertheless, at the Centre-stage Roy places Velutha against the odds who is crumpled to death. In Arundhati Roy's fictional world, man and woman remain only islands and fail to shape up as continents, because their relationship lacks mutual love, understanding, and adjustment. On the contrary, her flourishing business and growing popularity intensify his Jealousy and desire for retaliation. The edifice of their marriage survives, but its essence crumbles totally when Pappachi, cautioned against beating, pull out all communication with his wife. Arundhati Roy presents a panoramic view of the social order and comprehends the effect of history on the individual. The emphasis of her entire work is the idea of the struggle between individual freedom and physical, psychological, political, and social restraints.

The God of Small Things deals with the tribulation of women as daughter and wife in a patriarchal society. Women have become victims of gender oppression. Gender, in our male-controlled society, plays a very vital role in discriminating between the powerful and the helpless. According to the ideology of male superiority and feminine inferiority, all men are empowered to exercise "right" over all women. Though Mammachi belongs to the better socio-economic class she has no right at all in her husband's family. She is beaten, ill-treated. In a sense, the story of Ammu and Velutha is not a story of Ayemenem alone. Even after seven decades since India achieved Independence, Dalits are still oppressed in one form or another. If Dalits in villages are subject to punishments such as lynching death, rape, and other humiliation, Dalits in urban spaces face a 'white-washed' form of caste-based discrimination. If feudal society is responsible for the injustices meted out to the Dalits in the rural setting (as seen in *Untouchable*), crimes, committed on Dalits in urban spaces are perpetrated by the state (as seen in *The God of Small Things*). Arundhati Roy takes her involvement with the life around her a stage further. Social commitment is almost a trait of her personality. The very title of the novel, *The God of Small Things* implies the nature of her commitment. Shashibala Talwar and R.S. Sharma (1999) have concluded from the author's own explanation that *The God of Small Things* "stands for the life of the weak and the helpless, whether they are small creatures like blue bottles, frogs and ants or human beings such as the victims of Hollick's lust or the women who supply Chacko's 'man's needs' or the children like Estha and Rahel.... *The God of Small Things* represents all those people who are victimized by the forces of history, dead convention, false pride and respectability, the tyranny of the state and the politics of opportunism and andro-centric order" (Roy 130-35).

But "small things" need not refer to inanimate objects only. There is no lack of selfish, cruel people in our society who treat the poor and the powerless no better than "small things". They reduce beings or persons to objects which can be broken, crushed, thrown away or destroyed at the sweet will of the powerful. Their fate, nay even their life, is immaterial to those who wield power. They are unable to raise their voice against the injustice done to them. As they are voiceless, as they cannot resist, they are but "small things". We are now in the position to conclude that Arundhati Roy has a deep concern for the "small things" and her commitment is related to them. We have seen what the "small things" mean. They are the victims of the state, society and sheer will of the unthinking powerful. Though the term "small things" implies a lot and defies an exhaustive enumeration and elaboration, we can broadly put it in the following four categories:

1. Women who are placed in a subordinate position by society and left defenceless by the state.
2. Children who are unable to defend themselves and suffer a lot to survive.

3. The workers and the Dalits who are downtrodden, exploited and abused traditionally.
4. The environment which is subjected to wanton acts of manipulation and destruction.

These writers stand principally as social realists who revolted contrary to man-made, unreal, anti-human establishments. They demonstrate a keen interest in the eradication of social evils and their novels are nothing but creative efforts to stimulate the slumbering conscience of the individuals to trigger them to remove these evils. They are voiceless, starting from Mulk Raj Anand to Arundhati Roy and many more authors have raised their voice for them. It is not our intention here to go into every single socially committed novel or novelist in Indo-English literature but to point how a rich tradition does belong here and that every single socially committed writer deserves a place within this tradition. Their novel is concerned about the inhuman behavior that springs from caste prejudices, but the atrocities committed and the suffering caused are no less palpable.

Thus, we find that communalism injected in the youth poisons their minds. Anger and frustration lead them astray and culminate in violence, loot, and even murder. Politics under the circumstances becomes a weapon of prolonged social turmoil. The message of the chapter is simple: humanity is "the best of all religions rather than the only religion like Hinduism, Islam or Christianity, Sikhism". In other words, we need a non-sectarian approach in individual as well as in national life. Not a false secularism but a broad, secular outlook is the remedy of the social malaise that has been tormenting our nation ever since.

4.12 Anand the Novelist with Purpose

This conflict cannot last long. Anand and other writers advocate different approaches for solving this impasse. Anand believes in 'bhakti' which means selfless action for the betterment of society, Anand expects every oppressed individual and group to engage in affirmative action for social transformation or universal liberation. He believes in a socialist, egalitarian, fraternal and caring society which will emerge from the embers of the vanishing society. The writer has an important role to play in exposing these contradictions and clarifying alternatives. He/she has to be the spokesperson or the 'fiery voice of the voiceless. In other words, he has to play a prophetic role. Achebe too believes in the unique role of a writer or intellectual in the emerging social change. He/she acts as a pivotal point in the process of education and liberation.

Therefore, the writer becomes a teacher or educator according to Achebe. The writer becomes the conscience of the people. They have to educate and pull up the drooping confidence and morale of the people. Struggles at all levels need to be carried on if the ultimate triumph has to be a historical reality. Anand condemns caste and class discrimination as a pernicious, shameful and inhuman practice. Class and Caste consciousness are so much a part of our cultural and religious heritage that it devolves on every Indian, particularly the victims of this system to raise their voice of protest. Anand's commitment to humanism shines through each of his novels and underlies his powerful indictment. Neither Anand nor any other writer is an obscurantist. They all appreciate and welcome the revolutionary changes in lifestyle, and modes of thinking introduced by the processes of modern scientific and technological development. In fact, they are complementary and mutually enriching. Even the Marxist critics and theorists concede the autonomy of art and therefore a committed writer need not neglect art or make it subservient to content or subject matter. Anand's subject matter reveals his profound involvement in the lives and fortunes of the people, especially the oppressed masses, Anand's language, style, and fictional techniques reveal certain flaws thus inviting unfavourable critical review.

Societies of all civilizations have retained traditions passed down through numerous generations. These long-established and inherited ways of thinking and behaving are patterns which allow for the perpetuation of cultural beliefs and practices. Often considered in contrast to traditional customs are ideas that are regarded as modern. In mid-twentieth century India, including the latter time of its occupation and post-independence, there was tension concerning conflicting ideas; a number that was considered time-honoured versus those which were new and unusual. Mulk Raj Anand was impacted by this collision of beliefs. Anand was raised as a child in India but spent his impressionable and malleable young adult years in England where he was educated and exposed to Western thoughts and ideologies. He acknowledged that during his school years at the British Indian schools he attended, he was taught everything English: ideas, history, philosophy, etc.

Anand never really felt a deep and passionate attachment to ancient Indian beliefs and traditions; he did not feel as if they were a part of his essence. He was, however, cognizant of the denigration of some of these time-honoured and customary traditions and ways of life and the impact they had on citizens of India. Some reflected shame on the country and Anand believed that they needed to be eliminated or corrected. Anand recognized the limitations of the Indian past and found it crucial and essential to correct these wrongs rather than to celebrate its achievements. As a philosophy student, Anand showed a preference toward the concreteness and provability of the sciences over romantic attitudes. This caused him to question the base of Indian wisdom and some philosophies that he considered faulty. Anand felt that it was the responsibility of the writer to illustrate the entirety of man's existence in an objective manner, compelling him to act in accordance with his point of view whether he maintained it or changed it.

Anand believed that the archetypical Indian author must analyze all the influential societies; evaluate them for their achievements as well as consider their defects, then present the findings to the Indian world. This would affect the Indians and so stir their emotions that they would seek to act in favor of the total human experience and modify their attitudes and adjust their beliefs to change any shortcomings and to establish a supreme and unsurpassed way of life. The preeminent Indian author, Anand hoped, would be the vehicle of progress that would make a case for the traditional ways of life; citing its limitations and its strengths. The enlightened author would address the out-of-date political and social attitudes while presenting more current and acceptable points of view. The finest author would speak to the theme of modernity while focusing on the impact that modernity would have on the long-established and accepted ways of life. An astute author would, through the amalgamation of India's rich history and traditions and contemporary ways of thinking, provide India with the tenets necessary to evolve into a progressive and contemporary culture.

His novels *Untouchable, Coolie, Two Leaves and a Bud,* and *The Road* displayed numerous instances where long-established and accepted behaviours clashed with modern thought. It was Anand's hope that through his work, India would be able to meld the past with the current mindset and technologies and incorporate them to find a new, advanced and enhanced, superior, human-centered India. Thus, arises the question of the relevance of literature to life and to society. Social writers like Mulk Raj Anand, who finds kinship with Charles Dickens, are expected to effect social change. In their hands, literature is propagandist and meant to stir society's conscience against the terrible hurts and pain they depict. Anand's *Untouchable* won acclaim in India and abroad for its treatment of the caste problem. Yet caste is still a burning issue in India today. Likewise, *Coolie* is clearly anti-child labour in its stance, yet child labour is rampant and appears to be well on its way into twenty-first century Indian society. Literature or legislation? Which will it be to ultimately change society? Can we depend on literature to awaken social conscience and volunteer for shaking the undesirable attitudes and practices in society; or does it take legislation to enforce the change? Then again, when legislation fails, is it the artist who must appeal to the emotions for a change of heart? If the success of the novel is judged by its effectiveness in achieving social change, Mulk Raj Anand's two best novels *Untouchable* and *Coolie* must be considered failures. As tools of societal change, they have accomplished little. To what then does Anand's work own its reputation and worldwide acclaim having been translated into thirty-eight languages and attracted prestigious awards?

Writing at a time when the underdog was not a persona for celebration or even representation, Anand looked upon the poor, the downtrodden, the outcaste with rare eyes of compassion. In a society that only accepted but, in fact, thrived on inequality and injustice, Anand saw people as people and recognized the human soul in the lowliest individual. Religious sanction backed caste-based inequalities and the colonial set up did not require moral questioning of attitudes and treatment toward the servitor. Into such society, Mulk Raj Anand focuses the search light of his perception, bringing into perspective the possibility of a renewed vision of the poor, the helpless and hopeless. His work follows in the tradition of Pro-Black writers awakening the conscience of white America, smug in the complacency of the slave run economy of the south, where the Black was not recognized as human. We notice that Anand shows a deep social awareness and exposes a system that enables the powerful and the rich to oppress the weak and the poor.

Literature and society complement each other the way the human heart and mind do. The superiority of one upon the other can be established in a hurry. Literature records dreams and desires, fears and furies, fact and fiction in the minutest details to soothe and soften mankind in hours of agony and anguish. It also creates the background of numberless games, which decide the fate of individuals and society. It brings a change, which keeps germinating, in the minds of man for years. The saga of man's emergence from the savage to the civilized stage is nothing but the result of the transforming power of literature.

Works Cited

Adiga, Arvind. *The White Tiger*. New Delhi: Harper Collins Publishers, 2008. Print.

Anantha Murthy, U.R. *Samskara*. Trans. A.K. Ramanujan. New Delhi: Oxford University Press, 1976. Print.

Arnold, Milliard. "Introduction." *Black Consciousness in South Africa*. New York: Vintage Books, 1979. Print.

Chaitanya, Krishna. *Kerala*. New Delhi, 1979. Print.

Choudhry, Monika. "The Other Half of Indian Writing in English". *International Journal of Reviews, Surveys and Research*. Web. 3 April 2016.

Deshpande, Shashi. *That Long Silence*. New Delhi: Penguin Publishers, 1988. Print.

——. *The Dark Holds No Terrors*. New Delhi: Penguin Publishers, 1980. Print.

Folorunso, Femi. *Works from a Country in Progress: Nigerian Literature*. Washington D.C: World Press Review, 1993. Print.

Gaidzanwa, R. *Images of Women in Zimbabwean Literature*. Harare: College Press, 1985. Print.

Gordimer, Nadine. "Relevance and Commitment." *The Essential Gesture: Writing, Politics and Places*. New York: Penguin Books, 1988. Print.

http://irckigalirw.pbworks.com/f/African-American+Literature.ppt. Web. 30 June 2015.

Iyengar, K.R. Srinivasa. *Indian Writing in English*. New Delhi: Sterling Publishers, 1985. Print.

Kumar, Raj. *Dalit Literature and Criticism*. Hyderabad: Orient BlackSwan Private Publication, 2019. Print.

Lockwood, Elizabeth McClearyCale. *Sites of Resistance: Writing as Protest in Black Anti-Apartheid South Africa*. Mount Holyoke College, 2008. Print.

Mazuruse, Mickson. *The Theme of Protest in The Post-Independence Shona Novel*. University of South Africa, November 2010. Web. 30 June 2016.

Mishra, Dr. Jugal Kishore. "A Critical Study of Dalit Literature in India". Web. 3 April 2016.

Mistry, Rohinton. *A Fine Balance*. London: Faber and Faber Limited, 2006. Print.

Morrison, Toni. *Sula*. London: Triad Grafton, 1982. Print.

Sawhney, Hirish. "India: A View from Below". *Express India,* September, 2008. Print.

Saxena, Shobhan. "Fact not Fiction", *Sunday Times of India*, October 19, 2008. Print.

Sharma, R.S. and Shashibala Talwar. *Arundhati Roy's The God of Small Things: Critique and Commentary*, New Delhi, 1998, 84-

95. Ed. Indira Bhatt and Nityanandam, Explorations: *Arundhati Roy's The God of Small Things*. New Delhi, 1999. Print.

Thiong'o, Ngugi wa. *Writing against Neo-Colonialism*. Middlesex: Vita Books, 1986. Print.

Zott, Lynn M. "Nineteenth-Century Social Protest Literature Outside England—Introduction", *Nineteenth-Century Literary Criticism*, Vol. 124. Gale Cengage 2003eNotes.com 1 Jan, 2019 http:// www.enotes.com/topics/ nineteenth-century-social-protestliterature#critical-essays-introduction. Web. 1 Jan. 2019.

5

Conclusion: The Vicious Circle Continues

Recent Headline of the newspaper created an uproar of the caste discrimination occurrences in the state of California in Cisco organisation against Dalit Indian American employee who was harassed to accept a caste hierarchy within the workplace where he held the lowest status within a team of higher-caste colleagues (*The First Post*). It is seriously alarming and proves that caste plays an indelible mark at global level. In a society in general, discrimination continues in the form of honour killings, and other caste-based crimes like untouchability, etc. Discrimination is a part of the lived experience of Dalits; others can be sympathetic to their cause, but cannot feel what they feel. Even dignity after death is being denied to marginalised communities. In August 2019, at Vaniyambadi taluk of Vellore district in Tamil Nadu, a man's dead body was seen in a viral video as it was being lowered by his kith and kin over a bridge as part of his last rites. The funeral procession of 46-year-old N. Kuppam had been blocked by members of dominant castes, which forced them to use the bridge (*Newsclicks*).

Anupama Rao writes in her book *The Caste Question: Dalits and the Politics of Modern India* (2010):

> ...expands caste, community, and subaltern historiography across the religious-political and colonial postcolonial divides and beyond its usual focus on the figure of the peasant, indigenous idioms of protest, and on a clean opposition between an anthropological conception of community and a Marxist distrust of

> state power. At the heart of my analysis are caste subalterns who positioned themselves at the center of the debates about inequality and discrimination in India from the late colonial period, and who transformed conceptions of nation, citizenship, and political rights by working *within*, rather than outside, state institutions. Their conceptions of power, like their desire for rights, derived from colonial liberalism, yet enabled Dalits to step outside the suffocating embrace of a cultural nationalism dominated by upper caste elites. Addressing caste radical's understanding of caste as a distinctive form of power allows us to see how, in western India, caste radicals articulated a critique of Brahminical hegemony and religious superstition with a powerful socioeconomic evaluation of caste as a material structure of exploitation, to develop a theory that traversed the realms of the experiential, the political, the epistemological, and the ethical. Their focus on the existential aspects of caste subalternity—on questions of the caste body, violence, language, and experience—addressed matters of personhood and self-making typically elided in critiques of colonial and anticolonial thought. Analysis of caste radical's thinking and action animates this book because it is their unique understanding of the manner in which the caste Hindu order was reproduced, coupled with vital efforts to bring into being a new political subject, that defines the trajectory of Dalit emancipation. (11-12)

Writing history from below in her book *The Caste Question* Anupama Rao says:

> tracing long term developments in the thought of radical anti-casteism that culminates in the political philosophy of B.R. Ambedkar during the interwar years allows me to illuminate distinctive aspects of the caste question and their potent translation into categories of democratic thought and practice. Subalternity itself stands to be reconceived in the process of understanding how Dalit's ideas, actions, and political interventions altered the

> content of caste and challenged the organising principles of colonial liberalism and democratic processes in India. (12)

Babasaheb Ambedkar criticized Indian communists because they did not fight against the caste system. He preferred Buddhist thought, which promoted democracy and non-violence, and rejected Marx's thought, because Marx accepted the use of violence in the struggle against capitalism. Believing that Marxist thought was incomplete as far as the Indian situation was concerned, Indian Marxist thinkers adopted, after Babasaheb's death and in response to the criticisms, a possibility of positive relationship in thoughts of Phule, Ambedkar, Marx and Buddha. Dalit issues are not only social; they are economic as well. It becomes apparent from a serious examination of the caste system that a very powerful, inequitable economic system is functioning behind it. Dalit minorities on their own will not be able to destroy this entrenched unequal system. Those who accept the thoughts of Marx as well as Ambedkar have argued that, for this unequal system to be annihilated, there needs to a meeting of Ambedkar's anti-caste thought and Marx's anti-class thought.

While the cause of Dalit's economic slavery is hidden in the Indian social order, the ultimate path to liberation will be found only through the convergence of Marxism and Ambedkarism. A class system is coming into being in the villages with mechanization and the laws. However, the fissures appearing in the traditional caste system have not brought an end to caste spirit. While caste spirit has gained strength in society, a class spirit is also on the rise due to the exploitation of the oppressed and the bond of common interest. According to Limbale every thought that expresses opposition to inequality is Ambedkarite thought. When the idea of opposing inequality emerges in our Dalit colony, it is called Dalit thought. When it is expressed inside the mill, it is called Marxist thought. When it is applied to white racism, it is called the Black revolution. The labels may be different, but the idea is the same, that is, opposition to inequality.

His preoccupation with history is a dominant trend in all post-colonial writing and it often acquires the nature of being an alternative discourse offering a variation to the official accounts of history. In fact, post-colonial fiction offers an invaluable archive of indigenous historiography. Anand's work exemplifies this trend: he is interested in providing yet another saga of the heroism of the nationalist leaders adding to the nationalist discourse of history. His focus, to use a phrase from the parlance of subaltern historiography, is on "the politics of the people." His novels cover a major part of the colonial history of India tracing the emergence of modern India; and they touch upon all the important social, and political events of the first half of 20th century, such as land reform of the British, the spread of industrial capitalism, repercussions of the world war on Indian economy, the Indian freedom movement, the partition of India and the abolition of princely states. These events are important to Anand not in themselves but in their relation to the life of the common people. It is important to note in this context that the principal actors in Anand's fictional world do not come from the dominant groups of the indigenous society but the subaltern classes and groups such as untouchables, coolies, farmers, and industrial labourers. It is history as it affects these large masses that are narrated in Anand's text. History here is not the representation of the glorious achievements of the heroic, but documents the suffering of millions of poor and helpless people who had no place in earlier, elitist historiography. Anand is sensible of the detachment that is between him and the folks whose lives he has tried to represent. He articulates that he might not be able to sense the miseries of the underprivileged straightly since he had always been relatively at an advantage as said by many Dalit writers later. He says continuing, mine was a secondary mortification, the mortification of seeing other people suffer. He, therefore, uses a variety of strategies in order to create a space for the subject position of his subaltern characters.

Anand's emphasis on socio-political praxis as the appropriate context for exploring the peculiarities of individual experience, and his preoccupation with fiction as an instrument of social transformation shape the distinctive features of his art. In his novels, individual human experience is always circumscribed by historical and political events and is linked to the development of plot and character. In fact, character and action frequently embody the problems of social and political confrontation around which the plot develops. This allows him to portray the complexities of the entire society within the parameters of personal and social relationships among a representative community. In the novels as *Untouchable, The Road*, Anand builds up a binary form in the narrative—in replication of the touchable/untouchable binary in the narrative—and destroys it towards the end. In doing so he performs in writing what he urges the untouchable to do as political activism: the old order must change yielding place to the new. He performs social writing as a correctivist activity and advocates 'social righting'. The form seems clearly inspired to show how the body can be a site of social performance, resistance, and aspiration while reifying notions of morality. How Mulk Raj Anand complicates the site by introducing a moral disjunction between what lies on the surface and what lies beneath. The concepts of alterity, of binary opposition and of the body as a social construction (borrowing from the disability studies inaugurated by Lennard J. Davis) which are post-modernist. This may apparently seem anachronistic to a novel written when modernism had just reached its apogee. The term 'alterity' may be defined as the 'otherness' of people, events, ideas that are radically different from those or of those who are in a position of power and has been used by theorists, especially those who are post-colonial, such as Gayatri Chakravorty Spivak and Homi K. Bhabha. The idea of the binary opposition is a corollary of alterity because the cleaving of any narrative into two sides, one in opposition to the other, is the way in which the nature of alterity in that narrative can be detected. It is such a binary, such as a detection of alterity that operates in the disability studies of Lennard J. Davis. He suggests that human bodies have been binarized into normal and abnormal, ideal and less-than-ideal by forces starting from the eighteenth-century eugenics to today's Hollywood movies. The disabled body is therefore marginalised, just as the able-bodied is centered. Mulk Raj Anand may be continuing this binarized valorization of the ideal body at the cost of the less-than-ideal, but he effects a twist in the binary by situating the able-bodied protagonist in the margins and the 'little' people in the centre. He disrupts the stereotypical conjunction between the ideal body and socio-economic centrality. It is this disjunction which gives the binary oppositions in the novels a complexity it would not have had otherwise. As we see all Anand's protagonists are finest specimen of physicality by nature.

Anand's fiction typically presents the complexity of the warring elements in contemporary society. Any conflict involves two groups or institutions. So also, in Anand's novels, two polarities are introduced and all the characters fall into either of the groups. In *Untouchable* and *The Road,* the conflict is between the caste Hindus and the Untouchables; *Coolie* presents a class struggle between the haves and the have-nots; *Two Leaves and a Bud* deals with the confrontation between British plantation owners and the Indian labourers. The two groups involved, therefore, turns into victims and victimizers, and the writer's sympathy for the former becomes obvious. Anand has stayed close to the contemporary social and political developments, studying keenly their impact on the lives of common folk. His concern with the structure of power and how it affects the individual and the society has a direct bearing not only on his novels, themes, but on their structure, and the particular fictional elements he employs—character, setting, plot, narrative, and language.

The thematic, as well as technical contours of his texts, are shaped by his political and social concerns. The caste system was a product of the Hindu obsession for mental and physical immaculacy. The function and position of each Hindu person were based solely on his attachment to a specific caste. Interestingly, the caste system was believed to be sincere and unwaveringly faithful. It has been formed with gallant objectives and was too kept in accordance with the directives of the Vedas, the sacred writings of the ancient Hindus. This, however, was actually in violation of, and contradicted these scriptures. V. Jayaram, noted author and writer on Hinduism and other related religions, maintains in his article "The Hindu Caste System" from the Hinduwebsite.com that "the Hindu caste system was a clever invention of the later Vedic society. The higher castes found it expedient to retain and uphold their social and sacred otherness with political and economic advantage" (Jayaram). By maintaining this categorical divide among members, those with the power were able to sustain their prominent positions.

Untouchable, a world classic translated into more than thirty-eight world languages cannot be equated with a less well-known novel like *The Road*. But all his novels are, undoubtedly, the creations of a great artist who has discovered the effectiveness of novel form and efficiently employed it to express his passionate love for the suffering people, who after long struggle managed to get political freedom but not yet, in spite of the continuous struggle, have succeeded in getting freedom from caste and class feeling, freedom from the belief in Karma and superstition, freedom from religious hypocrisy, parochialism and fanaticism, freedom from poverty and exploitation, freedom from sexual discrimination and so many other freedoms. In fact, Anand's social concerns are the driving force behind all his writings. They act as a catalyst to his creative output. In a nutshell, this research thesis gives us a faithful picture of the exploitation of the underprivileged. Anand was successful in producing works which genuinely and passionately depicted his basic life experiences but they also represented universal experiences. Anand proclaimed an uprising, an artistic mêlée, to bring about a fresh social order. While in pursuit of maintaining Indian conventions that support an egalitarian perspective of being, Anand predominantly concentrated on promoting expansion in the realms of thoughts and ideologies dealing with the progress of humanistic and technological varieties.

The caste system provided that the members of the various castes were born into their specific category and that they were not permitted to elevate their status. A person born into a lowly status remained there because the members of the more noble castes forbid the improvement or elevation of status in order to keep their position of exaltation intact. Munoo and Hari, in *Coolie* and Gangu and his family, in *Two Leaves and a Bud*, on the other hand, were not victims of caste discrimination like

Bakha; instead, they suffered due to class inequity brought on by the capitalistic drive for wealth. Both Munoo and Gangu came to understand that their abject poverty and deprivation were responsible for their predicaments, not the evils of the caste system. It was not caste that set these people apart, it was the capitalistic greed that formed and polarized the class system that exploited the penniless laborers. Earning the greatest profit possible was the main objective of the factory and plantation owners in Anand's works. In this context, we can refer to Prof. Raj Kumar who in his book *Dalit Literature and Criticism* observes the same as what is said by Mulk Raj Anand:

> Ever since the Dalit panthers coined the term 'Dalit', its connotation has been changing. The term is evolving and has acquired new meanings across academic boundaries. For example, Namdeo Dhasal, the well-known Marathi poet and one of the leaders of the Dalit Panthers movements, infused the term with a leftist vision to include not just the scheduled castes but also economically oppressed classes, including the scheduled Tribes, Neo-Buddhists, landless labourers, and all those who are economically exploited. Dhasal was heavily influenced by Marxist ideologies and he defined the term 'Dalit' in terms of Class, generally including women, tribals, workers in industries and agricultural workers, along with the untouchable communities. (8)

In the context of above lines, they all are Dalits. They were forced to live in unsanitary conditions where they were exposed to horrible diseases such as malaria and cholera. The selfish actions of not taking proper health precautions confirmed the parsimonious and avaricious mindset of the managers and plantation owners. Anand demonstrated how the drive and desire for wealth created a way of life where scores of humans were made to suffer inhumane treatment. This was in direct opposition to his belief in the ethical theory of humanism. The lack of sensitivity and compassion and the basis of taking advantage of other human beings infuriated Anand. The majority of the coolies, specifically on the Assam plantation but also across the subcontinent, were enticed to travel there to work on the promise of being given land to cultivate and therefore procure them independence. Gangu and his family had been forced to surrender their land to pay off a debt incurred by his dead brother. The brutal mistreatment of the poor workers initiated by a small fraction of elite and self-serving British plantation owners formed the theme of *Two Leaves and a Bud.* The sadistic cruelty suffered by these low-class members of society was in complete opposition to Anand's belief in charitable and humanitarian treatment for all human beings, and Anand sought to bring these cruelties into the light. Anand believed that if the lowest of the social classes banned together and stood up for their rights that they could reap the benefits of controlling their future. A component of Anand's idea of eliminating these abuses was to remove the social classes brought on by capitalism. If the community collectively controlled the means of production, distribution, and exchange of goods, and produced what it needed rather than based on its profitability, the shared wealth would be equally distributed among all the members of the community, therefore, eliminating the social class divisions. It was only through organization, struggle, and revolt that these lowly people would have an aspiration to rescue themselves as said by B.R. Ambedkar.

Anand also felt that by accepting modernity and the machine man would be able to progress into a human-centered society. He believed that the world could be transformed by human intervention and would, therefore, be able to liberate mankind from ignorance and irrationality. He felt that the present was discontinuous with the past and that through a process of social and cultural change, life would be different than in the past. His greatest desire would be for an egalitarian society that would remove all economic inequalities and emphasize the equality of all people socially, politically, and economically. Equality and human rights were the cornerstones of Anand's humanistic ideology that would solve India's humanitarian problems. His philosophy of humanism demonstrated support for the second-rate citizens: It condemned the caste system; criticised destitution and poverty; expressed disapproval of dehumanizing shortcomings such as greed and vanity, corruption and selfishness, censure of feudal values and practices, and demonstrated admiration for women through courage and the power of endurance; emphasized the love of the machine; and contained an insight into the psychology of children.

He believed that sympathy for the suffering of others included a desire to help. While he blamed the advantaged and fortunate community of their heartlessness, he also held the oppressed people responsible because of their tolerance and acceptance of such cruel treatment. He denounced fatalism and its attitude of resignation and passivity that resulted from the belief that people are powerless against fate and believed that man had control of his life to make decisions and choices that could change his life. He believed that man was indeed the center of the universe and that morally, all men are equal. He believed that with the acceptance of modern technology in combination with compassion, it was possible to lessen the anguish and cruelty suffered by man. Anand had confidence, faith, and trust in the human race. He hoped and believed that as an entity, humanity would prevail and triumph over all that impeded its progress. He wanted humanity to succeed in its plan to prove its superiority over everything else in the world.

He believed that among the primary principles, the dignity of man was of utmost importance. Anand is a humanist, a proletarian who does not believe in the "Art for Art's sake", but writes to awaken the social conscience. He is audacious enough to admit that he is using literature as a means to some other end, and this end is the alleviation of the suffering of fellow human beings. Mulk Raj Anand has written novels and short stories with a view of teaching men to recognize the fundamental principles of human living and exercise vigilance in regard to the real enemies of freedom and socialism. It has been a life time apostolate for him to help raise the untouchables, the peasants, the serfs, the coolies and the other suppressed members of society to fight for human dignity deliberately denied to them by the privileged sections of society. Anand appears in his fiction as a crusader against the injustice of every type. He steadfastly opposes the exploitation of the poor by any class and caste. This includes the imperial masters, the village money-lenders, the unscrupulous traders, the native rules, priests, tea-planters, politician, and government. So deep is his concern for the poor and the underprivileged that in his novels we find him cry with anguish against the injustice so prevalent in those days as well as today. Popular cinema's like *Aakrosh* (2010) staring Ajay Devgan, Akshaye Khanna and *Article 15* (2019) staring Ayushmann Khurrana realistically depict the recent state of affair in our country and is the vindication of Anand's writings. According Prof. Raj Kumar:

> Dalits constitute about sixteen percent of the country's population, numbering more than 220 million and spread over India. Apart from India, Dalits are also native to other parts of South Asia, such as, Pakistan, Bangladesh, Nepal, Sri Lanka and Myanmar. As a diaspora community they can be found in the United States of America, United Kingdom, Singapore, Malaysia, South Africa, Canada and the Caribbean... Dalit still suffer the sigma of untouchability even after caste discrimination has been declared an offence under Article 17 of the Indian Constitution. They are socially frail, economically needy and politically powerless. Even though a small section of Dalits have proposed under government patronage—thanks to reservation policies in education, employment and politics—and have moved up economically and professionally, socially they remain unaccepted. It does not seem to matter that Dalits are politically and economically the equals of anyone in free India. When they try to rise up the social scale, they are often brutally crushed by the upper castes and sometimes by the state machinery. Their oppressors resort to mob-raids, murder, arson and rape. Dalits, however, are now conscious of their rights to live with dignity and self-respect and, therefore, have been interrogating and challenging the hegemony of upper castes and classes. This has clearly been reflected in the recent emergence of Dalit literature, which is a part of the liberation movement. (03-04)

The focal point of Ambedkarism is the common person. The focus of Marxism also rests on the exploited, suffering common person. The essence of the thoughts of Babasaheb Ambedkar, Karl Marx and Gautama Buddha, Mulk Raj Anand are the same—the liberation of human beings from exploitation. Given this similarity, it seems that there should be a blending of the thoughts of Marx and Ambedkar. But Raja Dhale does not support this possibility. According to him:

> It is not true that we are poor therefore we are untouchable. The truth, he believes, is that we are untouchable therefore we are poor. Otherwise, every poor person in India would be untouchable! Rather than the root of our untouchability being in poverty, the root of our poverty lies in our untouchability. Marxism in the Indian context had to fight for the end of both the caste system and the feudal system. (66-67)

In Dhale's analysis, the source of untouchability lies in Indian history and the Hindu religion, and not in present day capitalism:

> The poverty and untouchability of Dalits is rooted in history and religion, and from that root has emerged a great tree. Untouchability has been replaced by discrimination based on caste. But it needs to be remembered that this discrimination is not located in history or religion, but in today's politics. Though the origin of Dalit's poverty is in untouchability, it cannot be said this is its only cause. Untouchability is now coming to an end due to transformations in social life brought about by inter-caste marriages, religious conversion, laws, Dalit agitations, progressive ideas, science and technology. However, the demon of caste discrimination is now raising its head, further sharpening the social issues confronting Dalits. (12)

Besides this, the inevitable unemployment, corruption, rising population, high costs of living, concentration of the organised production sector and political power in a handful of the rich, deserted villages and increasing number of filthy slums in the cities, have further trampled and oppressed Dalit life. These aspects of current reality cannot be ignored on the basis that they are rooted in history and religion. We must recognise that the source of such problems are today's inequitable arrangements. The origin of Dalit's poverty may well be in religion and history, but its present face is fundamentally different. Further, Dalit poverty has become a far more complex phenomenon on account of the government's public welfare schemes, reservations and the emergence of new Dalit middle class.

The relevance of Mulk Raj Anand's novels can be found in the recent statement of The UN High Commissioner on Human Rights Mr. Zeid Ra'ad Al Hussein who mentioned caste discrimination still stands as a root cause of human rights violations. Manjula Pradeep, Executive Director of the Indian Human Rights NGO, Navsarjan, outlined a number of key issues in the struggle for Dalit rights. These include a high level of violence against Dalits, multiple forms of discrimination against Dalit women and limited access for Dalits to resources, development, health and education. According to UNHR Special Rapporteur Rita Izs'ak Ndiaye report titled "Minorities and discrimination based on caste and analogous systems of inherited status" (2016) states that caste discrimination is also embedded in interpersonal and communal relationships that overcoming it will require not only legal and political responses, but also community-based approaches aimed at changing the mindsets of individuals and the collective conscience of the local communities. The report also highlighted that over 27% Indians admit practicing untouchability but it is likely to go high. The report also stated that more than 160 million Indians are engaged in manual scavenging and many lose their life due to choking cleaning the drains manually. Though India is applauded for its Reservation policy or positive discrimination for the weak classes by international communities and agencies but still much more is left to be accomplished in the future for a just society. A paradigmatic shift is already visible within society with the positive change and also voices against different forms of oppression related to class, gender, ethnicity, language, religion and other frameworks besides caste.

Works Cited

Anand, Mulk Raj. *Apology for Heroism: A Brief Autobiography of Ideas*. New Delhi: Arnold-Heinemann, 1975. Print.

Chakravarty, Uma. *Gendering Caste through a Feminist Lens*. Kolkata: Stree Publications, 2003. Print.

Chatterjee, N.R. "The Great Little Man: The Body As A Structural Motif in Mulk Raj Anand's *Untouchable*". *Untouchable*. Noida: Longman Study Edition Pearson, 2008. Print.

Gatade, Subash. "No-End-Humiliation-Dalits-After-Death". Newsclicks. Web. 22 July 2020.

Gupta, G.S. Balarama. "Towards a Closer understanding of Anand." *Perspectives on Mulk Raj Anand*. Ghaziabad: Vimal Publication, 1978. Print.

Jayaram, V. "The Hindu Caste System." *Hinduism, Buddhism, Jainism, Sikhism, Zoroastrianism and Other Resources*. http:// hinduwebsite.com. Web. 23 April 2016.

Jeenger, Kailash. The First Post. https://www.firstpost.com/india/ abolition-of-caste-based-reservation-untenable-as-long-as-dalits-suffer-atrocities-prejudice, 2020. Web. 4 July 2020.

Kumar, Raj. *Dalit Literature and Criticism*. Hyderabad: Orient BlackSwan Private Publication, 2019. Print.

Leitch, Vincent B. *The Norton Anthology of Theory and Criticism*. New York and London, 2001. Print.

Limbale, Sharankumar. *Towards an Aesthetic of Dalit Literature*. Hyderabad: Orient BlackSwan Private Limited, 2004. Print.

Paul, Premila. *The Novels of Mulk Raj Anand: A Thematic Study*. New Delhi: Sterling Publishers, 1983. Print.

Rao, Anupama. *The Caste Question-Dalits and the Politics of Modern India*. California: The University of California Press, 2010. Print.

Zoroastrianism and Other Resources. http://hinduwebsite.com. Web. 23 April 2016.

Bibliography

Primary Sources

Adiga, Arvind. *The White Tiger*. New Delhi: Harper Collins Publishers, 2008. Print.

Anand, Mulk Raj. *The Bubble*. New Delhi: Arnold Heinemann, 1984. Print.

——. "The Story of My Experiment with a White Lie". *Critical Essays on Indian Writing in English*, ed. M.K. Naik. Madras: The Macmillan Co. of India Ltd., 1977. Print.

——. "why I write". Ed. K.K. Sharma. *Indo-English Literature*. Ghaziabad: Vimal Prakashan, 1977. Print.

——. *Apology for Heroism*. New Delhi: Arnold Heinemann, 1986. Print.

——. *Apology for Heroism: A Brief Autobiography of Ideas*. New Delhi: Arnold-Heinemann, 1975. Print.

——. *Author to Critic: The Letters of Mulk Raj Anand to Saros Cowasjee*, ed. Saros Cowasjee, Calcutta: Writers' Workshop, 1973. Print.

——. *Confession of a Lover*. New Delhi: Arnold Heinemann, 1976. Print.

——. *Coolie*. New Delhi: Penguin Books, 1993. Print.

——. *Gauri*. New Delhi: Arnold Heinemann, 1981. Print.

——. *Lajwanti and Other Stories*. New Delhi: Orient Paperbacks, 1999. Print.

——. *Morning Face*. Bombay: Kutub Popular, 1968. Print.

——. *Mulk Raj Anand Greatest Short Stories*. Mumbai: Jaico Publishing House, 1999. Print.

——. *Seven Summers*. New Delhi: Orient Paperbacks, 1970. Print.

——. *The Big Heart*. New Delhi: Arnold Heinemann, 1980. Print.

——. *The Bride's Book of Beauty*. Bombay: Kutub Publishers, 1949. Print.

——. *The Invincible will to Live*, Congress Socialist (29th May, 1937). Print.

——. *The Lost Child and Other Stories*. New Delhi: Orient Paperbacks, 2004. Print.

——. *The Road*. Bombay: Kutub Popular, 1961. Print.

——. "The Story of My Experience with a White Lie", *Indian Literature,* vol. 10, no. 3, 1967. Reprinted in *Critical Essays on Indian Writing in English*. Macmillan, Silver Jubilee Students Edition, 1977. Print.

——. *Two Leaves and a Bud*. Bombay: Kutub Publisher, 1946. Print.

——. *Untouchable*. Gurgaon: Penguin Books India Ltd, 2001. Print.

Anantha Murthy, U.R. *Saṁskara*. Trans. A.K. Ramanujan. New Delhi: Oxford University Press, 1976. Print.

Berry, Margaret. *Mulk Raj Anand: The Man and the Novelist*. Amsterdam: Oriental Press, 1970. Print.

Cowasjee, Saros. "Anand's *Two Leaves and a Bud*". *Indian Literature*, vol. xvi, nos. 3 and 4 (July-December 1973). Print.

——. *Coolie: An Assessment*. New Delhi: OUP, 1976. Print.

——. *So Many Freedoms: A Study of Major Fiction of M. R. Anand*. New Delhi: Oxford University Press, 1977. Print.

Deshpande, Shashi. *That Long Silence*. New Delhi: Penguin Publishers, 1988. Print.

——. *The Dark Holds No Terrors*. New Delhi: Penguin Publishers, 1980. Print.

Gautam, G.L. *Mulk Raj Anand's Critique of Religious Fundamentalism*. Delhi: Kanti Publisher, 1996. Print.

Ghurye, G.S. *Caste and Race in India*. Bombay: Popular Prakashan, 1969. Print.

Gupta, G.S. Balarama. "Towards a Closer understanding of Anand." *Perspectives on Mulk Raj Anand*. Ghaziabad: Vimal Publication, 1978. Print.

——. *Mulk Raj Anand: A Study of His Fiction in Humanist Perspective*. Bara Bazar, Bareilly: Prakash Book Depot, 1974. Print.

Iyengar, K.R. Srinivas. *Indian Writing in English*. New Delhi: Sterling Publishers, 1985. Print.

Limbale, Sharankumar. "Akkarmashi". Translated edition (Hindi). New Delhi: Granth Akademi, 1991. Print.

Mistry, Rohinton. *A Fine Balance*. London: Faber and Faber Limited, 2006. Print.

Naik, M.K. *Mulk Raj Anand*. London: Arnold Heinemann; India: New Delhi, 1973. Print.

Niven, Alastair. *The Yoke of Pity: A Study in Fictional Writings of Mulk Raj Anand*. New Delhi: Arnold Heinemann, 1978. Print.

Packman, Gillian. "Mulk Raj Anand And the Thirties Movement in England." *Perspectives on Mulk Raj Anand*. Ghaziabad: Vimal, 1978. Print.

Paul, Premila. *The Novels of Mulk Raj Anand: A Thematic Study*. New Delhi: Sterling Publishers Pvt. Ltd., 1983. Print.

Roy, Arundhati. *The God of Small Things*. New Delhi: India Ink, 1998. Print.

Sharma, K.K. *Perspectives on Mulk Raj Anand*. Ghaziabad: Vimal Prakashan, 1978. Print.

Sinha, K.N. *Mulk Raj Anand*. New Delhi: Kalyani Publishers, 1995. Print.

Secondary Sources

Abraham, Francis and John Henry Morgan. *Sociological thought from Comte to Sorokin*. London: Wyndham Hall Press, 1989. Print.

Alavi, Seema. *Sepoys and The Company Tradition and Transition in Northern India*. India: Oxford University Press India, 1998. Print.

Anand, Mulk Raj. "I want to be born as untouchable". *The Hindustan Times*. New Delhi, Sunday Magazine, 26 January 1992. Print.

——. *Untouchable*. "Introduction" by Nandini Bhattacharya. Noida: Longman Study Edition Pearson, 2008. Print.

Apte, V.M. "Social and Economic Conditions". *The History and Culture of the Indian People*, vol. 1, Ed. R.C. Majumdar, Bombay: Bharatiya Vidya Bhavan, 1965. Print.

Arnold, Milliard. "Introduction." *Black Consciousness in South Africa*. New York: Vintage Books, 1979. Print.

Bagul, Baburao. *When I Hid My Caste: Stories*. Trans. Jerry Pinto. New Delhi: Speaking Tiger, 2018. Print.

Balewa, Alhaji Sir Abubakar Tafawa. *Shaihu Umar.* Translated from the Hausa by Mervyn Hiskett. London: Longmans, 1967. Print.

Bhatnagar, Manmohan K. and M. Rajeshwar. *The Novels of Mulk Raj Anand—A Critical Study.* New Delhi: Atlantic Publisher, 2000. Print.

Bhattacharya, S.K. *Bengal Renaissance: Social and Political Thought*. New Delhi: Classical Publishing Company, 1986. Print.

Bouglé, Célestin. *Essays on the Caste System*. London: Cambridge University Press, 1971. Print.

Briffault, Robert. *The Mothers: A Study of the Origin of Sentiments and Institutions*. New York: Vol. I, 1952, 345; for the original text, vide, *Manusmriti*. Print.

Chaitanya, Krishna. *Kerala*. New Delhi, 1979. Print.

Chakravarty, Uma. *Gendering Caste through a Feminist Lens*. Kolkata: Stree Publications, 2003. Print.

Chandra, Bipin. *India's Struggle for Independence*. New Delhi: Penguin India, 1992. Print.

Chatterjee, N.R. "The Great Little Man: The Body as a Structural Motif in Mulk Raj Anand's *Untouchable*". *Untouchable*. Noida: Longman Study Edition Pearson, 2008. Print.

Chokhamela. *On the Threshold: Songs of Chokhamela*. Trans. Rohini Mokashi-Punekar. New Delhi: The Book Review Literary Trust, 2002. Print.

Choudhry, Monika. "The Other Half of Indian Writing in English". *International Journal of Reviews, Surveys and Research*. Web. 3 April 2016.

Dangle, Arjun, ed. *A Corpse in the Well: Translations from Modern Marathi Dalit Autobiographies*. Hyderabad: Disha Books, 1994. Print.

Das, A.N. *The Republic of Bihar*. New Delhi: Penguin India, 1992. Print.

Dayal, Har. *Hints for Self-Culture*. Bombay: Jaico Publishing House, 1983. Print.

Desai, A.R. *Social Background of Indian Nationalism*. Bombay: Popular Prakashan, 1966. Print.

Deshpande, Manali S. *History of The Indian Caste System and Its Impact on India Today*. California Polytechnic State University, San Luis Obispo Fall, 2010. Web. 3 April 2016.

Edward, Paul. Ed. *Encyclopaedia of Philosophy*, vols. 3-4, New York: Macmillan Co. and the Free Press, 1967. Print. https://www.encyclopedia.com /people/philosophy-and-religion/philosophy-biographies/immanuel-kant.

Folorunso, Femi. *Works from a Country in Progress: Nigerian Literature*. Washington D.C: World Press Review, 1993. Print.

Gadhvi, Praveen. *The City of Dust and Lust*. Trans. Praveen Gadhvi. Delhi: B.S. Publishers, 2010. Print.

Gaidzanwa, R. *Images of Women in Zimbabwean Literature*. Harare: College Press, 1985. Print.

Ganguli, Dwarakanath, *Slavery in British Dominion*. Calcutta: Jijnasa, 1972. Print.

Gatade, Subash. "No-End-Humiliation-Dalits-After-Death". Newsclicks. Web. 22 July 2020.

Gautam, G.L. *Mulk Raj Anand's Critique of Religious Fundamentalism (A Critical Assessment of His Novels)*. New Delhi: Kanti Publishers, 1996. Print.

Ghosh, B.K. "Language and Literature". *The History and Culture of the Indian People*, vol. 1, ed. R.C. Majumdar. Bombay: Bhartiya Vidya Bhawan, 1965. Print.

Gordimer, Nadine. "Relevance and Commitment." *The Essential Gesture: Writing, Politics and Places*. New York: Penguin Books, 1988. Print.

Gramsci, Antonio. *Selections from Prison Notebooks* (trans.) Quentin Hoare and Geoffrey Nowell Smith. London: Lawrence and Wishart, 1971. Print.

Guha, Ranjit. 'Preface'. *Subaltern Studies,* vol. I (ed.), Ranjit Guha, Delhi: Oxford University Press, 1982. Print.

Hemenway, Stephen Ignatius. *The Novel of India*, vol. II. Calcutta: The Writers' Workshop, 1975. Print.

Hopkins, Edward W. *The Ordinances of Manu*. New Delhi: Oriental Books Reprint Corporation Book Publishers, 1971. Print.

http://irckigalirw.pbworks.com/f/African-American Literature. ppt. Web. 30 June 2015.

https://www.researchgate.net/publication/261778600. *The Weave of My Life a Dalit Woman.* Memoirs by Urmila Pawar translated by Maya Pandit. Web. 23 May 2018.

Jadhav, Narendra. *Outcaste: A Memoir*. New Delhi: Viking, 2003. Print.

Jayaram, V. "The Hindu Caste System." *Hinduism, Buddhism, Jainism, Sikhism, Zoroastrianism and Other Resources*. http://hinduwebsite.com. Web. 23 April 2016.

Jeenger, Kailash. The First Post. https://www.firstpost.com/india/abolition-of-caste-based-reservation-untenable-as-long-as-dalits-suffer-atrocities-prejudice, 2020. Web. 4 July 2020.

Khan, S.A. *Mulk Raj Anand—The Novel of Commitment*. New Delhi: Atlantic Publisher, 2000. Print.

Krishnan, Dr. Radha. *Indian Philosophy*, volume I. London: George Allen and Unwin Ltd., Humanities Press Inc. New York, 1920. Print.

Kumar, Raj. *Dalit Literature and Criticism*. Hyderabad: Orient BlackSwan Private Publication, 2019. Print.

Leitch, Vincent B. *The Norton Anthology of Theory and Criticism*. New York and London, 2001. Print.

Lexicon Universal Encyclopaedia. Volume 4, New York: Lexicon Publication Inc, 1987, Print.

Limbale, Sharankumar. *Towards an Aesthetic of Dalit Literature*. Hyderabad: Orient BlackSwan Private Limited, 2004. Print.

Lockwood, Elizabeth McClearyCale. *Sites of Resistance: Writing as Protest in Black Anti-Apartheid South Africa*. Mount Holyoke College, 2008. Print.

Marx, Karl and Frederic Engels. *Selected Works*. Moscow: Progress Publishers, 1977. Print.

Mathew, Philip and Ajit Muricken. *Religion, Ideology and Counter Culture*. Bangalore: Horizon Books, 1987, print.

Mazuruse, Mickson. *The Theme of Protest in The Post-Independence Shona Novel*. University of South Africa, November 2010. Web. 30 June 2016.

Mishra, Dr. Jugal Kishore. "A Critical Study of Dalit Literature in India". Web. 3 April 2016.

Mookerjee, R.K. "Social Condition". *The History and Culture of the Indian People*. ed. R.C. Majumdar. Bombay: Bharatiya Vidya Bhawan, 1968. Print.

Morrison, Toni. *Sula*. London: Triad Grafton, 1982. Print.

Naik, M.K. "Infinite Variety: A Study of The Short Stories of Mulk Raj Anand." *Perspectives on Mulk Raj Anand*. Ghaziabad: Vimal, 1978. Print.

Oyono, Ferdinand. *Houseboy*. translated from the French by John Reed. London: Heinemann, 1966. Print.

Parameshwaran, Uma. *A Study of Representative Indo-English Novelists*. New Delhi: Vikas Publishing House, 1976. Print.

Patel, S.J. "Agricultural Labourers in Modern India and Pakistan". *Indian Journal of Economics*, Vol. XXXIII, July, 1952. *The World of the Rural Labourer in Colonial India*. Ed. Gyan Prakash, Delhi: OUP, 1992. Print.

Prabhu, P.H. *Hindu Social Organisation*. Bombay: Popular Prakashan, 1962. Print.

Rao, Anupama. *The Caste Question—Dalits and the Politics of Modern India*. California: The University of California Press, 2010. Print.

Rawat, B.K. *Mulk Raj Anand—A Critical Study*. New Delhi: Omega Publishers, 2011. Print.

Robertson, R.T. "*Untouchable* as an Archetypal Novel". *Kakatiya Journal of English Studies*, 2.1 (1977). Print.

Roy, Amitabh. *The God of Small Things—A Novel of Social Commitment*. New Delhi: Atlantic Publishers, 2005. Print.

Sawhney, Hirish. "India: A View from Below". *Express India,* September, 2008. Print.

Saxena, Shobhan. "Fact not fiction", *Sunday Times of India*, October 19, 2008. Print.

Sharma, K.L. *Indian Society*. New Delhi: NCERT, 1998. Print.

Sharma, R.S. and Shashibala Talwar. *Arundhati Roy's The God of Small Things: Critique and Commentary*, New Delhi, 1998, 84-95. Ed. Indira Bhatt and Indira Nityanandam, Explorations: *Arundhati Roy's The God of Small Things*. New Delhi, 1999. Print.

Shastri, Shakuntala Rao. *Women in The Sacred Laws*, Bombay, 1959. Print.

Singh, Yogendra. *Sociological Bulletin*, Vol. xvii. No. 2, 1968. Print.

Social Welfare, vol. xxxiv, nos. 11-12, Feb-March, 1933. Print.

Srinivas, M.N. *Caste in Modern India and Other Essays*. Bombay: Asia Publishing House, 1972. Print.

The Editors of Encyclopædia Britannica. http://www.encyclopedia.com/social-sciencesand-law/sociology-and-social-reform/sociology-general-terms-and-concepts/class-0. Web. 14 July 2017.

Thiong'o, Ngugi wa. *Writing against Neo-Colonialism*. Middlesex: Vita Books, 1986. Print.

Valmiki, Omprakash. *Amma and Other Stories*. Trans. Naresh K. Jain. New Delhi: Manohar, 2008. Print.

Vivekananda, Swami. *Caste, Culture and Socialism* (Published by Swami Ananyananda). Calcutta: Ashutosh Lithographic Co., 1983. Print.

Wakankar, Milind. *Subalternity and Religion: The Prehistory of Dalit Empowerment in South Asia*. London: Routledge, 2010. Print.

Walsh, William. *Indian Literature in English*. London: Longman Group, 1990. Print.

Wikipedia contributors. "Manual scavenging." *Wikipedia, The Free Encyclopedia*. Wikipedia, The Free Encyclopedia, 20th April 2017. Web. 20 April 2017.

Yadav, Shiv Kumar. "A comparative study of Mulk Raj Anand's *Untouchable* and Sharankumar Limbale's 'Akkarmashi'". Ed. T.M.J. Indra Mohan. *The Novels of Mulk Raj Anand*. New Delhi: Atlantic Publishers, 2005. Print.

Zelliot, Eleanor. *Ambedkar's World: The Making of Babasaheb and the Dalit Movement*. New Delhi: Navayana, 2016. Print.

Zott, Lynn M. "Nineteenth-Century Social Protest Literature Outside England—Introduction", *Nineteenth-Century Literary Criticism*, Vol. 124. Gale Cengage 2003eNotes.com 1 Jan, 2019 http:// www.enotes.com/topics/ nineteenth-century-social-protestliterature#critical-essays-introduction. Web. 1 Jan. 2019.